Implementing Lean

Lean is about building and improving stable and predictable systems and processes to deliver to customers high-quality products/services on time by engaging everyone in the organization. Combined with this, organizations need to create an environment of respect for people and continuous learning. It's all about people. People create the product or service, drive innovation, and create systems and processes, and with leadership buy-in and accountability to ensure sustainment with this philosophy, employees will be committed to the organization as they learn and grow personally and professionally.

Lean is a term that describes a way of thinking about and managing companies as an enterprise. Becoming Lean requires the following: the continual pursuit to identify and eliminate waste; the establishment of efficient flow of both information and process; and an unwavering top-level commitment. The concept of continuous improvement applies to any process in any industry.

Based on the contents of ***The Lean Practitioners Field Book***, the purpose of this series is to show, in detail, how any process can be improved utilizing a combination of tasks and people tools and introduces the BASICS Lean® concept. The books are designed for all levels of Lean practitioners and introduces proven tools for analysis and implementation that go beyond the traditional point kaizen event. Each book can be used as a stand-alone volume or used in combination with other titles based on specific needs.

Each book is chock-full of case studies and stories from the authors' own experiences in training organizations that have started or are continuing their Lean journey of continuous improvement. Contents include valuable lessons learned and each chapter concludes with questions pertaining to the focus of the chapter. Numerous photographs enrich and illustrate specific tools used in Lean methodology.

Implementing Lean: Converting Waste to Profit explores implementation methods, line balancing methods, including baton zone or bumping, and implementing Lean in the office and machine shops. The goal of this book is to introduce the balance of the tools and how to proceed once the analysis is completed. There are many pieces to a Lean implementation and all of them are interconnected. This book walks through the relationships and how the data presented can be leveraged to prepare for the implementation. It also provides suggest solutions for improvements and making recommendations to management to secure their buy-in and approval.

BASICS Lean® Implementation Series

Baseline: Confronting Reality & Planning the Path for Success
By Charles Protzman, Fred Whiton & Joyce Kerpchar

Assess and Analyze: Discovering the Waste Consuming Your Profits
By Charles Protzman, Fred Whiton & Joyce Kerpchar

Suggesting Solutions: Brainstorming Creative Ideas to Maximize Productivity
By Charles Protzman, Fred Whiton & Joyce Kerpchar

Implementing Lean: Converting Waste to Profit
By Charles Protzman, Fred Whiton & Joyce Kerpchar

Check: Identifying Gaps on the Path to Success
By Charles Protzman, Fred Whiton & Joyce Kerpchar

Sustaining Lean: Creating a Culture of Continuous Improvement
By Charles Protzman, Fred Whiton & Joyce Kerpchar

Implementing Lean
Converting Waste to Profit

Charles Protzman, Fred Whiton, and Joyce Kerpchar

Routledge
Taylor & Francis Group

A PRODUCTIVITY PRESS BOOK

First published 2023
by Routledge
605 Third Avenue, New York, NY 10158

and by Routledge
4 Park Square, Milton Park, Abingdon, Oxon, OX14 4RN

Routledge is an imprint of the Taylor & Francis Group, an informa business

ISBN: 978-1-032-02918-4 (hbk)
ISBN: 978-1-032-02917-7 (pbk)
ISBN: 978-1-003-18580-2 (ebk)

DOI: 10.4324/9781003185802

Typeset in Garamond
by KnowledgeWorks Global Ltd.

This book series is dedicated to all the Lean practitioners in the world and to two of the earliest, my friend Kenneth Hopper and my grandfather Charles W. Protzman Sr. Kenneth was a close friend of Charles Sr. and is coauthor with his brother William of a book that describes Charles Sr. and his work for General MacArthur in the Occupation of Japan in some detail: *The Puritan Gift: Reclaiming the American Dream amidst Global Financial Chaos.*

Charles W. Protzman Sr.

Kenneth Hopper

Contents

Acknowledgments

There are many individuals who have contributed to this book, both directly and indirectly, and many others over the years, too many to list here, who have shared their knowledge and experiences with us. We would like to thank all of those who have worked with us on Lean teams in the past and the senior leadership whose support made them successful. This book would not have been possible without your hard work, perseverance, and courage during our Lean journey together. We hope you see this book as the culmination of our respect and appreciation. We apologize if we have overlooked anyone in the following acknowledgments. We would like to thank the following for their contributions to coauthor or contribute to the chapters in this book:

- Special thanks to our Productivity Press editor, Kris Mednansky, who has been terrific at guiding us through our writing project. Kris has been a great source of encouragement and kept us on track as we worked through what became an ever-expanding six-year project.
- Special thanks to all our clients. Without you, this book would not have been possible.
- Russ Scaffede for his insight into the Toyota system and for his valuable contributions through numerous e-mail correspondence and edits with various parts of the book.
- Joel Barker for his permission in referencing the paradigm material so important and integral to Lean implementations and change management.
- Many thanks to the "Hats" team (you know who you are).
- I would like to acknowledge Mark Jamrog of SMC Group. Mark was my first Sensei and introduced me to this Kaikaku-style Lean System Implementation approach based on the Ohno and Shingo teachings.
- Various chapter contributions by Joe and Ed Markiewicz of Ancon Gear.

For the complete list of acknowledgments, testimonials, dedication, etc. please see The Lean Practitioner's Field Book. The purpose of this series was to break down and enhance the original Lean Practitioner's Field Book into six books that are aligned with the BASICS® model.

Authors' Note: Every attempt was made to source materials back to the original authors. In the event we missed someone, please feel free to let us know so we may correct it in any future edition. Many of the spreadsheets depicted were originally hand drawn by Mark Jamrog, SMC Group, put into Excel by Dave O'Koren and Charlie Protzman, and since modified significantly. Most of the base formatting for these spreadsheets can be found in the Shingo, Ohno, Monden, or other industrial engineering handbooks.

About the Authors

Charles Protzman, MBA, CPM, formed Business Improvement Group (B.I.G.), LLC, in November 1997. B.I.G. is in Sarasota Florida. Charlie and his son, Dan along with Mike Meyers, specialize in implementing and training Lean thinking principles and the BASICS® Lean business delivery system (LBDS) in small to fortune 50 companies involved in Manufacturing, Healthcare, Government, and Service Industries.

Charles has written 12 books to date and is the coauthor of Leveraging Lean in Healthcare: Transforming Your Enterprise into a High-Quality Patient Care Delivery System series and is a two-time recipient of the Shingo Research and Professional Publication Award. He has since published *The BASICS® Lean Implementation Model* and *Lean Leadership BASICS®*. Charles has over 38 years of experience in materials and operations management. He spent almost 14 years with AlliedSignal, now Honeywell, where he was an Aerospace Strategic Operations Manager and the first AlliedSignal Lean master. He has received numerous special-recognition and cost-reduction awards. Charles was an external consultant for the Department of Business and Economic Development's (DBED's) Maryland Consortium during and after his tenure with AlliedSignal. With the help of Joyce LaPadula and others, he had input into the resulting DBED world-class criteria document and assisted in the first three initial DBED world-class company assessments. B.I.G. was a Strategic Partner of ValuMetrix Services, a division of Ortho-Clinical Diagnostics, Inc., a Johnson & Johnson company. He is an international Lean consultant and has taught beginner to advanced students' courses in Lean principles and total quality all over the world.

Charlie Protzman states, "My grandfather started me down this path and has influenced my life to this day. My grandfather made four trips to Japan from 1948 to the 1960s. He loved the Japanese people and culture and was passionate and determined to see Japanese manufacturing recover from World War II."

Charles spent the last 24 years with Business Improvement Group, LLC, implementing successful Lean product line conversions, kaizen events, and administrative business system improvements (transactional Lean) worldwide. He is following in the footsteps of his grandfather, who was part of the Civil Communications Section (CCS) of the American Occupation. Prior to recommending Dr. Deming's 1950 visit to Japan, C.W. Protzman Sr. surveyed over 70 Japanese companies in 1948. Starting in late 1948, Homer Sarasohn and C.W. Protzman Sr. taught top executives of prominent Japanese communications companies an eight-week course in American participative management and quality techniques in Osaka and Tokyo. Over 5,100 top Japanese executives had taken the course by 1956. The course continued until 1993. Many of the lessons we taught the Japanese in 1948 are now being taught to Americans as "Lean principles." The Lean principles had their roots in the United States and date back to the early 1700s and later to Taylor, Gilbreth, and Henry Ford. The principles were refined by Taiichi Ohno and expanded by Dr. Shigeo Shingo. Modern-day champions were Norman Bodek (the Grandfather of Lean), Jim Womack, and Dan Jones.

Charles participated in numerous benchmarking and site visits, including a two-week trip to Japan in June 1996 and 2017. He is a master facilitator and trainer in TQM, total quality speed, facilitation, career development, change management, benchmarking, leadership, systems thinking, high-performance work teams, team building, Myers-Briggs® Styles, Lean thinking, and supply chain management. He also participated in Baldrige Examiner and Six Sigma management courses. He was an assistant program manager during "Desert Storm" for the Patriot missile-to-missile fuse development and production program. Charles is a past member of SME, AME, IIE, IEEE, APT, and the International Performance Alliance Group (IPAG), an international team of expert Lean Practitioners (http://www.ipag-consulting.com).

Fred Whiton, MBA, PMP, PE, has 30 years of experience in the aerospace and defense industry, which includes engineering, operations, program and portfolio management, and strategy development. He is employed as a Chief Engineer within Raytheon Intelligence & Space at the time of this book's publication.

Fred has both domestic and international expertise within homeland security, communications command and control intelligence surveillance and reconnaissance sensors and services, military and commercial aerospace systems, and defense systems supporting the US Navy, US Air Force, US Army, US Department of Homeland Security, and the US Intelligence Community across a full range of functions from marketing, concept development, engineering, and production into life cycle sustainment and logistics. Fred began his career as a design engineer at General Dynamics, was promoted to a group engineer at Lockheed Martin, and was a director at Northrop Grumman within the Homeland Defense Government Systems team. As vice president of engineering and operations at Smiths Aerospace, he was the Lean champion for a Lean enterprise journey, working closely with Protzman as the Lean consultant, for a very successful Lean implementation within a union plant, including a new plant designed using Lean principles. Prior to joining Raytheon, Fred was a senior vice president within C4ISR business unit at CACI International and prior to joining CACI was the vice president and general manager of the Tactical Communications and Network Solutions Line of Business within DRS Technologies.

Fred has a BS in mechanical engineering from the University of Maryland, an MS in mechanical engineering from Rensselaer Polytechnic Institute, a master's in engineering administration from The George Washington University, and an MBA from The University of Chicago. He is a professional engineer (PE) in Maryland, a certified project management professional (PMP), served as a commissioner on the Maryland Commission for Manufacturing Competitiveness under Governor Ehrlich, as a commissioner on the Maryland Commission on Autism under Governor O'Malley, and as a member of the boards of directors for the Regional Manufacturing Institute headquartered in Maryland and the First Maryland Disability Trust.

Joyce Kerpchar has over 35 years of experience in the healthcare industry that includes key leadership roles in healthcare operations, IT, health plan management, and innovative program development and strategy. As a Lean champion, mentor, and Six Sigma black belt, she is experienced in organizational lean strategy and leading large-scale healthcare lean initiatives, change management, and IT implementations. Joyce is a coauthor of Leveraging Lean in Healthcare: Transforming Your Enterprise into a High-Quality Patient Care Delivery System, Recipient of the Shingo Research and Professional Publication Award.

She began her career as a board-certified physician's assistant in cardiovascular and thoracic surgery and primary care medicine and received her master's degree in Management. Joyce is passionate about leveraging Lean in healthcare processes to eliminate waste and reduce errors, improve overall quality, and reduce the cost of providing healthcare.

Introduction

This book is part of the BASICS Lean® Practitioner Series and was adapted from The Lean Practitioner's Field Book: Proven, Practical, Profitable and Powerful Techniques for Making Lean Really Work. In Book 4, we continue begin the I or Implementation Step of the BASICS Lean® Implementation Model. These steps include discussion of various implementation methodologies, implementing Kanban and line balancing as well as real-life examples of implementing Lean in machine shops and applying Lean to transactional processes.

The books in this BASICS Lean® Implementation Series take the reader on a journey beginning with an overview of Lean principles, culminating with employees developing professionally through the BASICS Lean® Leadership Development Path. Each book has something for everyone from the novice to the seasoned Lean Practitioner. A refresher for some at times, it provides soul-searching and thought-provoking questions with examples that will stimulate learning opportunities. Many of us take advantage of these learning opportunities daily. We, the authors, as Lean practitioners, are students still thirsting for knowledge and experiences to assist organizations in their transformations.

This series is designed to be a guide and resource to help you with the ongoing struggle to improve manufacturing, government, and service industries throughout the world. This series embodies true stories, results, and lessons, which we and others have learned during our Lean journeys. The concept of continuous improvement applies to any process in any industry. The purpose of this series is to show, in detail, how any process can be improved utilizing a combination of tasks and people tools. We will introduce proven tools for analysis and implementation that go far beyond the traditional point kaizen event training. Several CEOs have shared with us: had they not implemented Lean, they would not have survived the Recession in 2008 and subsequent downturns.

Many companies prefer not to use their names in this book as they consider Lean a strategic competitive advantage in their industry, and some of these companies have now moved into a leadership position in their respective markets, thus, we may refer to them as Company X throughout the series. We explain to companies that Lean is a 5-year commitment that never ends. About 80–90% of the companies with which we have worked have sustained all or some of their Lean journeys based on implementing our BASICS® Lean approach that we will share with you in this book.

The BASICS Lean® Implementation Series discusses the principles and tools in detail as well as the components of the House of Lean. It is a "how to" book that presents an integrated, structured approach identified by the acronym BASICS®, which when combined with an effective business strategy can help ensure the successful transformation of an organization. The Lean concepts described in each book are supported by a plethora of examples drawn from the personal experiences of its many well-known and respected contributors, which range from very small machine shops to Fortune 50 companies.

The BASICS Lean® Implementation Series has both practical applications and applications in academia. It can be used for motivating students to learn many of the Lean concepts and at the end of each chapter there are thought-provoking questions for the readers to help digest the material. The investment in people in terms of training, engagement, empowerment, and personal and professional growth is the key to sustaining Lean and an organization's success. For more on this topic, please see our book Lean Leadership BASICS®. Lean practitioners follow a natural flow, building continually on previous information and experiences. There is a bit of the Lean practitioner in all of us. Hopefully, as you read these books to pursue additional knowledge, as a refresher or for reference, or for academia, it can help expand your knowledge, skills, and abilities on your never-ending Lean journey.

Chapter 1

Lean Implementation Methodologies

If you are not working at your very best, you are literally stealing from the company.

Henry Ford

Vision without execution is just hallucination.

Thomas Edison

BASICS®: How to Implement

This chapter is about the I in the BASICS® model, which stands for implement (see Figure 1.1).

There are some improvements which we should just implement. These are simple improvements which, following the Lean philosophy, just make sense. For example, labeling tools, fixing a safety issue, and implementing a tooling improvement to a machine. For larger improvements, however, if the project scope requires a team or multiple stakeholder input, one must consider some type of event, project, or system implementation. The implementation model below describes the different approaches to Lean and compares them to Toyota (see Table 1.1). This discussion is often confusing as the word kaizen appears in all four methods. To clarify, let us examine each implementation method:

- Method 1 is made up of strictly implementing point kaizen events for organizational transformation. This process will be discussed in detail in this chapter.
- Method 2 is the initial transformational model we have been promoting in this book based on the BASICS® model and followed up with PDCA.
- Method 3, we believe, should be the true implementation goal of a Lean culture. This is where 80% or more of the ideas are generated from the floor every day and implemented by the team leader and/or group leader/supervisor.
- Method 4 is composed of high-level chartered teams looking at benchmarking the rest of the world and constantly assessing the overall continuous improvement strategies for the company.

DOI: 10.4324/9781003185802-1

Phases

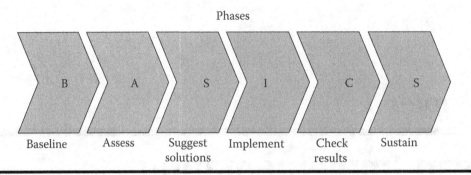

Baseline — Assess — Suggest solutions — Implement — Check results — Sustain

Figure 1.1 BASICS® model.

Table 1.1 Lean Implementation Methodologies—Differences in Kaizen Approaches

	Method 1	*Method 2*	*Method 3*	*Method 4*
Type	*Point Kaizen Events*	*BASICS Lean® Implementation*	*Toyota's Pure Kaizen Philosophy*	*Toyota's Great Idea (GI) Club*
% Consultants utilize for initial implementation	95% of consultants use today for batch to flow conversions with 50% sustain rate	>5% of consultants today use for batch to flow conversions with a 95% sustain rate	Less than 20% of consultants use this as the primary implementation Lean Culture goal	Less than 1% use this Toyota methodology
How implemented	Cross functional teams and KPO office	Value stream teams using BASICS® model	Ideas flow from the floor and implemented by the team, led by the team and group leaders	Board/ executive level chartered strategic kaizen teams
Best used for	Best used for initial sell/ sustain	Best used for batch to flow conversions	Primary vehicle for CI system	Current events continuous learning
How Toyota uses it	Toyota's uses 10% kaizen events for sustaining	Toyota's original implementation approach 100%	80% of Toyota's ideas come from the floor	10% of Toyota Ideas come from GI club
Timeline	1 line—7 kaizens 2 years	1 Line— implementation avg. 8–12 weeks	Ongoing—this is the goal! CEO & HR should own	Ongoing—this is the goal! CEO & Board should own

Source: BIG Archives.

Method 1: Point Kaizen Events

Over the many years we have been implementing Lean principles, we have identified the following approaches listed above used throughout the industry today. Most companies and 95% of consultants have been using method 1 to convert from batch to Lean. Most of their training material and certifications are developed around this point kaizen approach. A traditional point kaizen event requires a team of 6–8 people dedicated for a week, with the first day being training, the next 3 days on the floor or in the office making changes, and the last day ending in a report out and celebration. We have found that kaizen events can range from 1-hour events to the typical 5 days but sometimes longer, although this is rare. Point kaizen events require very specific, focused, realistic goals that can be accomplished within the event's time horizon. These are typically sold by consultants as ready-fire-aim events and contain the same day of training for each point kaizen event forever. Ready-fire-aim means you implement the changes without any or minimal planning. This is a just do it approach, which can easily result in chaos. There is just enough time to blow up current state and no time to complete future state. The perception is the event was done to rather than with the employees.

Why Is the Point Kaizen Approach So Prevalent?

Point kaizen events are great marketing tools for consultants and are easy to sell to management and companies. They are quick and easy and only need 4–6 people dedicated for 1 week. It is amazing what a group of dedicated, smart, talented, and knowledgeable people can accomplish in a 3–5-day time frame. Kaizen consultants encourage the team to stay up very late on Thursday night to put the presentation together. Then the team reports their successes to the senior leadership on Friday morning. Included in the team reports are the reductions in cycle time, distance traveled, work in process (WIP), and space. The management then salivates over these ready-fire-aim improvements and schedules more events. Not only do the point kaizen events or blitzes become a very easy sell but it is also easy to quickly train new consultants in this approach. The drawback is they are only trained in the approach itself and not the full blown Toyota Production System (TPS) management system.

Hit and Miss Method

This method was deployed by one of the big eight accounting firms and consists of assembling a team, maybe providing some basic Lean training for half day, or so, and then sending the team to the floor to make an improvement. There is no formal data collected, and participants make observations and pick one idea to improve. When the improvement is made, everyone celebrates the success and is then sent out to make another improvement until the week is over. This is a ready-fire-aim approach.

Kaizen Event Dilemma

> At Company X, we were told the sheet metal supervisor had purchased new setup reduction tooling with a plan to cut the internal setup time by 80%. He wanted to know when the company was going to have a kaizen event so he could implement the improvement! What's wrong with this picture?

Potential Pitfalls of the Traditional Point Kaizen Approach

We estimate 95% of consultants use point kaizen events today to implement Lean. The comments below are based on my past experience with AllidSignal and other companies we have toured over last 30 years. We spent 2 years implementing kaizen events getting very little to the bottom line.

A pitfall of kaizen events is that the dedicated teams are only put together for a week and there is no one left to follow up on the 30-day action list. The company typically assigns the list to the area supervisor, but this doesn't work either as the supervisor is too busy fighting day-to-day problems and was not part of the initial Lean training and cannot connect the dots and their role as a Lean leader. As a result, many point kaizen events don't sustain the improvement. The other problem of using point kaizen events as an implementation strategy is there is only so much the team can accomplish in the scope of a 1-week event. Point kaizen events are designed to make small and large improvements within the week and, by themselves, rarely lead to organizational cultural transformations.

On larger lines, only a small part of a line can be attacked in a point kaizen event. Therefore, if you don't target a process that is on the critical path, the results don't go to the bottom line. In addition, the old processes still exist. In many cases, you are still batching into and out of the improved area. This also makes it difficult to sustain because there is limited time and leadership commitment to develop concurrently the sustainable systems required to be successful from an enterprise perspective. We often hear comments from management and employees like:

- "Our results are not getting to the bottom line…."
- "We are having trouble sustaining the improvements…."
- "We are not able to complete our kaizen newspapers and 30-day lists…."
- "I can't put that many people in the kaizen promotion office or run all the events required based on 1 event per 100 persons in the company."

These comments were common. Weekly events were very successful in the short term but difficult to sustain in the long term or even the week after the event. Consultants often describe these results as normal. We were also told by our point kaizen event consultants that we may end up changing the layout up to 10 times a year, and that was normal because each event is looking at a different piece of the process. The important thing was to just go out and change something; don't study it, just do it.

Suppose you are a manager and just imagine we come to you and say, we are going to do a point kaizen event in your area this week. We are going to change your whole process design around and it may or may not work when we get done; but this is normal. This is called ready-fire-aim. Ready-fire-aim means we don't need to study or plan for it; after all, it just might work.

Consultants kept telling us it is not unusual to take three steps forward and two steps back. Doesn't this type of logic sound absurd? Yet, we have all embraced this type of approach with traditional point kaizen events for over 20 years. Sound management techniques and training typically would reject and, at least, discourage this type of thought and approach. When we explain this approach during our point kaizen event training sessions, it is often met, at first, with disbelief and amazement; however, owing to the reputation of kaizen consultants and films showing great results, we are often misled to believe this panacea exists and our sound judgment should be replaced with a just do it philosophy. The films do not show where these efforts fail and the potential costs of failure.

We believe, as a stand-alone improvement philosophy, that the point kaizen approach to leaning out entire companies is dangerous not only to American but also to global manufacturing, health care, and service industries. If the point kaizen event approach is not completely understood, or if it is implemented by poorly trained consultants internal or external, it can result in the opposite of the desired effect. It then becomes a futile effort, or a very expensive yet failed proposition.

We believe many companies have failed and scrapped Lean initiatives owing to their experiences with the traditional point kaizen event approach. We have often heard, "Oh, yeah, we tried that Lean stuff before and it won't work here!" It then makes it twice as difficult to try to implement the next time. We estimate over 40% of companies have tried and failed using solely this approach.

This does not mean the point kaizen approach cannot work. A fundamental cornerstone of Lean employs a scientific approach called PDCA not only for improvements but also for coaching and mentoring. This provides for both a planning and execution phase to obtain desired results. Professor James Bond states, "At Toyota they were structured similar to a kaizen event but did follow the ready aim fire approach albeit not as structured".

The point kaizen event approach was later popularized by a Japanese global consulting group in 1987 and an American spin off company. They turned the ready-aim-fire approach into the ready-fire-aim approach. For many years during this process, some companies have had much success with this approach, as outlined in the book by Art Byrne and Jim Womack, Lean Thinking and The Lean Turnaround: How Business Leaders Use Lean Principles to Create Value and Transform Their Company, McGraw-Hill, 2012. However, this approach was strategically implemented companywide, with an overarching plan and led by the CEO (leading and participating in events) along with their management team and ongoing outside consulting group over many years.

Most companies, however, do not keep the consultants engaged that long, or the CEO does not lead or participate in the events. When the efforts fail, most companies end up modifying the approach over time because it is not working for them. Like any good system, if the company receives poor training, tries to short-cut it, does not want to really lead it, and does not understand it, they cannot sustain it.

Back in its heyday in the early 1990s, this just do it approach was growing so fast that consultants were coming out of the woodwork with very little experience, sometimes with only two to four kaizen events under their belts. This led to consultants who when asked a probing question would respond with "You are not ready for that yet," which was code for —they did not have an answer.

As a comparison, good consultants, who really did have an answer, would respond with a question back to you, like "Why don't you think about it and come back to me with your ideas," and then they would discuss it with you. These consultants challenged their clients to begin to think and to come up with their own solutions, which could then be used to begin to look at things differently and at a much higher level of detail. The Association for Manufacturing Excellence (AME) was very good at encouraging this type of thinking back then.

In many companies after only four-to-seven point kaizen events, one could be deemed and certified as a Lean master! Therefore, we would like to change the nomenclature to Lean practitioner (LP). We do not know anyone who can be considered a Lean master after four to seven kaizen events. It takes years of training. Most LPs who have been practicing all their lives do not consider themselves Lean masters. It is to some extent an impossible title to achieve as we are always learning how much there still is to learn. As LPs we never stop learning. Not only are we teachers but we are students as well. We strive for perfection, which is always just out of our reach. Like any effort that grows too fast too quickly, this point kaizen approach led to some very poor consulting experiences for many companies and does not necessarily lead to a pure kaizen culture. As a side note, we have never come across the term "kaizen event" in any Toyota literature; it is always just "kaizen." As with any kaizen consideration, the implementation is made based on a collaborative approach based on consensus following the PDCA cycle to implement any kaizen. If a kaizen is to be implemented on the line, all stakeholders are consulted before any action is taken, to prevent obstacles, which might occur in either upstream or downstream processes.

Disadvantages of Point Kaizen Events Used for First-Time Implementation

1. Many kaizen events succumb to the combat 2-week rule—something improves and goes strong for 2 weeks—then goes away (flavor of the month perception by those in the organization).
2. The term, event, in and of itself does not signify continuous improvement, and the typical point kaizen event approach is ready-fire-aim, not ready-aim-fire. The point kaizen event must be scoped to something that can be accomplished in a week (really three working days), but, typically, companies try to tackle too much at once. They tend to suboptimize processes because only so much can be accomplished in a week. Sometimes, this is not enough time to make it work or for staff to understand or learn the new way. Staff members are typically not trained well in new procedures, and many times, the new procedures are poorly documented, if at all. The supervisor, if they do get it up and running and then find they have someone out sick, doesn't know what to do. The point kaizen event process has introduced so much variation to some areas that they have been shut down for days, weeks, or even months after a poorly planned event. Area staff are left with the results of a kaizen event (and in some cases, all the mess), but no support to clean it up. Many times, in people's haste to do it or make changes; we find safety, ergonomic, and local and state regulations are violated.
3. They are difficult to roll out as an overall system strategy. They are a slow approach and don't work well for initial batch to one-piece flow conversions. Changes to a system are not normally planned well, and opportunities exist for many unintended consequences after the team leaves (both upstream and downstream). During an event, there is only time to work on a piece of the process; we don't have time to take a step back to look at the whole process, that is, to look at the big picture. We found with point kaizen events, TQ teams, or Grass Roots Teams, sometimes we spent a week trying to improve a process; but had we looked at it from a system view, the process could have been eliminated. Instead, we wasted valuable time trying to improve it.
4. Most point kaizen events are based on what management thinks are the problems but have not collected data to know for sure. There are normally no audit systems to follow up.
5. Teams get in line for events, delaying improvements. Earlier we spoke of the machine shop supervisor who came to me and said, "I bought all the quick-change tooling we need for this one machine but I can't get on the kaizen event calendar to get it installed!"
6. There is normally not enough time to get a standard work in place and sustain it, and the supervisor doesn't know how to run it. Many companies form kaizen promotion offices. These contain the trainers for point kaizen events and people freed up as part of the past point kaizen events. While, in concept, the kaizen promotion office makes sense, they are seldom successful and become easy targets for layoffs. In addition, since kaizen trainers are

dedicated, they end up spending a lot of time in the office instead of on the floor making improvements or training line management how to lead events.

7. Kaizen events feed the CEO's desire for quick returns for little investment. They tend to turn into Friday shows for management and free lunch for the team, and a checkmark that the kaizen event has been completed for corporate.

8. Some companies are measured on the number of kaizen events instead of the continuous improvement measures they should be monitoring.

9. Some companies have initiativitis. They try to implement different pieces of the Toyota process system (TPS) separately. Over several years, a Fortune 100 company had launched separate initiatives with five S, focused factories, Kanbans, process flows (TQ speed), and process and wall mapping, not to mention the 4 days of TQ tools training, facilitator training, point kaizen events, etc. But they never put all the tools together and integrated them into a Lean culture. As a result, the improvements became difficult to sustain and most people figured they could just wait it out.

10. Many times traditional reward systems are not changed to support continuous improvement so it becomes difficult to sustain.

11. In many cases, the kaizen event approach typically makes one more dependent on consultants. Once management sees the first report out and the enthusiasm of the team, they are hooked. They immediately want to roll out more events. This is reinforced by the notion we only need to dedicate a team for a week to get great results. The consultants provide 1 day of the same training for every event, which is not enough to learn Lean or understand the philosophy behind it. Therefore, the teams become dependent on the consultants' knowledge or sometimes lack of knowledge. Since the consultants encourage the creation of a kaizen promotion office to coordinate the events and the company does not have enough trained personnel, the consultant can typically expect 1–2 years' worth of engagement.

Lesson Learned: Measuring the number of kaizen events can be a very misleading metric. The overall goal of any implementation system should be to expose the problems/waste remaining in the system.

Japan Benchmarking Trip

In 1996, I was invited along with others in AlliedSignal to attend a point kaizen event in Japan. We were also told we would see several world-class companies, including Toyota. The Japanese consulting sensei's, who were former Toyota employees, provided their day of training, which was translated to us. The trainer was great, although 90% of the training was what we already received on every other first day of the 5-day kaizen event training by their American consulting company. We spent three days working in Hitachi, a Japanese electronics surface mount technology (SMT) circuit board plant. To a novice, this Japan trip is phenomenal and can provide much needed paradigm shifts for traditional managers. Our Japanese sensei said, "Go find improvements, bring them back to us and we will implement them." When we asked if we could video, we were told "no time for videotape... go do..."

Please keep in mind we had over 10–12 years of Lean experience by this time, and our company back home was also an SMT and thru-hole electronics board manufacturer. As usual, Tuesday to Thursday, we found many opportunities for improvements. After talking with our sponsor consultant guides, we determined that any idea we thought of during our visit to Hitachi that Hitachi had already been thought of would be implemented quickly. If a tool or fixture was needed, it would appear overnight; however, when one of my colleagues came up with a modification to a machine which Hitachi had not thought of, we were told they had to study it first. On Wednesday morning, we spent several hours designing a new layout for their surface mount circuit board line. Once again, we were told they would have to study it first. We asked what happened to just go do it? Please keep in mind we had made similar equipment moves in our own surface mount plant overnight, so it was an achievable suggestion. Then our sensei consultant wanted us to stay up until midnight on Thursday when we had already finished our presentation by 8:00 p.m. We think this was just so they could say we stayed up late on Thursday night to do our presentation. The next surprise was that our sponsor wanted us to put results in our report that we did not achieve. We refused and said if they really wanted to do that then they could deliver the report. This cemented for me that ready-fire-aim approach was primarily designed to get Americans, Europeans, and other countries to just start making improvements. If this was the strategy, it worked, and they are still very successful with the point kaizen approach. However, it also taught me the value of the ready-aim-fire approach and that this was the approach which was really used by these former Toyota consultants when it came to applying Lean to their hometown plants.

During my 2 years on AME's Champions Club, the subject of kaizen blitzes came up during one of our meetings. Everyone at the table had just presented improvements they had done at their plants. They all had similar experiences with point kaizen events as we had at my old company and acknowledged they were not the right tool to convert an entire factory from batch to Lean. But kaizen blitzes sell and get companies involved, get initial results, and motivate them to start up Lean programs. There was no simple alternative, so everyone agreed to stay with kaizen blitzes because something was better than nothing.

Lesson Learned: The first lesson learned was to study new improvement ideas versus just doing them. Ready-fire-aim is a good way to get the management to do something and to start changing, but the point kaizen approach has a poor chance for true success as a stand-alone strategy unless the consultants stay with you for the many years required to give you all the pieces. A new approach is needed other than point kaizen events if the United States or any other country is going to be truly successful at sustaining Lean. Once the consultants leave, most companies revise their point kaizen event approach and kaizen promotion office because of the poor sustaining issue and lack of getting to the bottom line. I still hear the same complaints today from manufacturing and service line companies. The BASICS Lean® approach is the answer, but it takes time and resolve to implement because it is a ready-aim-fire approach and requires a significant commitment up front of project and training resources.

With all these negative comments, one might think we are against point kaizen events; however, we are not! We believe point kaizen events, if performed the right way, have their place and should be a part of your overall improvement strategy, but not your entire improvement strategy. We believe point kaizen events should be utilized as a management introduction to continuous improvement, to get people on board with Lean, and can be extremely beneficial as one of the tools for sustaining Lean to augment the continuous improvement program to foster the Lean cultural transformation.

Once the area has been converted to flow using the BASICS® model, we utilize method 1, but use the BASICS® point kaizen method of sustaining. This methodology follows the BASICS®

model with a ready-aim-fire approach. We also use point kaizen to introduce a new company to the power of what a dedicated team can accomplish in a week.

We will discuss the pros and cons of this as an approach to convert batch to flow. What took seven kaizen events and two years at one company to implement flow on one line using just traditional ready fire aim kaizen events, was surpassed at the same company using the BASICS Lean® approach during a one, 6-week system kaizen implementation (using method 2), by looking at the entire product line from beginning to end. It is a very powerful system. After that we used the BASICS® Point kaizen approach to continue ongoing iterations of improvement.

The traditional point kaizen approach seldom leads to method 3, which is the overall goal of a Lean culture, whereas as method 2, the BASICS® model leads directly to methods 3 and 4.

Advantages/Results of BASICS® Kaizen Events

■ If properly scoped and chartered with the right expectations and utilizing the BASICS® approach (i.e., analyze the product, operator, setup), kaizen events can provide great results, and significant changes can be accomplished in a very short time frame. We have completely changed entire layouts overnight.
■ More than 50% productivity and space improvements can be made within the specific area being targeted.
■ Kaizen events promote organizational team building.
■ Kaizen events offer visibility to the senior leadership team.
■ Kaizen events showcase the power of dedicated cross-functional teams to make quick changes, which help break down functional barriers.
■ Kaizen events can be a good training and sustaining tool to help develop a continuous learning organization.
■ We find that there are many projects that lend themselves to the kaizen event approach. Some of these are as follows:
  – Setup/changeover reductions
  – 5S
  – Poka yoke
  – Total productive maintenance (TPM) pilot
  – Visual displays or controls
  – Smaller area layout improvements
  – Processes that can be improved within the weeks' time frame, trained employees, and the supervisor leaving with a complete standard work package

To utilize point kaizen events as an overall implementation approach, there must be a cohesive strategy with multiple sequential events in one area and a ready-aim-fire approach. Toyota did not get Lean doing point kaizen events. Point kaizen events came much later, after the company was converted to flow. We have developed a new, revised kaizen approach to convert the point kaizen event to more of a ready-aim-fire style event with training tailored to the event. We recommend against generating a 30-day list, as it has been our experience that these are seldom followed up unless the proper resources are dedicated and management has the discipline to bring the outstanding items to closure.

Our revised kaizen approach is composed of the following:

- Senior leaders should lead the event and the training.
- Charter the team properly.
- State the target improvement and expectations up front.
- Focus the team and invest in the right team members and resources.
- The kaizen team must be dedicated during the event.
- Give the team priority over resources, especially maintenance.
- Act on fact, use the BASICS® tools, video, and utilize a ready-aim-fire approach.
- Provide the necessary training tailored to the event for all participants.
- Follow up at the end of each day with the team champion.
- Make sure all changes are documented in the standard work prior to the end of the event.
- Make sure changes are communicated to the product team ahead of time and secure their buy-in.
- Implement the changes.
- Report out to the senior leadership team at the end of the week's event.
- Make sure that any remaining action items are turned over as recommendations to the area or functions responsible.
- Have a follow-up meeting with the management to ensure all actions are closed out.
- Have a follow-up audit or review at 1-week or 1-month intervals (as needed) to ensure the improvements in the area are sustaining.

Point Kaizen Event Best Practices

- The facilitator must have a good working knowledge of the Lean principles and how to apply them.
- The team leader (or process owner) should lead the event.
- The active steering committee (leadership team) should be guiding the events and ensuring continuity.
- Maintain patience with the culture change and work toward self-sufficiency.
- Communicate a sense of urgency following the event with follow-up and removing ongoing barriers.
- Maintain a no layoff policy due to continuous improvement.
- Develop a matrix of people trained and participating in events.
- Managers must be change agents.

Method 2

Demand Flow Technology (DFT)

DFT was taught by the Worldwide Flow College in Denver, Colorado, and described in a book called Quantum Leap[1] by John R. Costanza. DFT was a ready-aim-fire approach. It involved following the product, following the operator, creating a sequence of events that merges the two together, and then developing a layout. The layouts are usually characterized by a middle conveyor line fed by individual branch conveyor lines. The main unit is assembled down the middle as sub-assemblies are completed on the branch lines (see Figure 1.2). These are normally sit-down lines

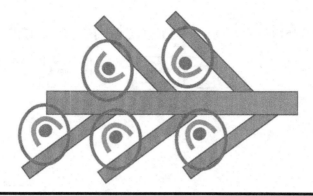

Figure 1.2   DFT layout.

with a focus on station balancing. The layouts are typically designed to create isolated islands on the branches where work cannot be flexed (see Figure 1.3). The lines are timed but are typically not balanced and contain excess WIP or idle time.

Each of these implementation methodologies will realize improved results. It is the degree of result realized that makes the big difference.

■ Point kaizen events and the hit and miss method generally have 50% or less chances of sustaining. When you are working on a piece of an area and batching into it and out of it, it becomes difficult to sustain.
■ The DFT process has a good chance of sustaining but is limited on making additional improvements based on the layouts.
■ The BASICS® approach has the best chance of sustaining as the entire product line or machining area is reviewed and analyzed versus just a piece of an area.

Figure 1.3   Isolated islands designed into the layout.

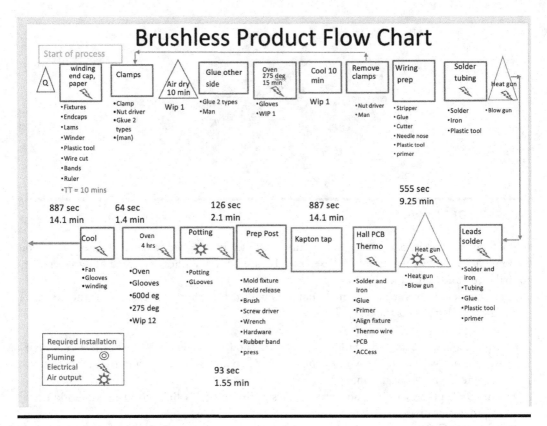

Figure 1.4   Process block diagram.

The BASICS® Implementation Model

This process, described in this book series, involves following the product and the operator and then analyzing any setups or changeovers for the overall value stream. We create a block diagram (see Figure 1.4) where the product flow is aligned such that the required assembling or machining the part is in order of assembly. Then we create the layout with a focus on baton zone balancing versus station balancing. This is structured, hierarchical, ready-aim-fire approach with some layout advantages over the DFT approach. It is like DFT but has subtle differences, particularly in the order of the steps along with the layout and line balancing, which differentiate the approach.

The BASICS® Implementation Model

For organizations serious about converting their old batch-driven systems to Lean, which could represent processes that would have significant challenges due to batch-type processing such as Biotech, FDA, and government agencies, we recommend the larger initial transformation approach or what we define as the BASICS Lean® implementation approach. This approach, which is aligned with PDCA, reviews the overall process from beginning to end and has proved sustainable across many companies worldwide. There are six phases that follow the simple acronym BASICS®. Each letter represents the main theme for the activities that occur in its phase: baseline, assess, suggest solutions, improve, check, and sustain. The first three letters equate to the P in PDCA, which stands for plan. The planning phase includes gathering the background and current condition, and developing a hypothesis.

Many organizations deploying both Lean and Six Sigma have standardized their improvement road map to the acronym DMAIC, which stands for define, measure, analyze, improve, and control. It works well for organizations implementing Six Sigma tools; however, it can be very confusing as the Lean tools overlap many of the DMAIC phases. We have found that remembering the acronym DMAIC and what each letter stands for can be challenging for some. We have opted for a more simplistic model, hoping that it may be easier for everyone to follow and remember as they go through the activities and steps. Within each of the six phases, we have highlighted, by category, what one may have to communicate and deliver while moving from phase to phase. The BASICS® model contains total quality (TQ), Lean, and Six Sigma tools. The overarching categories under each of the BASICS® phase are as follows.

The BASICS Lean® implementation approach follows the PDCA problem-solving model with a target condition of one-piece balanced synchronized flow regardless of the environments outlined earlier. It is based 50% on the principles of scientific management, developed primarily by Frank Gilbreth and Frederick Taylor and taught by Dr. Shigeo Shingo, and 50% on respect for people and change management, which is discussed throughout the book. This approach is utilized to convert processes from batch production to one-piece flow. It was originally designed by Toyota to work in the low-volume high-mix shop, but it also works well in low-volume low-mix, high-volume low-mix, or high-volume high-mix environments. Listed in the following text is a summary of the BASICS® steps to Lean implementation with the PDCA points noted. Lean is a combination of training, tools, and supervision to harness a new culture.

Pre-Implementation (PLAN)

- Prepare for the company rollout—generally done after the first pilot.
- Determine and scope the initial project.
- Charter the team.

Start of Implementation Team: BASICS® (B)

BASICS®: B (Baseline)

- Baseline metrics:
  - Calculate the customer demand
  - Calculate the takt time (TT)
  - Calculate the factory demand
  - Calculate the current productivity, that is, number of worked labor hours (direct and indirect) divided by number of units produced or stocked
- Video and photos:
  - Pan the area with the video camera
  - Take pictures of the area. Note: You can never take enough pictures!
- Value stream mapping (VSM) the process (optional, if applicable)
- Determine the customer demand and TT
- Calculate the current state cycle times

BASICS®: A (Assess/Analyze)

- PFA—become the product:
  - Video or walk the process
  - Current state analysis
  - Use the omits process
  - Create the new process flow
- Group tech analysis
- Full work analysis (FWA) of the operator/job breakdown sheet:
  - Video the process
  - Review the video with the operators
  - Complete the FWA sheet noting tools and parts used/or ten cycles for machining
  - Use the omits process
  - Develop the new process
  - Line balancing
  - Cross-training matrix
- Changeover analysis
- Ten-cycle analysis where applicable

BASICS®: S (Suggest Solutions)

- Block diagram:
  - Incorporate the new process flow analysis (PFA) process
  - Add the times from the workflow analysis (WFA)
  - Determine the standard WIP (SWIP) locations (from PFA)
  - Calculate the SWIP quantity from the WFA
- Layout planning:
  - Layout in computer-aided drawing (CAD); tape out on floor or cardboard mock-up
  - Workstation design
  - Fit up/flexible utilities
  - Make and approve recommendations
  - Create the optimal layout for the process
  - Design the workstations including parts and tools in-sequence of assembly
- Create and post standard work for the supervisor, create job breakdown standard work and training videos for the operators
- Determine the capacity and labor requirements
- Operator training—Legos
- Train the staff in the new process

BASICS®: I (Implement)

- Implement the new process—use pilots:
  - Setup the order staging rack
  - Setup the line
  - Setup the lineside materials
  - Setup the lineside warehouse (supermarket)
  - Setup the workstations

- – Create a day-by-hour chart with targets/actuals
- – Initial 5S
- – Initial visual displays
- – Create the Lean line package
- – Tie day by hour to safety, +QDIP
- – Take video and photos after
- – Pan the area with the video camera
- – Take before and after pictures of the area
- ■ Implement the Lean metrics
- ■ Incorporate the 5S and visual controls
- ■ Mistake the proof and TPM the process
- ■ Develop accountability systems to sustain activity/Lean initiative

BASICS®: C (Check)

- ■ Lean layered audits including senior leadership, +QDIP & huddles, and sustainability boards
- ■ Daily management
- ■ Visual management
- ■ Heijunka scheduling
- ■ Mistake proofing
- ■ TPM
- ■ Lean accounting

BASICS®: S (Sustain)

- ■ Kaizen, kaizen, kaizen.
- ■ Leadership development path
- ■ Daily suggestions implemented from the floor are part of the culture
- ■ PDCA cycles—over and repeatedly
- ■ Make sure updating standard work becomes part of the quality system

Post-Implementation: Other Necessary Lean Components

- ■ Lean materials:
  - – Lineside materials—two-bin system (see Figure 1.5) or set pallet system (SPS)
  - – Warehouse bins and shelf locations as needed and labeled
  - – Create the plan for every part (PFEP)
  - – Implement a milk run system
  - – Create a pull system from finished goods (FG) to the line and from the line to subassembly process or supplier
  - – Implement a vendor-managed inventory (VMI) system at the line
- ■ Work order/backlog planning status versus new cell capacity
- ■ Baton zone line balancing
- ■ Formalized line balancing/flexing
- ■ Cross-training
- ■ Visual management

Figure 1.5 Two-bin systems with standard work posted above the line.

- Six S the line and put six S sustainability boards in place
- Visual controls in place (andon lights, SWIP locators)
- Convert order staging to heijunka and past due rack
- Day by hour in place with a plan
- Month by day in place and tied to productivity
- Key performance indicators (KPIs) up and current
- Quick changeover setup flexibility
- Group technology:
  - Period batch
  - Location batch
  - Segmented batch
- Changeover analysis and implementation
- Lean management systems:
  - Run a QDIP meeting properly
  - A3
  - Assist in implementing Hoshin planning (optional)
  - Quality—zero defects
    - Control plan implementation (see Table 1.2):
    - Mistake proofing—implement a mistake proofing project.
  - Conduct six S, standard work, heijunka, and Lean line audits.
  - Implement a supply chain materials project.
  - Implement a sequenced material delivery system with a supplier (i.e., build to order—rotary)
  - Follow up on outstanding action items.

Table 1.2   Control Plan Example

Critical Process Step	Target Result	Measurement Techniques	Process Control Method	Verification/ Out-of-Control Action Plan
Machine settings	Amplitude = 0.070″ Clamp pressure = 20 psi Weld time = 1.08 seconds Hold time = 6 seconds	Branson Welder gauges and digital readouts: 1. Air pressure gauge 2. Analog gauge 3. F(3) digital readout in 0.001 units 4. F(2) digital readout in 0.01 sec units	Daily check of settings	Determination of exposure and severity of risk by burst testing multiple units welded w/mig welder. (sample pulled from lot of exposed material)
Weld	Welded parts without leaks and w/burst strengths in excess of 12 psi	1. Leak test 2. Vacuum chamber test	100% leak test 100% vacuum chamber	np-chart w/50 unit subgroup (UCL = 6 leaks) out of control-line stops for root cause analysis
Material	Ensure quality of raw plastic	Burst test	Preproduction run sample 100% burst tested	X-bar and R chart sub grouped on supplier lot (mean burst strength shift disqualifies supplier lot and necessitates corrective action)

Source: BIG Archives.

- TPM:
  - Create a TPM system in a plant
  - Audit the TPM system for compliance
- Lean office:
  - Implement Lean in the office environment

Case Study: The Grand Experiment: BASICS® Model versus the Traditional Point Kaizen

We ran an experiment at one of our clients in South Carolina. This client had dabbled with Lean for last 10 years. The company thought they were far down the Lean path. They had their own training materials and even their own Kanban and safety stock formulas contained within a 70 plus-page PowerPoint presentation. Their sites were measured on the number of kaizen events they held each year. Each plant we visited had all the trappings of Lean, and also the graveyards of failed kaizen events. They had what they called Lean cells, but very few really were very Lean and most were what we might today call Lean lite where there was some semblance of flow but still mostly batching within the Lean cell.

The plant manager (who had some training from a global Japanese consulting group) kicked off our event by setting expectations and goals for the team which was going to work on the assembly cell(s) he wanted us to tackle. He wrote down on the whiteboard the following:

1. 50% increase in productivity
2. 50% reduction in inventory
3. Reduction in floor space

He explained he thought there was an opportunity to combine two of their assembly cells and thought we should work on that as well during the week. He also showed us a new table he acquired that could be manually height adjusted and suggested we figure out a way to incorporate it into our ideas if it made sense. The plant manager had an automotive background and was aware of what could be accomplished and had conducted 20 hours of Lean training with every employee over his first year there. He assembled a great team with the engineering, materials, and manufacturing managers (his senior leadership team), along with the assembly manager and two operators that worked in assembly. I thought the goals were great but throwing a solution out such as combining the two cells was an issue because there was no data behind the suggestion as well as its being very ambitious for people who were never really exposed to problem-solving or the Lean approach we use in this book. Our experiment was to run the first day as a traditional kaizen event. In our introductions, we found out that each person had participated in the past in a kaizen event, if not at this company, at a past company, and all were familiar with the process. We ran the first day as a typical point kaizen event and asked the team to go out into the cell and observe the product flow and operators and describe what they thought they could improve that would yield 50% improvement in productivity and inventory. They were all provided key observations sheets to document what they observed. After an hour or so, they came back to the conference room with what they thought was an impressive list—see the following text:

- Ergonomic issue—way spanner wrench.
- Label maker—how many machines do we need?
- Tables—at the wrong ergonomic height.
- The position of the vice on the bench is not operator-friendly.
- A two-bin system needs to be put in place.
- Testing—could be improved by changing equipment (very minor cost).
- We should preassemble parts before the final assembly line.

Once the team presented their list of improvements, I asked them if they thought they could achieve the 50% improvement challenge (reduce operators from 4 to 3) from the plant manager. They all said absolutely. It is interesting to note that even though we had two operators on our team, no one bothered to ask them or the operators in the cell what problems or ideas they had. We then brought in the operators from the cell and asked them what they thought the problems were and what they would do to get the improvement outlined by the plant manager. They proceeded to rattle off fifteen problems they faced all the time, every day, so fast the assembly manager couldn't write them down fast enough. Once we had that list, I asked everyone again if they really thought we could get to 50% improvement in productivity and asked how long it would take. It was obvious many of the items were beyond the team's initial control and were not quick fixes (see the following):

1. Sometimes, Z numbers and S numbers and cover sheets don't come with work order packets.
2. 8 to 4:30 normal hours—we work on late parts first and then work on the day's stuff.
3. If they don't get it out, they get a red on the quality, delivery, inventory, and productivity (QDIP) board.
4. Plating builds up in the mounts, which prevents screws from getting in.
5. The supplier's parts are running out (VMI), but the supplier doesn't change the bin sizes like he is supposed to.
6. The VMI supplier must come into the cell to scan the parts and is in our way. Maybe he should do it after hours.
7. The warehouse person brings the inventory and sets it outside the cell, and we must stop to go get our own material.
8. When we run out of a screw used in the parts, we must search all the cells to find it and then steal some. Some cells don't have the bins of screws needed in the cell to build it.
9. We need quick connects and disconnects for testing.
10. Everybody has a stash of material just in case we run out.
11. Out of standard parts—min/max, vendor, or both.
12. We are always working on something but not necessarily the work on that day—normally future or late parts.
13. We need an automatic robot or assembler.
14. We need a designated spot for special tooling, maybe a rack on the outside, or we can keep it in a black box in the cell.
15. Some parts don't go through inspection. They were certified suppliers in the past. We have an approved supplier list but not a list of dock to floor suppliers.
16. The supplier has open purchase orders (POs) but can't upload all items into one big blanket PO. We must pay them whenever they deliver.
17. We need to lock up tools in drawer toolboxes.

They were all convinced, for sure, that with this new list, they would meet the 50% goal. We asked them to review the list and pick out what items they could complete that afternoon. They circled several of them. We asked them to go implement the items on the list. They left very excited and proceeded to make the changes.

Kaizen improvements implemented after the first day were as follows:

■ Lowered the assembly table.
■ The air pressure was fixed.

■ A better spanner wrench was introduced.
■ A new blowout nozzle was added.
■ Initial 5S of assembly tables.

Once the improvements were in place, we asked them to do a pilot run and see how the new improvements worked. We asked them at the end of the pilot run (over 10 cycles) how they thought they did. All but one team member was confident they had beaten the 50% improvement goal. We all went back to the room to review the film of the process.

Result: To their complete surprise, with all the improvements they made, it took the operator 18 seconds longer to assemble the parts. It resulted in an increase in total labor time (TLT) from 7 minutes 14 seconds to 7 minutes 32 seconds but was much better ergonomically for the operator. Why? Because generally just throwing solutions at a "results focused" problem creates variation and confusion. Filling out time observation sheets can be misleading because we don't truly understand what the operator is doing and how much work is required versus unnecessary. The process was better ergonomically but did nothing to truly make the operator's job easier. This shoot from the hip problem-solving is common. If we had not made the team baseline their metrics prior to starting the event, they would have thought and claimed they made a significant improvement with no data to back it up.

We then proceeded to use the BASICS® model approach during the remaining part of the week. After conducting 1/2 day of training the team performed the process flow analysis (PFA-following the product), we reduced the product steps in the process from 89 to 53 or a 40% reduction. We reduced the storage overall from 93% to 36% and increased the process time (both value-added [VA] and non-value-added [NVA]) from 2% to 45%. We drew a new point-to-point diagram. We analyzed the operator using the workflow analysis (WFA) tool and reduced the number of operator steps from 150 to 91 and cut the TLT from 432 to 188 seconds or 3.1 minutes (thus beating our 50% target by 6%). We discovered that there was a part preassembled outside the cell and then put in the stock room only to be reissued with the kit for the final assembly. We determined (with a couple of quick and cheap assembly table modifications) how to incorporate that product into the cell. This eliminated the preassembly (that was sometimes incorrectly built but not discovered until final assembly—where the whole batch was bad). We created the future state PFA and WFA and a new block diagram incorporating the subassembly, redesigned layout, and workstations. We were able to eliminate 8 of the 26 steps it took previously to put this preassembled (subassembly) part together and cut its time from 115 seconds TLT to 62 seconds. When we add the 62 seconds for this new assembly to the 188 seconds for the final assembly, we get 250 seconds versus 603 seconds prior to Lean (not including the time it took to package it up, take it to the stockroom, stock it, and issue it for final assembly). The improvement now was from 603 seconds to 250 seconds or a 58.5% improvement including the addition of the previous preassembled subassembly, and the correlating reduction in stockroom labor. The operator spaghetti diagram prior to Lean lived up to its name. In addition to the other lists of improvements from the kaizen event the first day, we added over 22 more ideas for improvement just from watching the videos. Listed below are some of the improvements made during the BASICS® approach:

- Downsized tool.
- Tilted grease can.
- Experimented with positioning of parts.
- Removed the inspection/clean table.
- Relocated label maker and moved cleaning to an in-line process based on PFA.
- Implemented short-term preprinting of labels by water spider—still needed a long-term plan.
- Reduced paperwork—eliminated inspection sheet.
- Reviewed cure time for Loctite®.
- Trial ran subassembly on the final assembly line.
- Eliminated measuring and tape measures from the cell.
- Laid out parts and tools in a proper sequence of operations.
- Started implementation of standard work.
- Shrunk the footprint of the cell by over 50% and eliminated the subassembly cell entirely.
- Ran a new line with one and two operators.
- 5S'd cell—removed drawers and removed excess tooling.
- Lowered table to make it more ergonomic for part insertion.
- Piloted two-bin system with water spider.
- Pre-greased O-rings.
- Permanently fixed and regulated air pressure also added water collectors.
- Removed Plexiglas® from the test table.

Listed below are the lessons learned from the team:

1. Best intentions don't always yield the best results.
2. Always video to be objective.
3. Right tools at the right place—eliminate centralized tooling/shadow boards—label tools instead.
4. Act on fact—data—compare before and after.
5. The people (front line) are our best resources (they are the money makers).
6. Solve problems together—80% of ideas come from the floor.
7. Levels of waste—hidden waste.
8. Cash is king (not inventory).
9. Following the PFA steps TIPS is exhausting.
10. Batching creates lot delays.
11. NVA ÷ VA = 10:1 or worse.
12. Lots of travel time and distance.
13. Lots of storage.
14. Hard to focus on product versus process.
15. Processes overlapped.
16. Compounding lot delays.
17. Operator said it could go either way (operation step sequence) versus routing.
18. Too many steps.

19. Set up tooling in order of usage and flow of parts.
20. Organization of flow.
21. Take out steps.
22. Operator FWA exposes all waste.
23. Placing bins in front of the operator in correct order of assembly.
24. The shaft seal needs a fixture.
25. Another tool is needed.
26. Operators assemble differently—need to agree on standard work.
27. Adding sub assembly messed up flow initially, cause for readjustment, now works great.
28. Distractions cause mistakes.
29. One-piece flow works—booyah!
30. There is still more to learn and try.
31. The BASICS® approach is much better than our old point kaizen event approach!

Lesson Learned: Using the ready-aim-fire BASICS® approach that can be done in the same amount or sometimes even less time than a traditional point kaizen event, ready-fire-aim approach will always yield better and more sustainable results.

We were then able to take these improvements and transfer them the next week to four other similar but different cells! During this week, we added day-by-hour charts, conducted more 5S, created the Lean line package and standard work for the first cell, and created Lean job duties. The result was a 1300 to 847 ft² space reduction (35%), with line of sight (OBA gauge), and moved the assembly manager's desk to the cell. Ergo mats were added, two-bin systems were installed on the lines, and we added a material warehouse next to the line freeing up space in the stockroom and making all the materials visual for the water spider (that was also added).

The lessons learned for week 2 were as follows:

1. Visual aids help the operators and management to see all the proper ways to work and expose problems.
2. Hidden waste is revealed—through video review.
3. Fixtures and tools improve the ergonomic conditions and can produce better and faster results.
4. Oba gauge—the line of sight through all assembly lines helps manage the work-flow better by the supervisors. Stay in the cells and be proactive. Able to see problems.
5. VMI—screws and seals.
6. Operators have a direction (plan)—they know what is expected.
7. Water spiders—how many—training.
8. Use video whenever possible.
9. Restructure and continuous improvement are a must.

Results: We freed up 1.2 of 6.8 operators of which one was made a water spider and one temp was laid off. Units per day increased from 233 to 281 and WIP was reduced from 687 units to 5 units. The cells overall ranged from 46% to 74.4% in productivity improvement that is measured by paid minutes per unit and overtime was reduced.

After ongoing kaizens, we reduced another 11 steps and realized 19% more in additional productivity improvement.

Lesson Learned: Lean is about ongoing iterations of improvement. The Lean journey never ends!

Method 3

What is Pure Kaizen?

The word kaizen had its origin in Chinese and has the same characters (gǎi shàn). Kaizen is taken from the Japanese words kairyo suru that mean to improve. Kaizen is a Japanese word, kai means change and zen means for the better. Kaizen is interpreted in English as continuous small or incremental improvements. The terms kaizen and point kaizen are often confused or used interchangeably. Point kaizen events and "kaizen" are different concepts. Toyota's kaizen approach is based on the Toyota House, with the two pillars of just-in-time (JIT) and jidoka supporting the roof (respect for humanity) and the foundation being standard work, heijunka, visual controls, total company-wide quality control (TCWQC), and TPM. Toyota did not get to where they are today by using point kaizen events. The key factors in Toyota's system development were:

- Toyota led by Toyoda Kiichiro's "just-in-time" philosophy—producing only precise quantities of already ordered items with the absolute minimum of waste.
- Taiichi Ohno's systemic implementation of that methodology.
- Shigeo Shingo's industrial engineering training known as the "P" Course to support that methodology which was provided to thousands of Toyota employees.
- Ohno also utilized the model line concept.

For the last 60 years, Toyota used the tools explained in this book based on Taylor and Gilbreth's Scientific Management (1911), Training within Industry (TWI—1947 to Japan and 1951 to Toyota), and the PDCA problem solving and Hoshin bottom up management which was part of the CCS teachings (1949) to implement the system companywide.

Pure Kaizen

Kaizen is the concept that every employee contributes ideas and small improvements every day. Group leaders (supervisors) and managers are given time, at least 50% of their day, to implement these changes. These daily small ideas turn into thousands of suggestions and significant bottom-line profitability on an annual basis. In a recent book, Management Lessons from Taiichi Ohno, Mr. Harada states that Ohno would work to free up a person on the line and when successful would pull the "best" person from the line and then dedicate them to 100% continuous improvement of that line by soliciting all the team members' ideas.[2]

Toyota and Kaizen

Toyota has five classifications of kaizen that are based on the following:

1. Improved quality
2. Reduced costs

3. Improved safety
4. Shortened lead time
5. Improved workability

The Toyota philosophy is you always have a chance to perform kaizen, no matter what area you work in or what position you hold in the company. There are various ways of carrying out kaizen at Toyota; however, it is built into the job duties of every employee starting during their interview process.

Method 4: Great Idea Club

The great idea club is explained in the book 40 Years, 20 Million Ideas.[3,4] Toyota talks about how it utilizes information teams outside work and how it is an honor to be selected for one of these teams. These teams would research and gather information on totally new ideas and technology and report back to the chartering body. One example was when MRP was first introduced, Toyota put together a team to explore MRP and if this was something it wanted to implement and if so how to implement it.

BASICS® Lean Implementation: Are You Ready for It?

To determine if you are ready to implement Lean, answer the following questions:

■ Do you have a compelling need to change your organization?
■ Do you have a fundamental dissatisfaction with how things are done today and the waste that is prevalent in all your processes?
■ Are you willing to involve the entire organization, including your board of directors?

If so, then you are ready to read on. If not, then in the long run, you will not be successful. Remember that 40%–80% of companies do not sustain the Lean journey or fail.

How to Implement Lean Methodology

> You can do it to them or with them. We would rather do it with them than to them.

Charlie Protzman

Lean consultants were typically brought into the organization through the middle management and were not widely understood by CEOs or market analysts. Even today, if you mention Lean thinking to most people or even kaizen, they don't know what you are talking about. But if you mention Six Sigma or Green Belts or black belts, they have probably heard of the terms. So, Lean consultants had to sell Lean to both the CEO and to the shop floor worker. This has proved to be very difficult. To even get in the plant, the CEO wanted to know what the return on investment (ROI) was going to be so they could figure out how many bodies they could lay off. However, the same challenges still exist today with getting to the top management and with their blind pursuit of dollar savings. The overwhelming pressure to generate savings has also led projects to pad their dollar savings with distorted definitions of what has been saved. Over the years, more and more pieces of the Lean system have become more apparent in the over 400 books published in the subject and with the end of the New United Motor Manufacturing, Inc. (NUMMI) experiment/ JV between GM and Toyota.

Today, Lean proponents, through the auspices of leading professional organizations LEI, AME, SME, and IIE have begun to standardize on a certification process[5]; however, some of these programs while valuable still do not necessarily provide the best way for companies to implement Lean. Lean is still largely misunderstood by most companies and the public at large. As an example, when I was in Japan, we would regularly hear the word kaizen on the TV. Japan has promoted continuous improvement for years through the Japan Management Association[6] that started in 1942 and organizations like PHP,[7] which started after the Civil Communications Section (CCS) course to keep the training materials alive. Now, there is a talk of plans to relaunch the CCS course to countries like Africa and other third world countries.[8] Most US companies struggle with Lean due to the misconceptions, and some companies over the years have tried to implement different pieces of Lean but not put them all together and of course they fail. These companies brush off the Toyota precepts as we already know all this.

Should We Start Our Overall Lean Implementation with 5S?

Many companies start with a 5S initiative (see Figure 1.6). While sometimes this can be successful, most find they do not have the accountability or discipline in their organizations to sustain even the simplest area that has undergone 5S (see Figure 1.7). This can be discouraging and sometimes significantly delays moving on to other Lean initiatives or converting product lines (assembly or machining from batch to flow). They figure if they can't sustain 5S, why bother going forward

Figure 1.6　5S posted at a major grocery chain.

Figure 1.7   Need for 5S someone wrote this with their finger in the dust that was never cleaned.

(see Figure 1.8). While this has some merit, the BASICS® approach starts with the final assembly line and does 5S as part of the implementation. This gives us a chance to get all the workers in the area involved and makes sense because we can't implement standard work until we get 5S in place.

This approach has a much better chance of sustaining now that the entire product is lined up in order of assembly, and we know exactly what is needed and where it is needed by each operator. This same discussion goes for tool boards as well. Many companies will start their Lean journey off by putting all the tools in the area on a tool board, in drawers with shadow boxes, etc.

Figure 1.8   Poor 5S makes assembling difficult and shows lack of pride in the workplace.

Figure 1.9 Tools in drawers are normally a mess, unorganized and have tools not needed and needed tools not included.

(see Figure 1.9). However, the operators find they must travel to the tool board to get their tools and then travel to put them back. So, to eliminate the travel distance, they will keep the tools with them or scatter these tools around the workstation until the end of the day when they must put them back. As a result, the lines are never set up quite right to have the tools available or in the exact order required to perform the next operation.

At Company X, tools were on a tool board, resulting in waste as operators moved back and forth to retrieve tools. We developed an operator tool cart that provided tools at the right time for the work to be performed. This was set up like a tool board, so identifying missing tools was obvious.[9]

Where to Start? Always Start with the Customer!

Implementation starts with understanding the customer (and other stakeholders) needs and the customer demand. This is the only way to start thinking about pull systems or level loading. We always start our BASICS® implementations on the shop floor, closest to the customer, which means a final assembly line for most companies.

Why start on the shop floor?

- It is closest to the customer.
- One-piece flow exposes most pressing problems to the surface immediately along with the real bottlenecks in the subassembly processes (if they exist).
- Provides tools to analyze the current condition that create the requirements or pull for the front-end processes and prior operations.
- Provides a tool to identify and prioritize problems with instant ROIs.
- Creates a system based on standardized operations and eliminates much of the typical variation in our floor processes and sometimes eliminates the need for some administrative processes.
- Helps free up factory and engineering support resources to work on integrated product design and the Lean value stream in the front end.
- Creates a pull-on upstream process to drive an improvement.
- Identifies supporting process opportunities and their impact to production (releases/ scheduling).

During our initial assessments, most companies want to start with what they perceive to be the bottleneck that is normally a subassembly operation. But we have never found, once we have done our analysis, what is initially perceived to be the bottleneck, not to be the bottleneck. If you start at the front office, you can't possibly determine what is truly needed by the production in terms of paperwork. If you start at a subassembly operation, you can't possibly know the true demand or sequence required to support the final assembly. We find most companies violate this rule.

Always Start Closest to the Customer

This rule has never failed us, but it is somewhat counterintuitive. People say if the sub-process isn't working, then each area should understand what it is they have in the way of the inventory of supplies and how much they use based on their demand (daily). In addition, for each part, they should understand (i.e., PFEP) the replenishment process from the supplier, including how it is supplied to them (i.e., by box and the number in the box or the unit) and the lead time to obtain additional supplies, which will impact the minimum, maximum, and reorder point of each type of the supply required.

The amount and size of supplies and bins or containers will determine the size and number of shelves required for the new layout. We need to right size the bins or containers so that supplies are utilized to the actual demand. If the containers or bins are too large, the tendency will be to overstock the bins. This can lead to organizational cash flow issues, due to money being tied up in excess inventory. In addition, over-ordering and overstocking raise the potential to purchase supplies that will only become expired or obsolete.

Implementing the Line: 3P Cardboard Simulation

A cardboard is a simple, inexpensive, quick, and effective way to help people visualize what the line will look like (see Figure 1.10). It is much easier to move cardboard versus moving actual machines. Cardboard simulations can be simple 2D models laid out on the floor or a more complex 3D full-scale mockup of the cell with identified utilities, outlet locations, tooling cabinets, etc. They can include the tooling parts used at each station and identify the in/out for materials replenishment. These efforts can take from an hour or less to several days depending on the extent of the simulation exercise. Many times, this becomes the heart of the product preparation process (3P) or layout design kaizen.

Importance of Lean Pilot Experiments

We recommend using Lean pilots. We start off with small pieces within the project, apply the Lean tools, and work out the kinks prior to converting the entire area. A phased approach gives everyone time to voice their opinions and secure the necessary staff buy-in from the area. We also suggest involving the engineering/maintenance and health safety and environmental departments on the team either full time or part time.

- When determining where to start the lean pilot, we have the following to consider:
- It should be a final assembly line or in an office, a transactional process, closest to the customer.
- It should prove the BASICS® tools and PDCA model work.

Figure 1.10   3P exercise on the floor. Laying out the new cell to scale. Operators get to experience the new layout first hand. Can also be done with virtual reality (VR).

- It should be a key product or process for the business.
- It should be a true test of the Lean principles.
- The result ideally will be transferable to other lines (YOKOTEN).
- It will require the supervisor or process owner to spend 100% of the time on the team.
- Most of all, it must be loaded for success.

Each of these is important to consider but the last is imperative. One must not only consider the product line but the culture of the area and personnel when choosing the first project. The best change management is built on a succession of ongoing small wins. We must first start with an open-minded leadership willing to participate on the team, take ownership, and drive and sustain the change.

Picking the Pilot Line

At Company X, we had a rather impassioned discussion on where to start. We had a choice between two facilities in two different but adjacent states, and several product lines for the pilot line. The vice president at the time wanted to pick a line at the headquarter plant, whereas we wanted to start with the line at a sister plant in the adjoining state. This was because from visiting and touring both plants, we knew both the culture, and the plant manager at the sister plant would be more receptive to the implementation. Then the Vice President (VP) decided he wanted to start at a subassembly operation but we stuck to our guns and insisted on starting with the final assembly operation first. After 6–8 weeks, the final assembly product line was up and running one-piece

Table 1.3 Results: 48% Increase in Productivity = $300,000 Contract Savings; 6× Return on Consultant Training Investment

	Before	After	After %
Operators	22.0	16.0	27
Pieces per day (includes OT)	4.8	6.0	25
DL per piece (hours)	41.0	21.3	48
WIP	10.0	3.0	70
Throughput time (hours)	18.0	3.5	81
Cycle time (hours)	1.9	1.2	36
Space final assy only	28,000	12,500	55
Space feeder cells	20,000	9,375	53
Units per person per day	0.2	0.4	72

Source: Big Archives.

flow with standard work, smooth materials flow, and baton zone balancing and became a huge success with 48% in productivity savings (see Table 1.3). It proved that the subassembly operation, while it had lots of room for improvement, was not the main bottleneck in the operation as everyone previously thought.

Once you make your first Lean pass at final assembly, the data and resulting Lean system will show where the next real bottlenecks reside and ultimately what paperwork or material requirement planning (MRP) system transactions are really needed (if any) to produce or track the product through the shop. In most instances, we turn off the shop floor tracking in MRP and utilize either the shop order release, or the stocking transaction to relieve the inventory and pay invoices. One can decide whether to backflush at either of these locations. Note: If you wait to backflush until you ship or stock the units and are not on Kanban, the system will think this material is still available depending on the software you are utilizing. However, beware as the MRP or computer system functionality and implemented or non-implemented modules can present significant challenges to Lean implementations.

We always try to strive to include sub assembly operations as part of our Lean lines, which means these are no longer pre-built or built off-line. For some reason, there tends to be this human desire or thought process that leads us to believe that to improve or speed up a manufacturing operation, we should pre-build part of the product or outsource it. While in some cases this may make sense, there can be many problems with this line of thinking. However, these problems tend to be counterintuitive.

Pre-building is defined as building ahead, which is batching. It is the number one waste of overproduction and is incurred whether parts (or paper) are built by one-piece flow or batch methods. In Lean, the only acceptable pre-building would be to get the SWIP in place that is technically still a batch-type buffer because we have not been able to solve the problem forcing us to carry that WIP inventory. It should be noted that we consider building a subassembly, in parallel, on the line as part of the one-piece flow process. However, the subassemblies should not be built way ahead of time (or more than the SWIP quantity) but should be timed to coincide with the final assembly product insertion.

Figure 1.11 Batching during Lego® car simulation.

It is surprising how many Lean experts or Lean masters we have had in training, building simple Lego cars that want to preassembe parts of the car prior to starting the exercise or batch them up during the exercise to improve their output (see Figure 1.11). One tends to forget that one still needs to consider when one builds ahead, all the problems that come with the batch system which accompany this pre-building. Any pre-building is the waste of overproduction even if it is eventually needed. In addition, the WIP talks to you. If you are pre-building, it means the line is either not balanced or is station balanced. This is all stored labor, which is WIP (cash) that should be output (sales).

Ohno spent most of his early efforts working on reducing the waste of overproduction first and this is why we consider it the most important waste. This is the framework or foundation on which JIT was built. The pre-built inventory still requires labor, space to build it and store it, and it results in problems or defects that won't be found until final assembly; which can get damaged in transit or storage; and must be inventoried, accounted for, and matched up to the top-level work order at some point. Sometimes, the parts are even taken off the line for another customer order!

Twelve Classic Implementation Pitfalls[10]

1. Lack of top management support, or lack of leadership and accountabilities in the plant
2. Underestimation of time required
3. Unexpected problems (i.e., unintended consequences due to lack of planning or communication)
4. Undercoordination
5. Competing distractions in the business, lack of alignment around top five goals
6. Inadequate capabilities and skills of employees, lack of cross training

7. Uncontrollable externalities (something outside the control of the team or the plant negatively impacts the implementation, i.e., sudden surge or drop off in demand)
8. Lack of support for change
9. Unclear goals and expectations
10. Lack of involvement of employees in the area
11. Dismissing any complaints outright—not listening
12. No full-time commitments by the entire team

Standard WIP and Workstation Design

SWIP is a key part of implementing Lean synchronous flow lines and is a very difficult concept for operators and supervisors to understand. Once the SWIP level is determined, the line must be run until all the excess WIP is worked off and the SWIP is in place. We call this wetting the line and sometimes this can take several days. The operators will naturally want to always finish these pieces. This means you must be there with them to teach them about SWIP and to help them get the line wet (Figure 1.12).

Lesson Learned: The Lean practitioner must stay with the line for at least a week or two, sometimes longer, depending on the complexity, to make sure the line continues to run properly. It is a very counterintuitive process, and if operators are left to their own discretion, they will not run the line properly (will revert to their previous ways).

Operators need to make sure the SWIP is maintained to the level posted while running the line and in place at the end of the day. When trying to baton zone balance the line, many times, operators will bump back to the SWIP instead of the preceding person when flexing on the line. This then results in drying up the SWIP. Many times, at the end of the shift, the operators will again try to dry up the line. This means they get more output on the day-by-hour chart, but since the SWIP was already assembled to some level, it is a false gain. The next day they must start over and wet the line again. This means they will have no output until all the SWIP is built up and back in place again. In some product lines, it is not possible to leave the line wet but that is not the norm.

Figure 1.12   Standard WIP locations to support one-piece flow with batch ovens.

Understanding Standard WIP

- You need to get the right amount of SWIP in place at the start. We generally set it at the maximum because operators and supervisors do not understand it enough to fluctuate it based on cycle times and demand.
- You must stay with them all the time to make sure they manage the SWIP correctly.
- You need to teach them how to add a piece into the system and take a piece out of the system.
- Teach them not to bump to SWIP.
- Teach them how to calculate SWIP based on the number of people on the line and post at each location.

True Pull System

At Company X, we implemented a true pull system from final assembly back to sheet metal raw material using visual controls (see Figure 1.13). To set up the line, we had to convert a functional factory to Lean. We put the final assembly line together first, which means we had to take the welding out of its functional area and put it at the start of the line. We then set up a one-piece flow, a VMI materials system next to the line (freed up that space in the stockroom without using any more room on the floor). We set up a Kanban pull system that started with shipping. When a unit was shipped, it triggered the paint area to grab the next final assembly in their Kanban. This triggered the final assembly to grab a unit from the welding Kanban to start the line. Welding pulled from a production ordering Kanban fed by sheet metal that triggered sheet metal to replace the part. All internal production schedules were eliminated and the production control people were freed up to do other tasks. This system worked all on visual triggers.

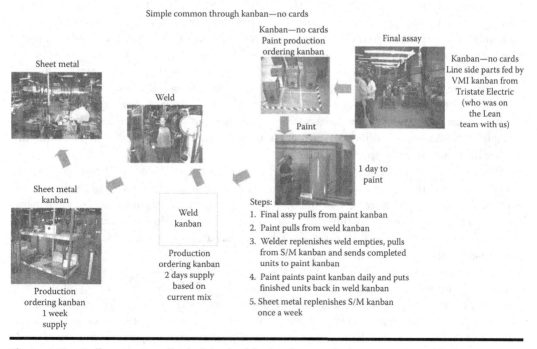

Figure 1.13 Pull system totally designed with visual controls.

Mixed Model Lines—Paperwork

When producing mixed model lines, there can be several work orders in process at one time especially when there are orders of one and two pieces. It is important to keep the initial work order with the first piece as it goes down the line and for all the operators to complete the initial paperwork (where applicable) as it moves through the line. The last operator needs to complete the final paperwork then box it up and prepare the parts for shipping. This also means that first in, first out (FIFO) must be maintained down the whole line so the various orders don't get mixed up. Operators, when given the chance and proper coaching, will figure this out and will get quite good at it. Barcoding, radio frequency identification (RFID), and other solutions exist to eventually replace the paperwork.

Lesson Learned: Everyone implementing must be very open-minded throughout the process and consider all operator suggestions in the spirit of continuous improvement.

Kaikaku

Kaikaku means reform or reorganization. It is a term noted in Jim Womack's book, Lean Thinking, and is the subject of a book of the same name. In the book, Kaikaku,[11] it is described as "a great transformation in awareness and in actual business. It is a large fundamental change of policy, practice, or awareness."[12]

Kakushin[13]

Kakushin is a serious blossoming improvement plan, defined as a revolutionary change driven by the leadership including the board level. An example would be in 2006, Toyota was even questioning its basic kaizen approach. The result was the initiative by then CEO Mr. Watanabe to cut the number of components in their car by half. This was on top of the 2004 initiative to improve system components and to cut procurement costs by 30%.

We use the BASICS® approach to transform cultures from batch to Lean described in this book which we have shown to be a different implementation approach than point kaizen events. It is more along the lines of the Kakushin and Kaikaku approach, utilizing Lean system implementations or what some call a system kaizen. These are typically 1–14-week implementations based on applying the tools of scientific management of both time and motion study while planting the seeds of Lean culture and respect for humanity.

When converting processes from batch to flow, we use the BASICS® tools to implement as described in the earlier chapters across the entire system. Then we use kaizen (method 3—ideas from the floor) and point kaizen events (method 1) to sustain and drive continuous improvement. The goal is to create a culture within the company, where most of the improvement suggestions emanate from the staff on the floor doing the job every day and then giving supervisors and managers time to implement the improvements.

When we do point kaizen events, we do them a little differently than traditional kaizen blitzes, in that we continue to use the ready-aim-fire approach in BASICS® versus the typical kaizen approach of ready-fire-aim. We pick an area to improve; assemble a team; video and analyze the product, operator, and setup; and then make the Lean improvements. We get more proficient in the tools each time we utilize them. In some cases, on smaller scope projects, we can get through all the necessary BASICS® tools in a day or less.

The Secret to Driving Continuous Improvement

At a well-known Japanese company, the team worked 9 hours per day. The group leader had to have an hour of planned downtime every day. This means the line was not producing for an hour each day. At first glance, this doesn't seem to make sense. To make matters more confusing, he was evaluated on that hour of downtime. If he did not incur it, he was reprimanded! It sounds kind of strange, doesn't it? However, this hour of downtime was specifically utilized to drive continuous improvement. How? You see, the company was manufacturing different types of seasonal vehicles on a paced assembly line. The way this process worked is as follows:

- Let's say the line ran at 90 seconds cycles. This means that every 90 seconds, a vehicle came off the assembly line.
- At some point during the day, the group leader changed the operating rate of the assembly line from 90 seconds to 89 seconds. He then looked for any operator or operation that couldn't keep up (bottlenecks the line).
- The whole line then had an hour to work together to fix it.
- If they couldn't fix it in an hour, he changed the rate back to 90 seconds.
- The next day, he repeated the process until it ran 89 seconds. The next day he would reduce it to 88 seconds…

Homework: How can you build this continuous improvement drive into your department or product line?

The real secret to driving continuous improvement is to develop a system where:

1. The employees own the job and are accountable to improve the job every day.
2. The employees are all taught how to solve problems using PDCA.
3. The leaders develop their employees and, in the process, develop themselves. We call this leaders developing leaders.
4. We embed daily routines to teach our leaders how to teach, sustain, continuously improve, and drive results focused on the customer.

What Type of Commitment Is Required?

We tell companies that Lean is a 5-year commitment that never ends! It is a journey, not a quick fix solution. It requires resources, a budget, a plan, and an unwavering commitment. We recommend budgeting up front for Lean and paying for it with savings from ongoing implementations. However, budgeting is necessary to define what constitutes savings up front. The term project is somewhat of a misnomer with Lean; the word project has an ending connotation to it. Technically, once we end a Lean project, we are just beginning the improvement that is necessary for the area, the process, or the changes to the overall system being implemented.

Lesson Learned: Whenever implementing Lean, people are going to resist changes. As leaders, you must hang in there and support the changes and, maybe even for a period, be prepared to brute force the changes for several years until the new culture sticks.

Hansei: The Check in PDCA[14]

Han means to turn upside down. Sei means to look back upon, review, or examine oneself. Hansei is going through the process of reviewing your past actions and the impact they had in hopes that you can learn from them. It is a time of reflection on past events. In the United States, we call this the learning organization, but not too many companies do it very well. In his book Execution, Larry Bossidy talks about the necessity of and being able to confront reality. In a sense, Hansei is confronting the brutal reality of the past. The key is to be able to learn from your past and change your behavior in the future. Toyota does this exercise even when things go right. It is part of the healthy paranoia they create in their culture. If it went well then why did it go well? Can we repeat it? There is a saying at Toyota: No problem is a problem. So, when doing Hansei, you have a paradox where you must look for the bad even in the good.

We use this tool in Lean when we roll out implementations. We always look back to ask: How can we do it better next time? How can we make the equipment flexible so we can move it twice as fast? There is a saying in the United States that goes something like "it doesn't matter what you've done for me in the past; what are you going to do for me today?" The goal is to create an environment of healthy skepticism where you treat your work as never being good enough. Toyota has standardized this concept by making it part of their day-to-day procedures. Next time you have a cause to celebrate, consider Hansei and figure out how to bake it into your culture.

Lean or Six Sigma, Which Comes First?[15]

I was talking with my friend Jeff, a production control supervisor with a US-based automotive battery manufacturing company. First, I was amazed that our discussion got me thinking about how many car and truck batteries are produced every day. Although this story goes back a few years, it really is timeless, and I am sure the magnitude of production quantities has not changed much. His factory shipped nearly 14,000 units per day, as did each of his company's nine other sites, give or take a bit. That equals 126,000 units times 240 days (not including surges, overtime, or the like), which is over 30 million batteries per year for cars, boats, motorcycles, trailers, and trucks. This is a staggering number when you think about it; and at that time, there were three other major domestic manufacturers doing the same thing for original equipment manufacturer (OEM) and aftermarket—that is nearly 91 million batteries per year; do we really use that many? I have not put a replacement battery in any of my vehicles in years!

We were discussing efficiency and problem-solving to meet production requirements when Jeff related a story that got me thinking about what should come first: Lean or Six Sigma. His plant was making daily JIT shipments to a Japanese transplant automobile manufacturer, one of their OEM customers. They were cross-docking pallets of wet cell batteries (so many high by so many wide) when a fork truck driver turned too fast and six batteries dropped off the pallet. They landed on their side on the floor. The Japanese transplant automobile manufacture staff arrived to find three batteries dripping battery fluid, while the other three were dry. Concerned, they called Company X engineers to help resolve the issue. Why did the three batteries leak fluid while the three other batteries remain dry? After careful measurement and contract specification consultation, the company's engineers reported that the battery leakage was well within the drops per minute allowed in the specification. Problem solved—right? …. Wrong!

The Japanese transplant automobile manufacture engineering staff's concern was not that all batteries were within specification, but rather why didn't the three dry batteries leak any drops at all? How could this happen? What is the difference? What caused this variance? Why didn't they all leak the same? Wasn't there enough fluid? What other features or performance criteria may be different between the leakers and non-leakers or, for that matter, all the batteries? What did the production do differently? You can see where this is going. What should a customer expect especially since they are (really a reseller) standing behind the field warranty costs? We may be concerned with the production cost; however, they are concerned about after the sale—total lifecycle cost.

I toured Company X's plant. Folks were working hard to meet production goals and to maintain quality levels. Many process steps, whether automated or manual, had some sort of quality specification monitored and methodically checked as prescribed. Many of those features required plotting on an XBar-R chart or P chart, and an appropriate action was taken according to statistical process control (SPC) protocols. When an out-of-control condition presented itself, someone was called to address it. Quality control seemed to be the production mantra of operations. So, what happened? Why did the three batteries leak and the other three batteries did not? The answer is not in either Lean or Six Sigma as we know it; it is the inverse of variation: consistency. The consistency of the product and how each product is produced should be the same as the one produced before or after. We come up with many reasons for the variance, that is, tool wear, we do not have time (to do it right the first time), people learn differently, and on and on. The real reason is we believe that specification tolerance is acceptable rather than specification target. We have been trained that things are always different, never the same; for us, the bell curve needs to be wide, because we believe the wider the three Sigma is, the lower the cost because it allows us to accept all the differences, and that will be good enough.

Okay, let us sort this out. First, some of our staff get it and are using tools to improve the process—while some staff may take a while and some staff (are so short-term oriented) never get it and are putting the company on a path to go out of business. This may be a strong statement but it is a possible outcome unless they get promoted first. In this business case, Company X's people got it. Maybe because of customer pressure, since it was such a big account, they had to. Second, what about this specific problem? Irrespective of the contract, Mitsubishi, and Company X's expectation of the differences between battery units were very different—all met spec, yet they were different:

■ What level of difference is acceptable?
■ Is the problem/solution an indicator or just a piece in a larger puzzle?

My thought is that the more consistent the product, the easier the future problem-solving becomes. The more stable the process becomes, the more repeatable the process and the easier it is to improve that process. A dilemma is as follows: do you spend the time to understand and solve the problem or is it whitewashed just to minimize the current budget expenses and the cost of goods sold to make the numbers (and bonuses)? The problem must be solved to gain knowledge to better understand and solve future problems; this will allow an improvement of product performance and production costs.

So how do Lean and Six Sigma fit into this? As I see it, they are both the means to an end, with the true end being (lower cost, higher efficiency) consistency. With consistency, it becomes easier to apply Lean techniques and to use Lean tools to achieve process improvements. At the same time, Lean applications will help establish consistent processes. Six Sigma tools also drive toward consistency and improvements, maybe more narrowly, but it does solve problems and achieve process control once the overall process (system) is stabilized. Interesting, both have the same resultant: more repeatable processes and a product with greater consistency at a lower cost. As I see it, improvement must drive toward consistency.

Lastly, we still have the three batteries that leaked and the three batteries that did not. Without getting into trends, runs, or order of production, let us just say with the variance extremes, they were unable to pinpoint the root cause. They probably just wore down the Mitsubishi engineers. The after-the-fact nature of defining these failures is costly to solve because there is so much investment inertia in the program.

Lesson Learned: Defining performance impact takes a lot of time, energy, and cost. Frankly, the easier (and by that, I mean total cost-effective) approach is to spend the time to stabilize the process first using Lean (that includes Six Sigma methods) with more well-defined rigid process steps up front. This will make future problem-solving quicker. The result is the same: lower cost and higher customer satisfaction.

Not Everyone Is Going to Buy in to the Changes

Implementing Lean changes is not easy. Not everyone is going to buy into the changes. Sometimes, in the early phases, there are some casualties who were too tied to the old ways of doing things. While it is important to coach and motivate to help these people buy in, it is not worth spending all your time on the 10% or so who will refuse to change.

Taiichi Ohno ran into the same problem when he first started implementing his new system. In his book, The Toyota Production System, Ohno states "One has to use your authority to encourage them."[16] When he (Ohno) introduced Kanbans to the Toyota production process, he was forced to resort to holding his position against many complaints from his foremen to his boss. He had to rather forcefully urge his foreman to go along with the system resulting in several complaints that he was doing something ridiculous and should be stopped. Fortunately, the top manager trusted him and told him not to stop.[17]

By sticking with his new system, he eventually introduced it companywide, even though it was not a smooth transition. If the Toyota leadership had not supported Ohno, the system we know as Kanban probably would not exist. Ohno now is considered the father of the TPS. The earlier passage supports the notion that top management must change its way of thinking, make an unwavering commitment, and show strong support for Lean to be successful. This means that the traditional system on which the top management has relied for so long must change.

Ohno goes on to say,

Organizational leaders must comprehend factors such as inner and outer environmental changes and the demands and directions of the times. Based on these factors, the corporation must indicate what must be done from the top down. In the production plant, from the bottom up, employees must propose ways to improve human relations, increase productivity and ultimately reduce costs through improvements to their own workplaces. I believe it is this harmony and discord, the magnified effect between the top-down and bottom-up styles that cause insanity in the minds of people working there. Based on my experiences in the production plant, I know that in the beginning, people tended to resist change, whether large or small, making the atmosphere not conducive to implementing change. However, if the employees were frantic, we were crazy! In the end, we forced our way through and persuaded the others. The whole process of developing the TPS took place this way. From the late 1940s to the early 1960s, with everyone in opposition, it was called the abominable Ohno Production System. People refused to call it the Toyota Production System. When I confirmed the validity of the system and tried to implement it, everyone objected vehemently. To overcome this resistance, I had to quarrel and fight. And since the numbers were against me, I had no choice—I went crazy. This differs from an "ambitious spirit."[18]

We think it is important for the reader to realize, whether it is manufacturing, government, service industries, or health care, Ohno's quote above applies. Lean is seldom easy to implement, and it is not always nirvana where people get together to sing the praises of the Lean implementation. If it was, every company would be Lean already. In the book The Birth of Lean,[19] it further validates that Ohno's approach was to implement the system rather forcefully while totally focusing on making the operators' jobs as easy as possible. It is somewhat of a juxtaposition that the operators who were not directly involved with Ohnosan always looked forward to his visits.

Lesson Learned: Many companies only use Lean to cut manpower; so now, people equate Lean with the loss of jobs, which is really the antithesis of Lean. If implemented properly, Lean saves money and creates jobs!

Importance of Involving Everyone

We work very hard over the course of the several-week implementations to find ways to involve everyone in the area in the process. This can take the form of contests, 5S, identifying materials needed and locations, etc. By getting others involved, it not only takes work off the core team but secures buy in from those in the area. We initially get their feedback on how things are going and continuously work to have them solicit and implement small ideas for improvements.

Keep the Ownership with the Line Organization

The Monkey

Many times, an organization holds the Lean practitioner responsible to implement and drive change through the shop floor and offices. This approach has a fatal flaw. In the United States, there is a reference to the person that has the responsibility of the monkey being on their back (Figure 1.14). The changes are in essence being pushed on the line organization by the Lean practitioner. This makes any changes very difficult (like banging your head against the wall) and creates an environment where the line organization takes a hands-off approach. After all, it's the Lean team's job to get Lean implemented. In this way, there is a built-in "cover your ass (CYA)" mentality because anything that goes wrong will obviously be the Lean team's fault! This means the monkey is on the Lean practitioner's back, versus where it should be which is on the line organization's back.

The real key to implementing and sustaining Lean is to create a pull for Lean from the top. The CEO needs to set goals and expectations for the line organization, which can only be met by implementing Lean and Six Sigma. It is important to keep the ownership with the process owner and not let it fall to the Lean team. The Lean team can unknowingly take the ownership by simply developing the team charter document for the process owner or doing the scheduled report outs. These tasks must stay with the line owners to be successful long term. The Lean practitioner's role is to support the line organization using facilitation and training to develop everyone into Lean practitioner where Lean becomes the way we do business.

Figure 1.14   Where is the monkey?

Where Is the Monkey?

During a kaizen event in Italy, the Lean team leader was told to make a 50% improvement in the setup time of a press machine. The Lean team leader put together a team and scoped the project. The manager over the functional setup department was asked to participate and include some of the setup operators. The first sign of a problem was when the setup manager said none of his people were available. "They were all too busy." Have any of us heard this before? The goals and scope of the team were reviewed and the setup training was performed on day 1. The next day, the videos were reviewed (without the operators), and every idea the team came up with was immediately dismissed by the setup manager as impossible. Any idea he came up with was okay; but everything else was shot down. We asked the Lean team leader, "where is the monkey?" He said it's on my back! We said we need to move the monkey to the setup manager's back. It took three meetings with the general manager and some other highly placed individuals to move the monkey. This became apparent when on the last day some of the operators suddenly appeared to review the standard work the team put together and the videos. The operators provided some great ideas and proceeded to break the record for the setup time by almost 50%.

Lesson Learned: The monkey must be on the line manager's back if the project is to be successful and even more importantly sustained.

Lean Implementation Cycles of Learning[20]

Having committed the past 14 years to what most would say are failed attempts at Lean implementation within Company X, I have learned each attempt was not a failure; but a step-in learning what was necessary. I am pretty sure there is no right way to shift an existing culture to one that can make use of the Toyota manufacturing system. Described in the following text is the path we followed at Company X; it was not the short path, and following this description, I will summarize the path that may have performed better in hindsight.

First, without the upper management being actively engaged and investing their time into this management system, forget about any installation being successful. We had a couple of years where our local management (being a global company) was highly engaged in Lean implementation and progress was made. We learned about single-piece flow, line layout, Kanban, lineside inventory, standard work, error proofing, and filming the work for analysis with the workers involvement. We made great improvements during this time.

We started this implementation in a factory composed of three buildings containing more than 200,000 ft^2. During 5S, we found items dating back prior to World War II; all were disposed of through sale and or trash. Some 60 dumpsters, 30-cubic yards each, went to the landfill. After our consultant delivered an intensive 1-week training to ourselves and the workforce, we worked to make our manufacturing cells highly configurable and Lean, allowing us to eliminate the need for all but one building. This activity was in preparation to move the entire factory over a weekend to a new location some twenty miles away. Our consultant helped with the new green field layout where we eliminated all the walls except for those required for a clean room.

After the move, the manufacturing area was doing very well. The local management thought it was time to branch out to the support functions with our Lean implementation. They decided accounting would be a good place to start. "Wow, what a mistake!" The accounting department had a reporting structure that went to the global organization level very fast. The global controller and some of his staff were on a plane and in our factory within a few days. They did not understand Lean manufacturing methods and were simply appalled. Within weeks, our local operations management suddenly announced they were seeking other opportunities outside of Company X.

The next couple of years, our Lean champions also were encouraged to find other opportunities outside Company X. For the next 5 years, the only department with a vision of continuous improvement that still had a Lean presence was my manufacturing engineering department. We did our best to influence the systems where we had control. Line layouts and processes were sharpened and we continued Lean training for our shop floor team members. People had the opportunity to see how the Lean manufacturing system could improve their work, but it came with a price as our people who grasped the Lean system became discouraged and disgruntled. Our past global president felt that change was needed so he hired an operations VP who trained at Toyota and spent many years at General Motors (GM). His agenda was a culture change modeled after the Toyota manufacturing system. The first directive was to create a measurement system that was to be displayed to all people. This display was used to run the business and to force correct behavior.

Then global management would meet with every factory each week reviewing the metrics and the supporting metrics and methods checking and offering help when required. These methods, designed to create an improvement were discussed in detail and everyone was aware that progress was expected. If there was no progress, or insufficient progress, then you could count on someone else doing your job the next month. This was very serious and in a high-pressure environment in the beginning.

These same methods flowed down to the managers and workers using daily communication meetings and whiteboards. The goals that supported the global requirements would be discussed each day and the progress measured. The plant operations director attended each daily team meeting and actively engaged all the workers attending the meeting.

Since some of us had been training in Lean for nearly 10 years, our factory made great strides and showed a massive improvement ahead of the other factories. Our progress was so-much-so that the global management started closing other sites and moving the work to our site. In the end, five factories were closed and consolidated in our location requiring us to acquire the adjacent building. The rapid growth soon overtook the support staff's ability to control the new production lines and processes, requiring us to adjust my manufacturing engineering organization. Unfortunately, this is where the story must end right now since it is still in progress.

At Company X, we were implementing Lean in a manufacturing environment. There were some rumblings from the corporate VP of finance. The VP showed up at the plant and spent some time with us. After that discussion and a tour of the facility to observe this Lean initiative, the VP was amazed at the results and was outwardly supportive of the activities. Their support was surprising but appreciated as they became a big proponent of these Lean initiatives at his facility.[21] As promised at the beginning of this story, here is a summary of what may have worked better for us from a hindsight vantage. I believe the VP of operations had the correct formulary to succeed with a Lean culture shift. The first order was to measure the business, and this is not a simple task as each business would argue for differences and, in some cases, unique measurements. What I have learned are as follows:

- Lean measures should deal with
  – Environment, health, and safety (EH&S)
  – Quality
  – Delivery/supply chain
  – Inventory
  – People
  – Productivity/cost
- Do not waste time making measurements unless you plan to use it to improve.
- Each measurement needs a goal and a set of ideas that will improve the goal toward infinity and beyond.
- If goals are achieved, the targets need to be reset trending toward perfection.
- The progress must be communicated with the general workforce at least monthly in front of the business development board.
- The general workforce will become the driver of the support staff because they will see the metric results and begin to ask why a lot.
- If we do a good job of training, the people will become very critical of the support staff and this may cause hostility.
- One must be careful to manage the expectations to prevent infighting that can derail your efforts. This is not an easy task as everyone has different triggers and requires a fine touch of highly involved managers. Each of them sees the process much clearer than you do for their piece of it anyway. They require attention, and your management team needs a lot of upfront training to be effective at keeping them engaged.
- The hard part is keeping up with the people when they catch fire. I think it is impossible to be ready for the rush of improvements that will follow. I would recommend preparing by going heavy on your support staff at this time.

Now that your people are in tune with the business and can follow the improvements and/or losses; they need a set of tools to help make improvements. We hired a BIG consultant to teach us the Lean process and tool kit used by Toyota. Our people all went through a 5-day training session and came out excited and expecting to make changes. We ended up stifling their efforts because we did not have enough support staff and resources to keep pace with all the ideas. This caused the general workforce to lose faith and give up (just something to think about). When your people start to produce ideas, it is important to not allow them to drop off the idea to the support staff and see what happens; this was the culture at our factory. The hard part is to turn the idea right back to the person with the empowerment to try it, with support, time, and, when required, capital. Once they understand that this is not a support staff-only process, they can make an improvement in their work and see the reward of recognition from their coworkers and managers; you will be at the real beginning of your journey where anything is possible.

This is a great place to introduce PDCA. Once we had some key measurements in place and our people had learned the Lean tools for improvement, we introduced the PDCA cycle and tied it directly to our metrics. Lather, rinse, and repeat forever. The simplicity of this improvement tool is amazing. Most of the metrics posted on the daily management board are of the run chart variety, and if trends or variation becomes apparent, the responsible team members would activate the PDCA process. At the end of the row, where the poorly performing metric is displayed, attach a PDCA sheet where the team publicly presents the countermeasures and results to improve the troubling metric.

When developing a plan, I always use the Toyota production vision taken from the book *Toyota Kata*[22] by Mike Rother. I use this method to determine if it is right to move forward with a plan. Does the plan support these values? These are very simple, yet impossible to achieve, thus leaving endless continuous improvement opportunities:

1. Zero defects
2. 100% value added
3. One-piece flow, in sequence, on demand
4. Security for people

Lesson Learned: Getting everyone looking for an improvement that supports your vision will improve your ability to please your customers and stockholders.

Team Charters

Team charters can be a helpful tool prior to starting any project. Team charters include entry and exit strategies, budgets, and detailed scopes. They are contracts with the teams, implementing department, and the leadership or steering committee:

Do I Really Need A Team Charter?

At Company X, Bill, the Lean practitioner, started working with his second plant. The first Lean implementation had been very successful and was even toured by other companies. Before the second plant kicked off, Bill met with the leadership to review the charter his team had prepared. The leadership took the position they had already done Lean in one plant, and there was no need for a formal charter for the second plant. How wrong they were! About 3–4 weeks into the project, the team champion/sponsor was on vacation for several weeks. During this time, certain members of the team took over, alienated Bill, and ostracized him from the management meetings. Meanwhile, the leadership team decided they wanted no part in the changes and the effort stalled. Because there was no charter (the result of an uncommitted leadership team), there was no escalation plan. As the problems surfaced, the team started infighting. It was further complicated by a new hire whose job was to project manage (micromanage) the team. The project manager was not familiar with Lean or Six Sigma. Instead of meeting with Bill and learning the Lean implementation process, the project manager met with the team and laid down his rules and how his project was going to run. It took almost a year to recover this plant and get the effort moving once again on solid footing.

Lesson Learned: The significance of the team charter is not just to provide a road map for the team but also to create a pull for the team, provide a structured approach for leadership interventions, and create a vehicle for leadership follow-up and sustaining during and after the initial Lean implementation. The charter is a symbol of management commitment and provides an escalation process and ultimate ownership for the team and its results in the event they run into any resistance to change.

Different Types of Teams

Many books have been written on all aspects of teams. Our purpose here is to differentiate between different types of teams utilized in or with Lean. We break teams into three categories:

1. Problem-solving teams: implementation teams (Kaizen or Kaikaku, Lean or Six Sigma)
2. Information-gathering teams
3. Leadership-chartered teams

Problem-Solving Teams

Everyone's job in the organization is problem-solving and continuous improvement, that is, developing new paradigms. The role of the problem-solving team is to solve the problem at hand utilizing the company's problems solving methodology.

Information Gathering Teams

The role of the information gathering team is to objectively collect the data and determine the facts. These can be through research, questionnaires, observations, supplier meetings and visits, focus groups, experiments, etc. The goal is to gather whatever information is necessary to make as much of an unbiased assessment and decision as possible.

Leadership-Chartered Teams

These are implementation teams, which are chartered by the board of directors, CEO, a senior level executive, or CEO-led process improvement committee, given a budget and empowerment level.

Team Stages of Development

As Lean is implemented throughout a facility, people must learn to work together as a team to accomplish their tasks. If the people assigned to an area are not taught how to work together, the performance can suffer and stress levels can increase. Teams go through four stages of development: forming, storming, norming, and performing.[23] During the forming stage, the team is going through an exploration period. Team members are cautious and guarded. Sometimes, confusion and anxiety are experienced as individual differences surface within the team. The team facilitator can help by sharing relevant information, encouraging open dialogue, providing structure, and developing a climate of trust and respect.

During the storming stage, the team feels defensive. Conflict cannot be avoided during this stage. The team must deal with the issues of power, leadership, and decision-making. They will challenge the wisdom of the leader. The team facilitator should engage the team in group problem-solving, establish norms for looking at different points of view, discuss decision-making procedures, and encourage two-way communications. At the norming stage, the team feels as though they have made it through the storm. Team members become committed to working with one another. Trust, the most essential ingredient in team dynamics, begins to evolve. The team facilitator guides the team to talk openly about issues and concerns. Positive feedback and support for a consensus decision-making process will help the team grow. The performing stage brings a sense of team identity and commitment to the team and its goals. The team has learned to work together. Communication is open and information is shared. The team facilitator should observe the team and offer feedback when requested. Encourage ongoing self-assessment and mentor the team to develop to its fullest potential.

Lean and Stress

A demand meter is a device installed in many retail stores and factories by the power company. Its sole function is to determine the peak usage demand of electricity. This peak demand is typically attained when someone unknowingly turns all the store circuit breakers on at the same time. It can also be triggered by a power surge such as during a lightning storm. You can watch the arrow on the meter rise to 3/4–7/8 of the top reading. The store is billed for this peak demand usage for the entire month, even though they probably only hit that usage once and on average were significantly below that demand. To prove this, have the employee turn each circuit breaker on one at a time but not until after each of the lights on that breaker are fully on. You will then see the peak demand meter at a mere fraction of its peak, normally 1/16th to 1/8th of the total on the dial.

I liken this analogy to leadership stress. I think that once you have worked for a boss that raises your stress level to say half of the dial, then any future stress that is under that level is no problem to handle. When you get a new boss, board of directors, some other leader, or are placed into a new situation in which your stress level exceeds that halfway point on the dial, you now feel it and must deal with it. If this new boss or situation takes you to three-fourths on your scale, you are now good up to that level. Sometimes, just having an awareness that this is the case can prove helpful.

Using the Future State "To Be" and Future State Analysis to Design the New Process and Implementation

The key elements that need to be considered in your optimal flow design are all derived from the analysis tools we described earlier:

- The future-state VSM helps provide a road map for areas and projects to focus process improvement, identify wastes and throughput opportunities, and our current state metrics.
- Knowing the current and forecasted customer demand and peak demand is critical. We should design our new processes and layouts to 50% of the current demand or to the demand forecasted in the company strategic plan to encompass future growth.

- Determine the available time, which is the amount of working time available to do work or perform an activity over the course of a shift or day (sometimes by hour).
- Understand the TT (customer demand divided by available time). This helps determine the beat or pace of the activity that needs to be performed as well as assists in balancing the workload.
- The future state or what we call the to be PFA and point-to-point diagram showed us how the flow should look. This is where we begin to design the new layout for the area. This can be done with a CAD system, but it is usually best to get a to-scale diagram of the area and use paper dolls or cutouts to see how everything fits. It is not unusual to go through many versions of the layout before getting it right. Each time we develop or change the layout, we need to draw a new point-to-point diagram of how things are going to flow using the layout guidelines we will discuss in more detail later. We need to optimize the layout and workstation design to create a Lean layout that places the sequence of steps/activities in the correct order.
- The full work of the operator analysis and spaghetti diagram showed us how to optimize operator walk patterns, locations for point-of-use storage, and workstation design. The workstation must have the right tools at the right place to perform the activities in the proper sequence within the process.
- The to be changeover analysis showed us what our additional capacity can be. The key now is to determine if we have the resources necessary and determine the time frame to implement the changeover ideas. We need to calculate the capacity for the areas before and, after, to determine if they can support the input to and from the area implementing the turnover project.
- Calculate the TLT from the WFA. The TLT is equal to the sum of the total VA and NVA labor time. It is the amount of time staff members spend to make "one" of the products or the activity taking place in the area. The demand, available time, and TLT will drive the number of staff or operators needed to run your process and impact your work area design.
- Understand the desired cycle time and new staffing model. The cycle time comes from the operator analysis, the demand, and the TT. We need to figure out how many operators are needed to support the current peak demand and forecasted demand. We need to make sure we can balance the workload for the staff. After balancing the workload, we will have the cycle time (the amount of time each person must meet to complete their part of the operation or activity within the process). It is calculated by dividing the available time by the volume demand of the new process. It also equals the TLT divided by the number of operators/staff members (if work is balanced evenly). The new layout needs to be reviewed to ensure we have room for the number of persons required to support current, peak, and future demand.
- Have the employees in the area help develop the standard work and train to the defined standard work. Make sure to plan for demand fluctuations related to staff and resource (supply) requirements. This often requires a new staffing model for the area. The plan should include how to run the area with one or two less persons in case the demand drops or one or two more persons in the event the demand increases.
- Adjust the inventory and understand the materials and supply chain management. Make sure the layout has enough room for the right amount of supplies available at the right time at point of use, in other words, available when needed and room to grow if necessary.
- Create a PFEP with a focus on how and where each item will be replenished. Some options for replenishment include fixed time or fixed quantity Kanbans.

■ The layout needs to be flexible. Put workstations on wheels, don't hard pipe machines, and install flexible utilities wherever possible, so if we must move equipment or workstations in the future, it is not a barrier. One can now see why we spend time analyzing the process.

■ The analysis of the data will lead you to the optimal solution.

General Overarching Lean Implementation Tips

1. Work hard to keep it simple.
2. Get as many people involved as possible. Make it their line, not your line!
3. Keep things the same or similar where possible to ease the change process.
4. Manage by exception wherever possible. Focus on the 80% where it can work on.
5. If you can't do it all at once, phase it in. Don't try to get it all perfect right away. It is okay to make mistakes.
6. Pareto rule (80%/20%). The Pareto[24] principle normally applies to Lean implementations. Focus on the 80% you can impact and save the 20% to work on later.
7. Skeptics are good; cynics are bad. We encourage skeptics. After all, they keep us honest. Cynics are convinced it will never work, thus anything you do will be wrong. If you can turn a cynic, they become zealots, but it takes a tremendous investment in time; but they can become your best salespeople.
8. Leverage your informal leaders as they can significantly influence your ability to achieve buy-in and acceptance.
9. Naysayers are not always against you. Many times, they just honestly believe it won't work. It is okay to be negative if they are not cynical. We can normally bring them along once the new process is up and running and they physically see it working.
10. Dedicate as many resources as possible. We find that each person you can dedicate to improvement pays for themselves ten times over. In the long run, we need to free up 50% of our supervisors and managers' time to implement improvements.
11. Convert indirect labor to direct labor as much as possible.
12. Going from two shifts to one shift is normally more productive.
13. Leaving or adding chairs promotes batching!
14. Allowing any preassembly promotes batching!
15. Start cross training and job rotation before you implement the line if possible. It is important for flexibility and bumping and to have backup people if someone calls out sick or on holiday.
16. Everything on wheels where possible creates flexibility.
17. Conveyors block the walking paths and end up storing materials.
18. Develop guidelines and standard work for all new processes and procedures.
19. Create sustainability systems concurrently with all Lean initiatives.
20. Encourage open communication and information flows.

Guidelines for the Group Leader/Supervisor

■ Be a leader and lead the work area.
■ Create an atmosphere that encourages adherence to the standard work.
■ Run the daily team meeting/huddle.
■ Make timely and effective decisions.

■ Be able to prioritize and delegate.
■ Be the role model for the work area (i.e., attitude and breaks).
■ Make the numbers and meet the schedule.
■ Understand how the line runs and run it properly. Make sure people have tools and materials to do their jobs. Know each job thoroughly and be able to train others in standard work and hitting the times. Manage the SWIP in the cell. Manage breaks, lunch, and start times.
■ Ensure the day-by-hour chart is filled out and the month-by-day chart is filled out.
■ Deploy people properly, make sure people stay in the areas, and flex as required. If you have extra people in the cell, make sure to move them to another area.
■ Discipline people as required.
■ Clearly display the supervisor standard work sheet in the area.
■ Keep the area clean. Make sure tools are put back after each shift.
■ Cross train everyone in the area and rotate jobs at some frequency—daily, weekly, or monthly.
■ Create a top 10 problem action item list for both the team and upper management.
■ Take swift and effective action on ideas generated by the team.
■ Update the standard work as suggestions are implemented.
■ Attend production meetings and update the management; escalate as appropriate.
■ Float into the line as needed or ensure someone is available to float.
■ Be responsible to immediately respond to problems in the area with appropriate action and document on the day-by-hour chart.
■ Demand meter analogy.
■ Be responsible to immediately respond to problems on the line with appropriate action and document on the day-by-hour chart.
■ Shut the line down if necessary to root cause problems.
■ Ensure your area is safe daily—safety is everyone's responsibility. It doesn't matter how much we produce if someone gets injured in the process.
■ Develop people within your area—help your team grow.
■ Create an environment of trust and respect (see Figure 1.15).

Business Environments

Listed in the following are the various environments in which we may work, and each requires different tools and skill sets when implementing Lean; however, all can still follow the basic Lean principles of:

■ Establishing as close to one-piece flow as possible
■ JIT materials
■ Jidoka
■ Standard work
■ Flexibility
■ Respect for people

Assembly

The assembly environment can be either for a single product model or for what we call a mixed model line where various products (generally but not always similar) are produced down the same line.

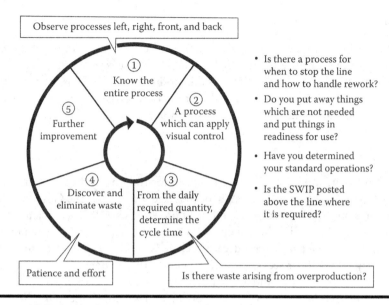

Figure 1.15   Guidelines for the supervisor.

Machine

A machining environment can be where one machine makes a single product and multiple products or where many machines are utilized to make parts for a single product or multiple products or where machines are grouped and organized in one or many cells to make a family of similar-type parts. Machine shops that make very low-volume, high-mix parts are generally referred to as job shops.

Automated Lines

Totally automated or lights out lines are used to describe lines that can run monitored but unattended.

Robots

Robots can be used in assembly or machining environments. We use this term to indicate a machine that generally assists in loading or unloading a part for a machine or in some cases may perform an operation (i.e., welding).

Hybrid

The hybrid environment can be any combination of the environments previously discussed.

Office/Transactional

The office environment is generally considered to be an environment where engineering or administrative work is performed. It can include jobs done in the field (i.e., EPA, person auditing a company, or checking on a site).

Health Care

Health care has its own set of unique environments and components. Emergency departments, surgery, and floors can all utilize the BASICS® model but have some unique conditions to consider. In health care, the patient, many times, is the product, and while hospitals for the most part don't produce things, they do spend most of their time testing, diagnosing, and repairing. Many times, the information component of the value stream paces the cycle time versus the patient.

Government

Government also has its unique challenges. Funding for training and consultants is sometimes very difficult to come by and to justify. Many of the functions within the Government are transactional; however, some involve field work and audit processes as well. There is a natural tendency for empire building, silos, and redundancy as the number of policies, and requirements have grown significantly over the past several decades. There is another issue related to staffing, as the Government rarely cuts staff or seeks efficiencies, noting that budgets are often reviewed based on the spend of the previous year, and are not developed from the bottom up, based on requirements, which often results in "I need to spend to budget or I will lose it mentality." The voice of the customer is often lost in the Government, which is a major piece of the Lean enterprise. Finally, political pressure often conflicts with Lean, and this leads to many inefficiencies.

Managing Variation during Lean Implementations

Variation in Assembly and Machining Lines

Most assembly lines have variation. The reasons for this variation can be as follows:

- ■ Everyone builds it a different way. This could be due to:
  - – Lack of or poorly documented work instructions
  - – Lack of supervision or discipline on the line
  - – Poor training
  - – Lack of process/manufacturing engineering support on an off shift
  - – Lack of proper tooling and fixturing on the line
- ■ Poor engineering designs, that is, designs that require tweaking or tuning
- ■ Lack of process capability
- ■ Inability to properly measure a specification
- ■ Inability to properly test a specification
- ■ Poor equipment maintenance
- ■ Lack of required skill set, that is, knack to complete task
- ■ Right- or left-hand process tendencies
- ■ Leadership that is not developing a team—lack of cross training

It has been our experience that it is virtually impossible to remove all the variation in a line when it is first implemented; however, we do address the lack of standardization and training and many of the test and equipment issues as part of the implementation. Tuning and tweaking generally involve engineering and result in many excuses such as "we don't have time" and "it has to be prequalified to make any changes." Therefore, Lean needs to be an overall company effort and not just a pursuit of the shop floor. Since a variation is part of the equation, we must learn how to handle balancing the line with the variation. This is a good thing in that it lets us keep the line running but a bad thing as we are masking the problem. This means that there needs to be a variation reduction or mitigation action plans assigned to the appropriate individuals who are held accountable to resolve the problems. As the problems are resolved (sometimes over many years), one will need to update and incorporate any necessary changes into the standard work.

Mixed Model Assembly Changeovers

The goal for mixed model assembly changeovers should be zero seconds (see Figure 1.16). Many times, this can be easily accomplished by having all the parts for each model available at lineside. We normally color code the bins for each model with another color for parts common across all models. Sometimes, we have each model's parts on a separate row of shelves and repeat the common parts on each shelf. In some cases, we have more models than shelves. Between all the parts and fixtures that had to be changed over, this line initially took 20 minutes to setup between models. After several iterations and employee ideas, it is now less than 1 minute between changeovers.

Figure 1.16 Used different color bins to store the parts for each model. Each shelf contains parts for different models.

Failure Mode Effect Analysis (FMEA) for Implementation

When planning your implementation, take the time to brainstorm with the team everything that could go wrong. Then consider each item as to the probability it could go wrong, the severity if it went wrong, why it might go wrong, how you will determine if it does go wrong, and what to do if it does go wrong (see Table 1.4). Most of the time, we do not impact production as moves are done off shift or over the weekends, or we figure out how to set up the new line while the old line is still running. This is the best possibility.

Lean Implementation Guidelines

Since the Lean system is new to the organization, we have learned the process owners do not have the discipline, Lean knowledge, resources, or accountability to hold the gains and continually improve. Therefore, it is necessary to include a strategy for accountability and sustaining as part of the Continuous Improvement Road Map. In the overall implementation plan, there must be a consideration given as to how the project will be followed up and sustained. Keep in mind that sustained means ongoing improvement. This is a very important statement...not well communicated or understood outside of the Lean practitioner circle.

We typically start out with a leadership training session centered around the change equation to determine what problems we have today and if there is a compelling enough need to sustain the change. We then use this session to create a contract for change which everyone signs and then identify the starting point for the pilot implementation. Part of the exercise is to create four plans:

1. Lean implementation plan
2. Training plan
3. Communication plan
4. Resource plan

Each project ends with reflection to develop lessons learned, and creating a sustain plan and system to check the ongoing progress.

Lean Needs an Owner

At Company X, sustaining became a big problem. The finance department said it was not their job to sustain the first lean line or make sure the team met the ROI, which finance drove up front. The process excellence staff organization said it was not their job to make sure it sustained because they were moving on to the next project. In addition, there was a major reorganization in the works within the company. This created quite a quandary, which, by the time we departed, was never resolved. Once the project was done and the Lean team moved on, we held several meetings to try to resolve the ownership issues for each line. The organization finally decided it was the process owner's job to sustain and continue to drive improvements. We agreed! But we brought up our concern that if the process owner, from a Lean maturity standpoint, doesn't know what needs to be done, and there is no one to coach them on their standard work, it will ultimately fail. There must be someone identified in the interim to make sure the process owners are first able and then do take the lead. Part of the Lean Roadmap must include this overall ownership accountability for the Lean initiative.

Table 1.4   FMEA Example

Failure Mode	Failure Effects	Causes	What to Do	Controls (Current)	Plans (Future)
People	Mistakes	Use A3 process	Root cause and mistake proof where possible	Inspection	Camera systems, Pick to light Bar coding systems
Personnel shortage	Less output Overtime Poor quality Imbalance of line	Layoff Poor attendance Tardiness	Look at day by hour chart and select one of the following options: 1. Can use a floater or team leader to fill temporary gap 2. Find additional staff from another area to add to line 3. Run the cell 4. Run balanced but less output (staff up next day to recover) 5. Run line on weekend	Accurate absenteeism projections Monitor individual attendance record Cross-trained floater Cross-training matrix	Overstaff to expected level Flexing over larger area and overtime.
Skills shortage	Poor quality Shutdown Immediate training need Production imbalance Not meeting cycle time	Layoff Poor attendance Tardiness New machine/ operation Inadequate training Not following standard	Process engineer monitor or train operator Use video as training aid	Cross-training matrix (consider seniority) Use periods of low demand to cross-train Flexible floaters	Train before need Ensure 3+ deep in all skills Use video for training Improve work instructions Employee suggestion plan

(Continued)

Table 1.4 (Continued) FMEA Example

Failure Mode	Failure Effects	Causes	What to Do	Controls (Current)	Plans (Future)
Learning curve	Poor quality Low output Imbalance of line	New product startup New employee Cross training	Add temporary staffing to supplement line Offset low output with excess work in process (WIP) Overtime	Offline training Associate certification WIP build up if it is known that the situation is imminent	Video of engineering tech implementing/new assay Assembly team participates in video review and idea formulation
Excess personnel	High automatic test inspection (ATI) Imbalance in line Excess production/WIP	Shutdown of other areas Material shortage Tools/equipment not available	Have staff 5s area (temp) Transfer personnel to another area Repair out-of-flow assemblies (if any) Cross-train	Staffing projection tool Alternative work plan Personnel deployment plan	Rapid response team to solve line stop problems
Planned downtime	Less output High (ATI) hours	Meeting time Training	Plan ot to cover production shortfall	Keep meeting time < 20 minutes per day Load planned downtime into line staffing tool	

Source: BIG Archives.

Don't let this happen to you. Include Lean accountabilities and escalation plans in your Lean leadership road map. Encourage HR to play a role by beefing up people development and assisting leadership in creating the culture of accountability and discipline. This is a new set of skills that needs to be taught along with the vision and expectations of the new culture we are trying to create.

Listen to Your Lean Consultants/Experts

Many companies get to a point after 3–6 months where they think they know enough to do it all themselves. Every company seems to go through this phase. People get to a point where they know enough to be dangerous. Why do companies hire Lean consultants? Many times, we have asked ourselves the same question. They refuse to put the Lean steering committee together; they stop listening to the Lean consultants and do whatever they want to do. Then, they come back to the Lean consultants and ask why Lean isn't working and blame it on the consultants.

So, what are we to do? As Lean consultants, we must occasionally let them falter. It is the only way they will learn. Any good Lean consultant (practitioner) will admit there is still much they do not know. We are always learning. When you think you know it all, it is time to quit!

Reasons Not to Try Lean Immediately on Your Own without a Sensei

Without a Sensei to share his/her experience, the company will fall back to what they currently know best. The company will not be able to interpret the tools fully and understand their flexibility. Initial projects work well because people listen to outsiders who have experience. However, people tend to focus on details instead of the big picture (systems thinking). If the current staff has no hands-on experience, they will easily start mixing people and machine activities (PFA and FWA) and try to just modify the current process instead of thinking outside of the box. Senseis have prior history implementing similar projects that cuts down on mistakes repeated in the past, transfers knowledge, and who can speak intelligently to upper management regarding the project. This cuts down implementation time frame and they can see outside the box because they are not part of your paradigm.

Adopt and Integrate Standard Work and Create a Suggestion and Reward System

Toyota first learned about suggestion systems from Henry Ford. Toyota's suggestion system is described in the book 40 Years, 20 Million Ideas.[25] It is a fascinating read. Their model is not based around a suggestion box, but by having suggestions encouraged from the front line every day by the team leaders and implemented in real time. If it doesn't work, they continue to try until it works, or they go back to the way it was before and try another improvement idea the next day. Once suggestions are implemented, the team leader updates the standard work to permanently capture the idea.

Continue Videoing after the Consultant Leaves

We worked with Company X for more than 2 years. They would invite us back quarterly for maintenance, which meant sitting down with their teams, reviewing their projects and events in the works, and offering suggestions. In addition, we would always pick out an area to work on improving while we were there. This was normally over a 1-week period. The first thing we would always do is baseline metrics and video following the BASICS® model. We would walk through the tools and make great improvements. Eventually, one of their process excellence people said to me, "I guess we should be videoing while you're gone" (i.e., not try to shortcut activities).

We are not sure why this phenomenon exists, but it seems once we leave, the day-to-day activities take over, and there seems to be no time to video. They tend to go back to shooting from the hip. We have always been successful using the BASICS® and PDCA models. It has never failed us.

Don't Leave Managers in Place Who Aren't Going to Get It

One of the biggest obstacles we face is the manager or supervisor who is just never going to get it. They don't buy into Lean. They are normally from the "my way or the highway" philosophy of managing (the command-and-control management style), or they just plainly look at this whole Lean thing as a threat to their job or this is the way they have just always done it before. Our policy is to coach and mentor, but eventually it becomes obvious the person is not going to buy in. Many times, they are always talking about how great Lean is and outwardly agreeing with the team, but behind the scenes, they are stalling and doing everything they can to thwart the team (Our 2 × 4 story).

Our experience is 40%–70% of frontline supervisors and managers initially can't make the switch from cop to coach and mentor. If you keep them, they will kill the project and blame it on Lean or Six Sigma. It is important to move them to another area where they can be an individual contributor or moved out of the organization. It is difficult to do, and most organizations wait way too long to address the problem and wonder why they don't get the results.

Lesson Learned: Caution—just moving these team leaders to another line only postpones the problem and rewards them for their behavior and others in the organization see this. What do you think the outcome of any Lean activity will be? Many times, additional training and super high-intensity training can sometimes help convert these folks from batch to flow but many will just never buy in.

These lead to ongoing reviews to see if we have the right people on the bus and if they are in the right seats to take us to the next level. With Lean, the need for the hero has gone away. It is also difficult when this person, who has so often been the hero of the month, must let go and focus on the process.

Don't Lay People Off after Lean Implementation

As stated before, our goal is to never lay off anyone because of continuous improvement. This does not mean there cannot be layoffs due to a recession or a major financial loss; however, this should be discouraged as well. Toyota and other companies have found a way to deal with recessions by hiring temporary part-time people. When you work for Toyota, they view the hiring decision as a lifetime commitment if the company is continuously improving. When you leave Toyota, they don't invite you back. An average of only 3 out of every 100[26] employee applicants is hired after an extensive interview process to assess the person's physical abilities as well as their ability to work and develop within a team environment. Team members must be able to follow the standard work and meet the times and be willing to volunteer problems encountered as well as ideas. Between companies like Toyota and Nucor, which have employees lined up to enter their organizations, where does that leave the rest of us?

Don't Shortcut the Tools

If we shortcut the tools, we shortcut the results. It is really that simple.

Encourage Lean Architectural Designs

Traditional architect designs are not Lean. If a Lean consultant is brought in, it is best to bring them in during the conceptual phase of the project prior to the architect creating any drawings.

Include a Go Forward Person on the Team

When implementing multiple sites or campuses, it works best if the prior campus team contains a person from the next campus to be implemented. We call this a go forward person. This is a great way to load the next team for success.

Train, Train, Train

One cannot train enough with Lean. There is so much to learn. There are more than 400 books on Lean as we speak, with many of the best now out of print. Creating a training plan up front and following it are critical to success. The training is no substitute for the experience of implementing on the floor, but good interactive classroom training does have a role with Lean. Initial training can be as short as an hour or up to as long as 3 months or more at different intervals. Training is an investment in your people and must be included as part of the budgeting process.

Ultimately, the training and ongoing continuous improvement culture becomes the role of the team or group leader with the assistance of the HR and management. You don't really learn the material until you must train the materials!

Create an Escalation Process

It is critical to have an escalation process in place to help the improvement teams or supervisors remove barriers to improvement. Many times, people are afraid to complain to their bosses or their bosses may be the problem. Failure to have this process in place will force these issues to be hidden and not surface. The escalation process should go all the way up to the CEO. Several times, we have had to go to the CEO during Lean implementations to make the final call.

Implementation and On-the-Fly Changes

As soon as you implement the initial change, you and others are going to see things that can be immediately improved. You may need to implement some changes right away for safety reasons, etc., but resist the temptation to continuously change things without getting input from everyone involved (especially other departments you may impact). Change is difficult enough without continually making a bunch of on-the-fly adjustments. Because of the on-the-fly changes, people get confused, frustrated, and sometimes combative. Without a fact-based problem-solving approach, it can have disastrous effects and even kill the implementation. As we tweak and refine the initial changes, we need to take time to analyze these situations as they occur as opposed to just reacting to them.

Identify the Process Owner Up Front

It is important to document and communicate roles and responsibilities for everyone in the organization. At Company X, we were speaking with a manager and asked to whom he reported. He said he reported to two different directors in the department. I asked each director who the manager ultimately reported to, and neither was sure. I asked the administrator over the area who the manager reported to. He said he reported to Director 1 and why was I asking. I told him that no one I asked was sure. Then he said, "well, he also sorts of reports to Director 2 as well." One director was administrative and one was clinical. This caused a lot of confusion and resulted in little accountability.

Lesson Learned: When all else fails, ask, "who owns it?" If there is even a moment of hesitation in the response, there is a problem (an opportunity).

Change the Reward System

If we implement the new Lean system but leave the old reward system in place, what will be the outcome? The new system will never sustain. We must change the reward system to align with the new desired Lean behaviors. This should be part of the Lean road map.

Lean Maturity Path

People and companies go through phases. These phases follow traditional change models. One can tell where a person or organization is in the Lean maturity path simply by the questions they ask. For example, if someone asks, "will Lean work here or will Lean work for us?" we know they have not started Lean. When someone says "we really aren't changing fast enough," we know they have moved into a new phase of their understanding of Lean. When they welcome and more importantly expect and insist on feedback positive and negative from any outsiders, we know they are in an even more advanced Lean state.

It Is Just a Bump in the Road

Many times, especially during the Suggesting Solutions, or implementation phase, the team will run into problems and setbacks. A legal or compliance person will tell you something can't be done, or somehow the team has inadvertently upset someone. We have come to refer to these as bumps in the road. At the time, they may seem like major issues or problems, but once we work through them, they become minor. This is a time to consider the communication model. Sometimes face-to-face communication is best during these bumps in the road.

Multiple-Site Rollout Strategies

Site/Area Selection

We generally suggest putting a cross-functional team of individuals together to form the team. We pick a pilot site and pilot line based on the following criteria:

- Most important, it must be successful.
- We must have an open-minded leadership willing to participate on the team, take ownership, and drive and sustain the change.

- We need the process owner to spend 80%–90% of the time on the team.
- The pilot should prove the BASICS® tools work.
- Where it makes sense, we should be able to transfer results to other plants and standardize the processes.

Trying to Implement Several Projects at Once without Sufficient Resources

Resources become a critical ingredient when implementing point kaizen events or system Lean implementations. If you can't resource it, don't launch it! We have seen and been part of many efforts that failed because the implementing area, while really wanting to make the changes, couldn't free up the necessary or the right staff to make the changes successful.

The Leadership Sets the Standard!

We have seen cases where one area had a lot of problems during the implementation and the leadership refused to buy in to all the Lean principles. The Lean team was told to move on to the next area to meet the schedule promised by the executive team. The team agreed only after much protesting. During implementation of the next area when the team tried to implement standard work, the new area refused to implement it because the first area never had to implement theirs. This resulted in a cascading of sustaining failures. Even though finally one area rose to the occasion and was hugely successful, the first area continued to slip backwards. If the management does not insist that Lean practices are followed, similar situations will occur. Therefore, it is so important for the management to be educated and trained up front.

Lesson Learned: If the Lean team moves on to the next project before ensuring successful sustaining of the first line, future implementations can and probably will be doomed to failure.

Beware of Conflicting Improvement Approaches, Multiple Consultants

There are pros and cons associated with multiple consultants working in the same area. If the consultants have clearly defined expectations that complement each other or implement with the same methodology, this is not a problem. But problems are created when each consultant is working on the same area with different implementation models, skill sets, or approaches. It is important when implementing, to standardize the approach and problem-solving model. One of the pros is that organizations will learn something different from each consultant. But one of the cons is that it can get very confusing to those implementing what process they are supposed to follow and which consultant is right when there is a difference of opinion. It is also difficult for the consultants because many consultants don't like to share their approaches, methodologies, and software or training materials.

Don't Try to Cut the Lean Implementation Timeline by 50%

Beware of always wanting to cut the implementation time on the next project by 50%. This seems to occur in every company and with every multisite implementation. While implementations can be sped up, it doesn't necessarily mean it is a good thing nor does it mean they can be cut in half. We need to take the time to get people involved, teach them the tools, and figure out those items unique to the next area in which we are implementing. Remember the people piece; change can be difficult and takes time. It seems this lesson always must be learned the hard way.

Lesson Learned: It is the people who drive the change, not the Lean tools, so invest the time to train your employees.

Beware of the Cookie Cutter Approach

While many areas across different companies are similar, we have found none the same. For this reason, we highly discourage cookie cutter type approaches. It is important to go through the analysis steps (BASICS®) in each implementation to obtain the buy-in from the existing staff. This does not mean that once the formula is created, it can't be implemented slightly quicker, but it is important not to try to implement it too quickly or it will not sustain. Remember that Lean requires people to think differently than they are used to. If they don't go through the process of seeing their wastes in the process for themselves, they will have difficulty in accepting any new process proposed.

Scripting and Customer Service

Our experience is there is a high correlation between those companies that embrace scripting and employee-centered initiatives and their customer satisfaction numbers. These companies also have leadership support from the top down to do whatever it takes to ensure customer satisfaction.

Chapter Questions

1. Describe some of the various Lean implementation methods.
2. What is the difference between a point kaizen event and a system level kaizen?
3. What are some of the pros and cons behind point kaizen events?
4. Why do a lot of companies start with 5S? What can be some of the shortcomings with this approach?
5. What is the best way to implement a Lean line? What do we have to work off first?
6. What are some of the guidelines for a Lean group leader/supervisor? How do they differ from a traditional supervisor?
7. What is the importance of a team charter? Construct a team charter for a real problem you have.
8. What role does variation play when implementing a Lean system?
9. Why is conducting a FMEA important before rolling out a Lean implementation?
10. What are two of the implementation guidelines?
11. What role does SWIP play in implementing a new line? Why is it so difficult for people to figure it out?
12. What was your favorite lesson learned in the chapter?
13. What is the problem with the cookie cutter approach to Lean implementation?
14. What is the escalation process and how is it used?
15. How is TLT calculated? Is this the same as total throughput time?
16. What did you learn from this chapter?

Notes

1. Quantum Leap: In Speed to Market, John R. Costanza, Jc-I-T Institute of Technology, ©1992.
2. Management Lessons from Taiichi Ohno, Harada, McGraw Hill, ©2015.

3. Yuzo Yasuda, 40 Years, 20 Million Ideas: Toyota Suggestion System (New York: Productivity Press), 1990.

4. Video by Joel Barker, The New Business of Paradigms, ©2001; Original Business of Paradigms, 1989, Charthouse International Learning, distributed by Star Thrower.

5. Gold Bronze Silver SME Lean Certification Program http://www.sme.org/lean-bronze-certification.aspx

6. http://www.jma.or.jp/en/about/history_jma.html

7. PHP started by Matsushita, http://www.php.co.jp/en/publications/PHP stands for peace and happiness through prosperity, which expresses the ultimate ideal of the PHP group to bring peace and fulfillment to human society by assuring both spiritual and material abundance. To this end, the group conducts studies on a wide range of subjects centered on man and society. It also organizes a variety of programs designed to promote the ideals of PHP and share the fruits of its research with people all over the world. The PHP group is a research organization as well as a humanistic, cultural, and social movement. It is not a mere think tank, insofar as we do not undertake research projects just for profit, nor is it a religion, as we do not advocate worship of any deity or deities. We have our own philosophy, but do not impose a set of teachings or a belief system on anyone. The group is open to all ideas, past or present, Eastern or Western, and scientific or religious, if they contribute to the improvement to bring different ideas, experiences, and traditions together in pursuit of better ways to achieve peace and happiness. Our goal is universal, a shared aspiration of all people. Likewise, activities dedicated to that goal are going on everywhere. The PHP movement, therefore, goes far beyond the bounds of the PHP group alone.

8. Conversation with William Hopper, October 31, 2012.

9. Story furnished by Professor James Bond during chapter review February 2013.

10. Allied Signal Training—compiled by Michael Chan.

11. James Womack and Dan Jones, Lean Thinking (New York: Simon and Schuster), 1996.

12. Norman Bodek, Kaikaku (Portland, OR: PCS Press), 2004.

13. Evolving Excellence, December 2006, http://www.evolvingexcellence.com/blog/2006/12/toyota question.html

14. Source—Lean Manufacturing Blog, Kaizen Articles and Advice | Gemba Panta Rei, Jon Miller, November 30, 2006.

15. Jeff Gilmore, interview by Alan Butki, St. Joseph, Missouri, June 1999.

16. Taiichi Ohno, Toyota Production System (New York: Productivity Press), 1988.

17. Taiichi Ohno, Toyota Production System (New York: Productivity Press), 1988.

18. Taiichi Ohno, Toyota Production System (New York: Productivity Press), 1988; Taiichi Ohno and Setsuo Mito, Just-in-Time for Today and Tomorrow (New York: Productivity Press), 1988.

19. Koichi Shimokawa and Takahiro Fujimoto (Editors), The Birth of Lean (Cambridge, MA: Lean Enterprise Institute, Inc.), 2009, Brian Miller and John Shook (Translators), ISBN-10:1934109223.

20. Story submitted by John Volz.

21. Story furnished by Professor James Bond during chapter review February 2013.

22. Mike Rother, Toyota Kata (New York: McGraw Hill), 2009; 40 Million Ideas in 20 Years Book, Yasuda, Productivity Press, ©1990, www.artoflean.com; Durward Sobek, Understanding A3 Thinking: A Critical Component of Toyota's PDCA Management System (Portland, OR: Productivity Press), 2008; Managing to Learn, John Shook, Lean Enterprise Institute, ©2008.

23. With permission of Bruce Tuckman 1965, original forming-storming-norming-performing concept, http://www.businessballs.com/tuckman-formingstormingnormingperforming.html. Four stages of teams. Psychologist, B.W. Tuckman in the 1970s, developed this model and Tuckman suggests there are four team development stages teams must go through to be productive. The four stages are forming, when the team meets and starts to work together for the first time; storming, when the members within the team start to jockey for position and when control struggles take place; norming, when the rules are finalized and accepted and when team rules start being adhered to; and performing, when the team starts to produce through effective and efficient working practices.

24. http://en.wikipedia.org/wiki/Pareto_principle. The Pareto principle (also known as the 80–20 rule, the law of the vital few, and the principle of factor sparsity) states, for many events, roughly 80% of the effects come from 20% of the causes. Business management thinker, Joseph M. Juran, suggested the

principle and named it after Italian economist Vilfredo Pareto, who observed in 1906 80% of the land in Italy was owned by 20% of the population. It is a common rule of thumb in business, for example, "80% of your sales come from 20% of your clients." Mathematically, where something is shared among a sufficiently large set of participants, there must be a number k between 50 and 100 such that k% is taken by (100 − k)% of the participants. k may vary from 50 (in the case of equal distribution) to nearly 100 (when a tiny number of participants account for almost all the resource). There is nothing special about the number 80% mathematically, but many real systems have k somewhere around this region of intermediate imbalance in distribution.

25. Yuzo Yasuda, 40 Years, 20 Million Ideas: The Toyota Suggestion System (New York: Productivity Press), 1990.

26. Validated in email correspondence 5/4/13 with James Bond, "Based on my experience, I would say yes to the 3%."

Additional Readings

Babich, P. 1996. Hoshin Handbook. Poway, CA: TQE.

Beauregard, M. 2000. Experimenting for Breakthrough Improvement. Tolland, CT: Resource Engineering.

Dennis, P. 2005. Andy and Me. New York: Productivity Press.

Duggan, K.J. 2002. Creating Mixed Model Value System. New York: Productivity Press.

Harmon, R.L. 1992. Reinventing the Factory. New York: Free Press Simon Schuster.

Hirsh, S.K. 1996. Work It Out. Palo Alto, CA: Davies Black Publishing.

Hyer, N.L. 2002. Reorganizing the Factory. Portland, OR: Productivity Press.

Jones, D.T. 2005. Breaking Through to Flow. Ross-on-Wye, UK: Lean Enterprise Academy.

Larco, L. 2008. Build to Order. Brentwood, CA: Oakley Press.

Monden, Y. 1986. Applying Just in Time. Norcross, GA: IIE Press.

Robinson, A. 1991. Continuous Improvement in Operations. Cambridge, MA: Productivity Press.

Rother, M. 2006. Creating Continuous Flow. Brookline, MA: Lean Enterprise Institute.

Standard, C. and Davis, D. 1999. Running Today Factory. Cincinnati, OH: Hanser Gardner.

Wheelwright, S.C. 1992. Revolutionizing Product Development. New York: Free Press Simon Schuster.

Chapter 2

Kanbans

Kanban is like the old time milkman. Mom didn't give the milkman a schedule.
Mom didn't use the material requirement planning system (MRP). She simply put
the empties on the front steps and the milkman replenished them. That is the essence
of a pull system.

Ernie Smith

Lean Event Facilitator in the Lean Enterprise Forum at the University of Tennessee

Kanban literally means "watch over a board for a period"; it is like a sign outside a business,
but with a soul. Kanbans facilitate inventory management by providing a sign or signal for
replenishment. According to Taiichi Ohno, the person credited with developing just in time
(JIT), Kanban is a means through which JIT is achieved.[1] The purpose of a Kanban system
(see Figure 2.1a) is to control the flow of material by providing inventory as a buffer to synchronize two disconnected processes. Kanban is a visual management tool, see Figure 2.1b,
to help prevent overproduction, the number one waste, and for detecting delays in the process
or when processes are producing ahead of schedule (a pacemaker to prevent overproduction—
i.e., produce only what is ordered, when ordered, and quantity ordered). There are additional
benefits of Kanban to include increased flexibility to meet customer demand, reduction in
scheduling by production control and manufacturing, and competitive advantage by sequencing shipments to customers to ensure they receive what they want, when they want it, and in
the order they want it.

Kanbans are inventory, thus we must constantly work to minimize the number of materials.
A Kanban trigger or signal can be an empty space, an empty bin, a piece of paper, an electronic
signal (lights, electronic data interchange (EDI), or an icon (e.g., rolling golf balls down a tube).
A Kanban is a signal designed to trigger an event. The term Kanban can initially be very confusing because the term Kanban itself is used in several ways. It is not only used to describe the
overall replenishment system but also the individual bins or cards used within the system (see
Figure 2.2). A Kanban card or empty bin can signal the need for the material to be replenished
or it can serve as an order for production to start the order to replenish the parts. In many years of
implementation, we have found that when using this simple system, we have never run out of parts.

DOI: 10.4324/9781003185802-2

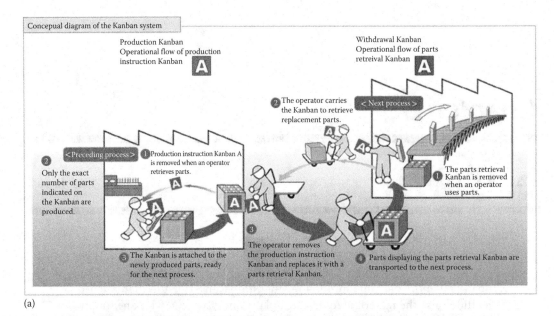

(a)

(b)

Figure 2.1   (a) Conceptual Kanban system and (b) Kanban squares outlined on the floor—Visual management vs. cards.

When you depend on a computer to manage when to reorder, we typically have many parts we don't need (excess inventory and additional cost) and we are out of the parts we do need. What are the impacts given this condition? Kanban is like the resupply of milk when the time-honored milkman would take your empties and replace them with full bottles.

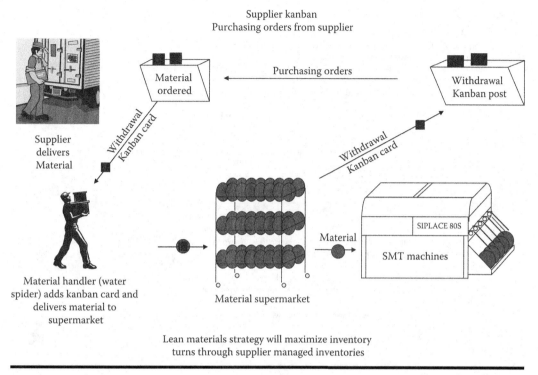

Supplier kanban
Purchasing orders from supplier

Figure 2.2   Kanban system with cards used for surface mount technology (SMT) machines.

Types of Kanban

There are several types of Kanban as shown in Figure 2.3 and explained in the first six chapters of the book entitled The Toyota Production System.[2] The main types are withdrawal (Toyota refers to this as retrieval) and production (Toyota refers to this as informative)[3] Kanban. Remember, Kanbans are triggers to cause an action or event to occur. Withdrawal means a person goes to a shelf with an empty bin, obtains a full bin, and leaves the empty. The empty may be replaced by an area, a stock room, or a supplier. If there is a card system, the person takes the card from the new bin and puts it on the empty bin. A production-ordering Kanban uses the empty bin to trigger the need for production.

The simplest type of Kanban is called a two-bin system (see Figure 2.4). A two-bin system is composed of two separate bins containing the same parts, with one bin placed behind the other. When the first bin empties, the next full bin slides down. The empty bin becomes the Kanban signal or trigger visually indicating that the bin needs to be replenished. The empty bins are collected, taken to the stockroom (or sent back to the supplier), and refilled. The new bin of materials is returned to the original location in the area. This is called a withdrawal Kanban system. Kanban systems regulate the inventory in a production system as the volume or rate of the process changes.

Kanban systems can also utilize card systems. In this system, the card is taken from the empty bin and placed in a holder (to be ordered). This is called a Kanban post. At certain frequencies during the day, the material handler or water spider comes and collects the cards in the post

Types of kanban

- Withdrawal
  - Interprocess: Specifies the kind and quantity of a product that the subsequent process should withdraw from the preceding process
  - Supplier: Specifies the kind and quantity of a product to be supplied from the supplier. All suppliers, kanban cards are bar-coded
    - Later replenishment system: Kanban are filled from suppliers' finished goods shelf
    - Sequenced withdrawal: Supplier sequences parts in reverse order for truck loading
- Production ordering
  - Specifies the kind and quantity of product that the preceding process must produce
    - Rectangle: One-piece flow production
    - Triangular: For small lot (segmented batch) production
- Job order
  - Issued for each job order
- Through
  - When two processes are very close, it doesn't make sense to issue two kanbans. Used where one process directly feeds (conveyor) the next process
- Common
  - Where a withdrawal kanban is used as a production ordering kanban if the distance between two processes is very short and share the same supervisor
- Emergency
  - Temporary, when there is a defect or problem, can be withdrawal or production
- Express
  - Temporary, issued when there is a shortage, can be withdrawal or production

Heat treat kanban system at company X

Kanban at McDonalds

Figure 2.3   Types of Kanbans.

Figure 2.4   Kanban—Two-bin system.

Figure 2.5 Materials visual controls—Empty cards were placed in "to order" post and once ordered place in "complete" post. When the parts arrived they were married up with the card in the "complete" post and placed back on the shelf.

(see Figure 2.5). The cards are used to reorder the parts from the supplier. Once the material is ordered, the card is placed back in the Kanban post in the ordered slot. When the new bin of materials arrives, the card from the reordered slot is placed on the arriving bin of materials. The new bin of materials is returned to the original location in the area. This is called a withdrawal Kanban system.

Another option for this system is to take the card off the bin of materials when it is empty and place it in the Kanban post. The water spider takes the card or the empty bin to the replenishment area and replenishes the bin or grabs an existing bin from the shelf. If the water spider replenishes the bin, the card remains on the bin and is returned to the shelf. If the water spider grabs an existing bin, the first step is to remove the card from the old bin and puts it on the new bin. The next step in the process is to take the card that was on the new bin and put it into another Kanban post to trigger replenishment from the supplier or production cell. If the card triggers production in the cell, it is called a production-ordering Kanban. Some jobs have non-common parts. For these jobs, we must create a special order Kanban card. These cards are typically generated once for a particular work order (see Figure 2.6). There are many types of Kanban systems that have been documented by Ohno, Dr. Shingo, and Monden.[4]

Failure Modes

Kanban systems have two major failure modes:

1. First, the Kanban system was originally designed in the plan for every part (PFEP) to support a certain maximum volume or customer demand. If this volume is exceeded, there will be parts shortages.
2. Second, if Kanban cards are lost, inventory will not be replaced. If there are too many cards in the system to begin with, it will create excess inventory.

Figure 2.6   Examples of Kanban cards.

Ongoing audits of the cards in a Kanban system are required to ensure all the cards are present. Some people will complain this takes extra time to find all the cards. If cycle counting of parts was done prior to Kanban, use this time to audit Kanban cards instead. Training of the entire area, discipline, and vigilance are necessary especially the first time the Kanban system is installed. The Kanban system can be a one-bin system as well if the parts are replenished every day. Normally in a one-bin system, the bins are refilled to the top, as one might refill bread in a store. It is still important to keep the earliest due date (EDD[5]/previously known as FIFO). This is called a breadman system. In some areas, parts are scanned into a bar code terminal as the quantity of supplies is taken. This information is passed immediately to the stock room or supplier as data for replenishment. This is called a point-of-sale system. Another way to trigger replenishment would be a water level line drawn or painted in the bin. When the parts go below the line, it needs to be replenished.

Kanban Calculations and Safety Stock

We have done significant research on Kanban formulas. Every book has a different formula for sizing Kanbans. The Kanban formula is the number of parts required to cover the time to replenish the parts + buffer stock + safety stock divided by container size.

Every company seems to have a different plan for safety stock. The safety stock can be calculated using coefficient of variation (CV) or probability statistics. We normally use standard deviation plots for parts and set safety stock based on the beta or risk assigned to the part. For low-risk parts, we may start with 10% of the demand based on the replenishment frequency.

Some formulas in a company drive a significant amount of extra inventory based on supplier delivery, performance, and CV. In any system, it is always best to start with more material than you need and then work to reduce the inventory levels. The reason for this is: if you run out of material, all the Lean naysayers will say, "I told you this Lean system would hurt our deliveries." When we implemented Kanban throughout Company X's first-tier supply chain, they went through three materials managers during the 4–6 months it took to implement the system. Every time they changed the materials manager, they had us change the safety stock formula to what the new materials manager was taught.

Safety stock formulas are confusing, and to understand the Kanban and safety stock formulas, you first need to understand that there are in essence two different minimums derived in the formulas. Some formulas drive you to the absolute minimum Kanban size, while other formulas drive you to a batch-based minimum, which is twice as many parts. The batch size formulas assume the parts cannot be replenished during hourly or daily consumption. For example, if there are parts that are used daily and there is a 2-week lead time from the supplier and 1 day of receiving time, the replenishment cycle is 1 day for manufacturing, 10 working days supplier time, and 1 day for receiving or 12 days. The minimum Kanban sizing is 12 days' worth plus safety and buffer stock divided by the container size. This assumes the supplier can deliver every day. The maximum (batch-based) sizing assumes the 12 days (2 weeks) is fixed and drives double or 22 days of material plus safety stock plus buffer stock divided by the container size. The analogy here is like standard work in process (WIP) with the oven. One formula assumes the oven can be opened each cycle, whereas the other formula assumes the oven can't be opened until the batch is completed, which doubles the amount of standard WIP required to manage the oven. In essence, RM Kanbans could be thought of as standard WIP for raw materials.

Some safety stock formulas assume significant supplier risk doubling or even tripling the 10-day portion of the sizing formula. We have seen Kanban sizing that results in three to four inventory turns that is exactly opposite of the JIT strategy. The goal of initial Kanban systems should be 12–20 inventory turns the first year and 40–60 by the third year.

How Do You Know If It Should Be a Kanban Part?

Kanban systems are sometimes referred to as supermarkets since they were the premise for the idea. Parts specially ordered or ordered once a year are normally not good candidates. Some companies utilize the CV[6] to determine which parts to Kanban or to set safety stock levels. This is computed by dividing the standard deviation of the usage by the usage mean.[7] More complicated factors can be considered such as throughput velocity, machine utilization, and autocorrelation processing time. One can also review the standard deviation of lead times to the CV based on statistics and probabilities of supplier capability and lead times. These formulas can drive much higher inventory levels than typically necessary. CVs less than 1 are considered candidates, between 1 and 2 are marginal candidates, and >2.5 remain on Materials Requirements Planning (MRP) system, which are push systems. We find it's easy to overcomplicate what should be a straightforward process.[8]

The simplest way is to consider any part for Kanban, which has a consistent demand over a user-defined period. This may be daily, weekly, monthly, or sometimes even quarterly. Parts that are considered special orders or ordered only once a year are not good candidates.

Kanban System Rules

Kanbans should only be used when we can't link processes directly together. Kanban cards should only be used when we can't use more simplistic systems, like an empty bin or space. The later process always goes to the earlier process to pick up material. The earlier process produces according to the Kanban quantity and sequence. If you are using cards, all parts must have Kanban cards attached, and parts must be supplied 100% defect-free. The goal is to reduce the number of Kanban cards over time through smoothing demand and shortening the cycle time. Kanbans have also been used in the traditional stock room where a minimum cycle count from a master bin signals the supplier from the warehouse management system to replenish the bin.

Kanban Replenishment: Constant Time or Constant Quantity

Kanbans can be replenished in two ways:

1. Constant time means they are replenished the same time each day or several times a day. This is referred to as breadman type replenishment, which is like grocery store shelves being restocked each night (see Figure 2.7).
2. Constant quantity is like the two-bin system (see Figure 2.8). It may empty out at any time, and we refill it with the same quantity every time.

Figure 2.7   Supermarket shelves replenished daily.

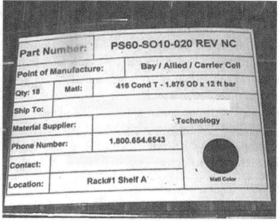

Figure 2.8   Finished goods Kanban with cards courtesy of Ancon Gear.

Sizing Kanbans: Calculating the Proper Quantity

Every book has a different formula for calculating the size and number of Kanban (see Figure 2.9). The simplest way to consider sizing a Kanban is to think about a two-bin system. When the first bin empties out, the second slides down to replace it. How much material do we need in the second bin? The answer is as much material as it takes to replenish the first bin and place it back

Kanban Sizing Traditional Calculations

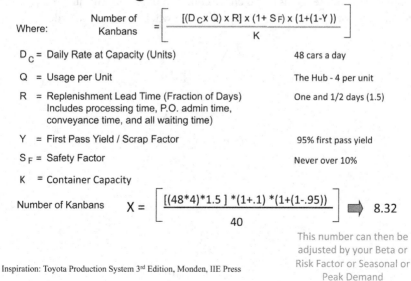

Where: Number of Kanbans $= \left[\dfrac{[(D_C \times Q) \times R] \times (1 + S_F) \times (1 + (1 - Y))}{K} \right]$

D_C = Daily Rate at Capacity (Units)   48 cars a day

Q   = Usage per Unit   The Hub - 4 per unit

R   = Replenishment Lead Time (Fraction of Days)   One and 1/2 days (1.5)
Includes processing time, P.O. admin time,
conveyance time, and all waiting time)

Y   = First Pass Yield / Scrap Factor   95% first pass yield

S_F = Safety Factor   Never over 10%

K   = Container Capacity

Number of Kanbans $X = \left[\dfrac{[(48*4)*1.5] *(1+.1) *(1+(1-.95))}{40} \right]$ ⇨   8.32

This number can then be
adjusted by your Beta or
Risk Factor or Seasonal or
Peak Demand

Inspiration: Toyota Production System 3rd Edition, Monden, IIE Press

Figure 2.9   Kanban sizing calculations.

behind the second bin. In addition, we need a small buffer of material to cover us in the event something goes wrong and the bin does not get replenished right away, which we define as buffer stock. We also carry some extra in case there are quality issues with the part of the process in which the part is used, which is called safety stock. It is normal to carry a small percentage of the overall quantity (up to 10%) to cover safety and buffer stock. There are many ways to calculate safety stock from standard deviations in current usage to z-scores. In statistics, the z-score (also referred to as the standard score) is used to compare means from different sets of data that are normally distributed. Safety stock ideally should be kept separate from the rest of the parts. The reason for this is that safety stock is excess inventory and we should keep it as a visual reminder that it is there due to a problem or quality risk associated with our process. The safety stock should be rotated with the regular stock so we don't lose the earliest due date (EDD). In many cases, it is not practical to keep the safety stock separate so we mix it in with the regular parts. In this case, we should note on the bin what quantity is a safety stock. Someone should own responsibility to reduce the safety stock as well.

Simple Kanban formula is as follows:

$$\frac{\text{Total Leadtime to Replenish} + \text{Safety Stock} + \text{Buffer Stock}}{\text{Container Size}} = \text{Number of Kanbans Required}$$

Kanban Maturity Path: Sustaining

Before implementing Kanbans, a system must be in place, and people must be trained (see Figure 2.10). We must be committed to the system and the idea that all excess inventories are bad or else the Kanban boards will end up in some storage shed (see Figure 2.11).

Kanbans are inventory and are by default created because we can't or have been unable to link two processes together. The first step in Kanbans is creating storage locations for the parts (see Figure 2.12). Other goals are to create common parts, but this just minimizes locations. The next step in the maturity path is job order Kanban where we make to order.

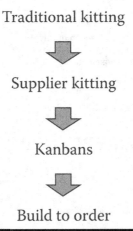

Traditional kitting

Supplier kitting

Kanbans

Build to order

Figure 2.10   Maturity path for Kanbans.

Figure 2.11 Kanban board not utilized but stored—Must have management commitment for Kanbans to work.

Transition to Lineside Materials and Material Warehouse on Shop Floor

At Company X, as we moved from traditional kitting to Kanbans, our first phase was to set up the lineside parts and material warehouses next to the lines. We then pulled all the material from the stockroom to the material warehouses located next to the lines. This was an interesting process as trying to find all the parts in the stock room that go to a particular line can be quite time consuming and difficult. Since this is a lengthy process, we find parts which simply turn up every couple of weeks that no one knew about. How can this be? As we continued down this path, we began to free up the stock room space, which was then used for more manufacturing, which increased their asset utilization and sales per square foot. The Kanbans were

Figure 2.12 Kanbans integrated into the cells.

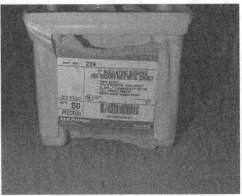

Figure 2.13   Examples of VMI inventory—Suppliers managed the containers and sizes.

in place for several years. The sheet metal shop and vendor-managed inventory (VMI) steel (see Figure 2.13) and hardware suppliers were replenishing the Kanbans based on a daily inventory of the warehouse Kanbans.

The next phase was to use group technology to see if we could improve the system. At Company X, we determined that instead of making a whole metal sheet of A parts, they could make a set of ABCDEF parts out of one or several sheets of metal for one unit. This created substantial initial resistance and a lot of effort to rewrite all the computer numerical control (CNC) programs but resulted in supplying a kit of parts to the floor sequenced by order of the units being produced based on customer demand. Once the parts were supplied on the kit cart and followed the unit, they were able to eliminate all the material Kanban warehouses and custom-made racks on the side of the line. This freed up the space on the side of the line to move their major subassembly lines that were now built JIT in sequence for each unit. The progression from traditional kitting to Kanban warehouse to build to order kits simplified the process and freed up a significant amount of waste and labor.

$$\text{Total Capacity} = \text{Output} + \text{Waste}$$

However, since none of this effort was budgeted, it took much perseverance and a solid management commitment and backing to make it a reality. If it wasn't for one of the plant managers who volunteered to figure out the sheet metal nests and revise all their CNC programs, it would have never happened.

Gas Gauge Visual Tool

A gas gauge comes in many forms but essentially is communicating when the item needs to be replenished. It is more of the breadman (or constant time) type of replenishment system. It can be green/yellow/red or a type of water level system. Some companies use golf balls. The water spider observes the shelves, and when they are in the green, no action is necessary. When it moves to yellow, it is time to replenish and red means you are into safety stock (see Figure 2.14).

Build to Order

Build to order is the goal in Lean, assuming we can build it and ship it the same day or hour required. This principle was proven during some episodes of a popular TV program called Top Chef.[9] After watching several years of episodes, we concluded that chefs that won always built

Figure 2.14 Examples of gas gauges—Green is ok, yellow means running low, and red means into safety stock.

their sandwiches or dishes to order. By building to order, their dishes were always fresh and hot. Those chefs that batched (i.e., made their dishes ahead of time) had soggy or dry bread, were cold, lost their texture, or had some other problem with the dish.

Subway® is a good example of the build to order process. Subway could not produce and store the large number of potential types of sandwiches and needed to perfect single flow Lean lines to maintain quality, reduce space, and ensure quick, affordable meals for customers. Upon entering the store, customers start in the single flow line, providing the sandwich operator specific details for each sub, including type of bread, meat, cheese, and condiments. There are some items that are supplied in batch because of the ovens, such as the bread; however, the assembly process is built to order, which provides the customer-made sandwich at a value-oriented price in just a few minutes. Using the Lean techniques for producing sandwiches, Subway has grown into a franchise system with over 35,000 stores located in over 90 countries.

Lineside Materials in Place and Labeled

The next step during implementation is to set up your lineside materials. These are materials generally in two-bin containers or in slotted sequence to the line. In an office, this includes any tools needed to do the job at that station such as a stapler, a three-hole punch, or a two-bin stack of blank paper.

On an assembly line, the bins should be labeled by location and in the order the product is produced. To do baton zone flexing (bumping), we may be required to add additional bins of the same part in the line at different stations (or sometimes even at the same station), which is also true for tools.

Lineside inventory can be sized differently for different applications, but the normal rule of thumb is to start out with a day's worth of product in each lineside bin. For large or bulky parts, this may require replenishing every hour or sometimes even every cycle (assuming longer cycle times).

Sometimes we must get creative on how to present the materials to the operator as it can get challenging with different types of parts or where there are hundreds of parts used in production. Sometimes we present parts from underneath the table. Sometimes we add chutes underneath the table for empty bins or they are placed on a designated shelf or rack at the station. There is no exact right or prescriptive way to handle empty bins if the process flow and Kanban strategy are maintained.

For mixed model lines, we may have parts for each model on a different row of shelves, or (see Figure 2.15) we may have shelves that roll up to the line. Don't limit yourself to what a book says on how to do it. Think about it and figure out what will work best for your situation. The goal is to make the operator's job easy. At Company X, they had several lines used for consumable type products. But they only received orders for these products three to four times a year. Once they received the order, it only took 2–3 weeks to finish the order. The company created complete lines on wheels including materials that they would literally roll in and out of storage when the orders were received.

There are some nonnegotiable points:

- The parts and tools must be placed on the line in order of assembly in correct orientation even if it means duplicating parts.
- The parts should be arranged to minimize operator motions such as reaching.
- There must be an established trigger and system in place for replenishment (worst-case scenario is the operator replenishing at the end of the shift).
- They must be labeled with the part number, revision level if applicable, and description along with both the lineside location on the front and replenishment location on the back such as warehouse, stock room, or supplier on the back. The front of the bin should include the quantity per unit (where it makes sense) and the back of the bin should include the quantity necessary to refill the bin from the material warehouse or supplier if VMI.

As stated earlier in the book, lineside materials are parts located at the operator workstation and within the normal reach of the operator. Generally, we utilize a two-bin Kanban system for

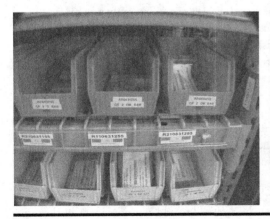

The legend sheet is color coded for each model which represents the same color bins in the rack

Figure 2.15 Mixed model lines Kanban supermarket.

these parts. Individual-type parts should be located at point of use (POU) in order of assembly, which means they may repeat several workstations. They should be located close enough to the operator, so they don't feel the need to pick up several parts and place them somewhere on their workstation prior to assembly. The parts should be picked up one at a time and placed immediately on the unit being assembled. If the parts are stored on shelves, there should be a vertical pattern starting from high to low for each column of parts. The operator should not have to go down an entire row of parts and then return to the front of the workstation to put in the next row of parts. This would necessitate the backward movement of the product, which is not acceptable.

Set Up and Label Warehouse Materials

The material warehouse on the shop floor is composed of parts kept next to or near the line, which are utilized to feed the lineside materials. The end goal is to eliminate these parts and have the vendor supply right to the line (vendor-managed products). The vendor becomes responsible and becomes the water spider for that specific product. Generally, these parts do not repeat, but there are exceptions. This can be a one-bin system with water levels, two-bin system, or multiple-bin systems with a visual trigger. Ideally, these would be flowed through racks like the lineside racks, but this is not always possible.

There are two strategies for the warehouse. It can be next to the line (see Figures 2.16 and 2.17) or in a centralized area off the lines (see Figures 2.18 and 2.19). Each strategy has pros and cons. If the warehouse is next to the line, it is easier for the team leader or group leader to see all their

Two bin materials warehouse next to the line (mostly VMI) behind this was a row for palletized materials

Two bin lineside materials

Back side of two bin lineside materials

Two bin materials warehouse next to the line

Figure 2.16　Lineside and warehouse materials next to line. (From BIG Archives.)

Figure 2.17 Material warehouses behind the line. (From BIG Archives.)

materials. The disadvantage is that it does add space to the cells, in that each cell has a space for the warehouse in between the lines. If the warehouse is centralized, it allows the cells to be placed closer together, but it is a longer walk for the water spider and team leader or group leader to check on their parts. This means a milk run must be made to the supermarket every hour or so depending on the replenishment times at the line. Some companies will leave these materials in the stock room and replenish them based on MRP or min/max. We recommend setting up the material warehouse next to the line if possible but generally the layout will determine the type of warehouse or supermarket. Placing the material near the line eliminates the milk run, starts reducing the stock room space (which can be converted to manufacturing space later), and reduces the reliance on any MRP or enterprise resource planning (ERP) system. The team lead or supervisor can see all the material in house by a visual check of the material warehouse and identify immediately where any shortages may occur or where there is excess inventory.

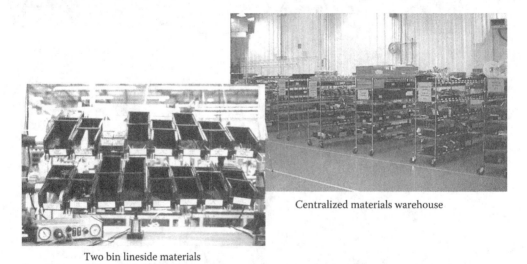

Centralized materials warehouse

Two bin lineside materials

Figure 2.18 Lineside and centralized warehouse materials. (From BIG Archives.)

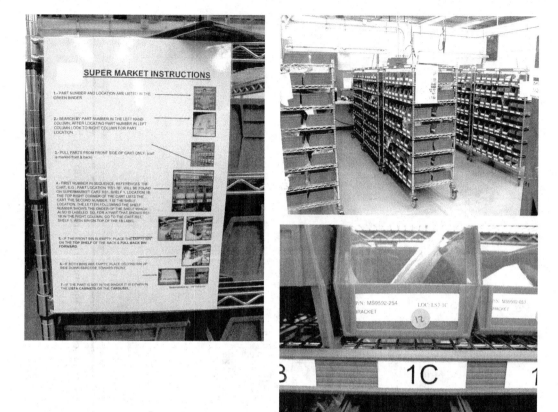

Figure 2.19   Centralized material warehouse. (From BIG Archives.)

Stock Room Transition

As discussed earlier, it is amazing when first transitioning a line how much excess inventory is normally found. There tends to be substantial initial resistance to pulling all the material out of the stock room. It is important not to let the resistance win out. The other problem is with MRP because we must rely on the planner to update the system and generate the work orders. If the planner is not there, the work orders don't get released or cut and we run out of parts. Mike Basler, Director of Materials and Logistics states: "Planning in most companies is like Whack-A-Mole. Every time you fix one problem, the next one rears its ugly head!"[10] It is not unusual to make the transition from stockroom to material warehouses on the floor to eventually VMI to the line side bins, in phases. Sometimes we end up supplying the material warehouse from the stock room until we deplete the excess inventory or get the supplier to buy it back. Over time, we work with suppliers to initially stock the material warehouse via Kanban and then VMI with the next step being direct to the line replenishment. We set up the quantities for both lineside and warehouse storage in the PFEP.

Material Plan

Once we determine the materials strategy, for larger implementations, we will create a material plan (see Figure 2.20) designating the locations of material warehouses along with their rack and shelf locations for each bin of material.

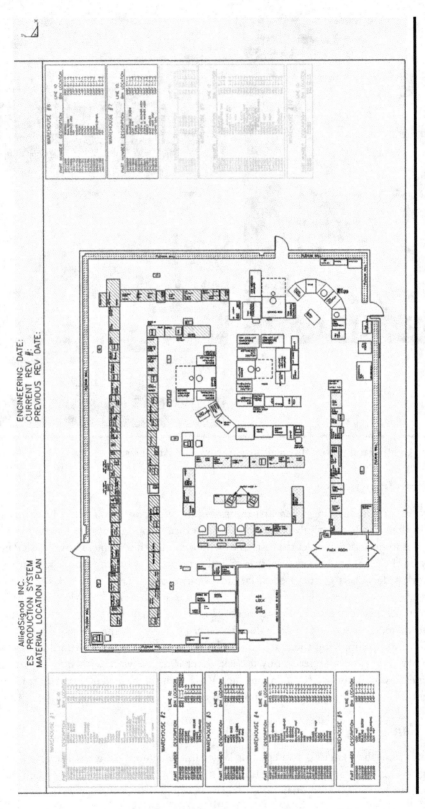

Figure 2.20 Material layout plan—Each color coded block corresponds to a rack with the material and location specified.

Supplies Needed and Placement

The supplies needed to perform a task and placement of the supplies are determined by videoing and observing staff members performing their task. As discussed earlier, a good operator will show us how to design their workstation. During the video analysis, we hold discussions regarding who uses the supply, why each supply is used, what it is, how it is used, and where within the workstation it should be placed for best access. The quantity needed may impact the location and/or timing of the replenishment of the supplies. Supplies and equipment should be placed in the order they are consumed. There should be agreement across all parties that share the workspace about the locations and quantity required. This is all documented in the PFEP. All shifts should have input into the workstation layout and design. This sounds simple; however, there can be a significant amount of change management with the people component involved. In addition, there are techniques utilized in Lean to help sustain workstation design, such as labeling and outlining, where supplies and equipment should be located to provide visual cues when equipment is misplaced. Supplies needed all the time should be at POU. Supplies needed once a day can be further away, and supplies used once a week or month further away still.

Labeling

Our next step during implementation is to set up and label the warehouse materials. The labeling of supplies and where they are placed, such as shelves and bins, is important because our goal is never to have to search for a part or tool. Labeling shelves should include a designation for the rack, shelf row, and position on the shelf row. In the example in Figure 2.21, the location for the top left box is A1A, that is, rack A shelf, row 1, in position A on the shelf.

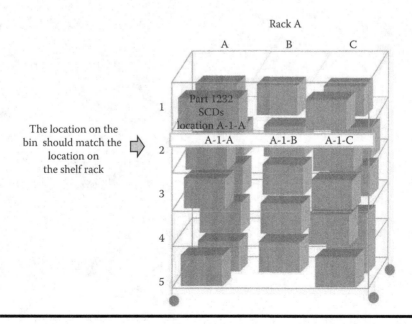

Figure 2.21   How to label racks—Should include the rack number, row number, and position in the row. If one starts labeling from the bottom up it allows for additional shelves.

It is important to label the bins. The front bin location should match the shelf location. This is true whether they are for the material warehouse or the lineside materials (see Figure 2.22).

The back of the bin tells how or where the bin is resupplied. Labeling is an important part of visual controls and is a critical component when implementing Lean initiatives to help eliminate the waste of searching (see Figure 2.23).

Some racks are not conducive to lineside inventory (see Figure 2.24). This type of hanging racks cannot be easily replenished from behind, which requires us to interrupt the operators to replenish the materials. This creates waste and confusion for the water spider and operators and results in mistakes by the operators as they lose track of where they were in their standard work.

Mistake-proofing elements can also be incorporated into bin labeling, for example, highlight metric versus English measurement systems or color codes (labels or bins or both) with geometric shapes (for color blindness) for common parts, or different model types (see Figure 2.25).

Figure 2.22 Locations on shelf—Bins location should match shelf location.

Figure 2.23   Examples of labeling.

Figure 2.24   Poor racking examples.

Figure 2.25   Metric parts well labeled so as not to use by mistake.

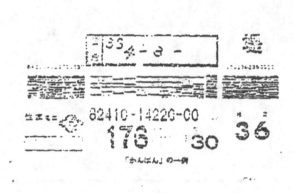

In the words of Ohno, "Subsequently, this was called the 'Kanban system' and it was felt directly that if this system were used skillfully, all the movements in the plant could be unified, i.e. systematized. After all, one piece of paper was providing the information of production quantity, time, method, sequence, or transfer quantity, transfer time, destination, storage point, transfer equipment, container, etc. clearly for grasping at one glance. At the time, I believed that this means of conveying information would certainly work."

Figure 2.26   Japanese first tier Kanban card example.

Kanban Cards

Kanban cards are normally paper-based cards in clear vinyl envelopes. They are used to disseminate three types of information (see Figure 2.26).

1. Pickup information
2. Transfer directive information
3. Production directive information

This is the same when using bins. The back of the bins shows the pickup information, the front of the bins shows the production information.

Water Spider Process

Water Spider for Replenishment

A nonstarter in manufacturing is to use your assemblers or machinists to retrieve their own parts or tools. After all, who adds value (increased revenue) for the enterprise? If the operator is standing in line at a stock room or tool room, they can't be working on/or producing parts for the customer; however, we find many companies violate this rule every day.

We must keep operators operating; thus, we add water spiders. Sometimes we call water spiders material handlers. The name water spiders come from the water beetle that frequently scurries around. The material handlers or water spiders replenish the parts when the bin is empty or when triggered by a Kanban card. This means the operators can continue to work on the product and not have to worry about replenishing their stock, enabling continuous productivity of the operators. The water spider concept can be deployed outside the materials supply system as well, such as transporting specimens around a laboratory from one area to another. Some hospitals, such as ACMH in Kittanning, Pennsylvania, use friendly, constantly monitored robots (such as Dusty in Figure 2.27) as water spiders to make deliveries. The goal is to enable our operators or staff members who are working with the product not to be interrupted or inconvenienced by having to search for supplies, this increases productivity and efficiency in the area.

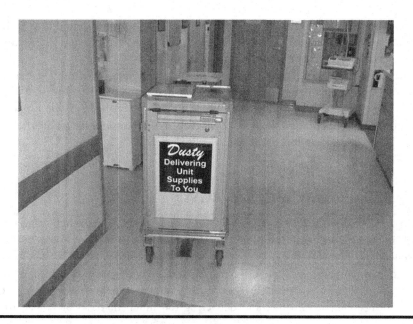

Figure 2.27   Dusty the water spider robot used at ACMH hospital in PA.

Water spiders (see Figure 2.28) can be used in assembly or machining. In machining, they can gather setup tooling and preset tools prior to the setup of a machine. Many times, we find that production can be significantly increased by taking a machinist and have them prep setups for other machinists. Some companies carry this application to the level of setup teams that descend on a machine when a setup is required. The team is notified in advance of the setup by a card, light, or

Figure 2.28   Water spider replenishing the bins.

signboard and works like a pit crew in a NASCAR® race. The operator should help with the setup or tend to another machine but not stand idly by watching the setup team. The setup team can also relieve for lunch or breaks or bottleneck machines.

In assembly, the water spider is used to replenish lineside materials from the materials warehouse. They are also used to sometimes perform off-line tasks or to relieve staff for restroom breaks. They can also be used to make sure incoming jobs (kits) have all the proper parts and quantities and stage those parts on the line where required. In automotive plants the water spider is a full time job critical to the success of the assembly lines.

Eliminating Auto Guided Vehicles (AGVs)[11]

The detailed vision in Figure 2.29 was designed and implemented to eliminate auto guided vehicles (AGVs), improve scheduling and planning, and reduce WIP via a pull system with a visual Heijunka scheduling in a very large electronics plant. Why eliminate AGVs? AGVs require technical support, maintenance upkeep, software upgrades, ongoing software reprogramming for changes, take too long to implement changes, require restarts when not working properly therefore not delivering material on-time, and delivering too much material or not all the material

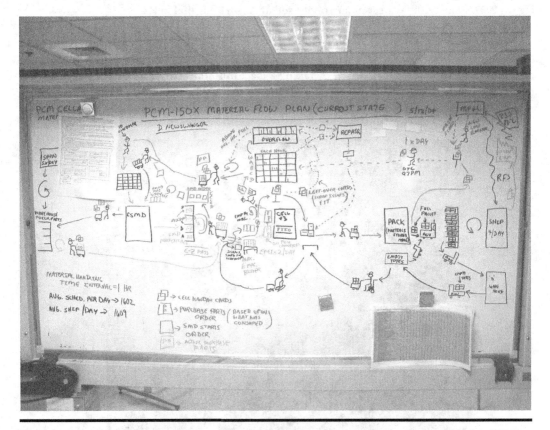

Figure 2.29   This vision was designed by Dean Newswanger to eliminate the need for AGVs.

needed when required. The above water spider route implemented eliminated all those issues as the water spider provided 1 hour material routes; replenishing only what was consumed from the POU locations. The water spider also pulled the Kanban cards from the Heijunka box to get the right circuit boards from the surface mounted device (SMD) supermarket for the assembly cells. The route ensured the water spider cart was never empty as it also ensured used dunnage pickup and removal while transversing to the warehouse supermarket utilizing the dunnage Kanbans to provide a signal to the 3PL (3rd party logistics) center.

This visual mapping was the key to a successful launch of the water spider and AGV reduction. Once it was implemented, the assembly cell operators never had to leave the cell, make calls to planning, deal with dunnage or parts presentation, or order material through an AGV material system allowing them to focus on being value adders. This significantly increased cell productivity, on-time delivery, and cut down overtime. The Heijunka box became the visual to tell the operators if they were ahead or behind and if they needed to run overtime and what to run if overtime was needed. This is just another example of how a simple visual system utilizing engaged employees can be better than someone trying to use a sophisticated technology just because it looks or sounds cool. The new system delivered material on-time, with only the right amount, and the right material every hour on the hour without all the technical and maintenance support & costs needed to support AGVs.

When this project was developed, there was a lot of skepticism on the elimination of AGVs throughout the facility as this facility spent multi-million dollars implementing AGVs. Once this project was piloted, it became obvious to go with a water spider system leading the way to the reduction in AGVs. As we like to say in the Lean World… Run the experiment!

Chapter Questions

1. What is the simplest type of Kanban? How does it work?
2. What are the two types of systems on which Kanban systems are based?
3. What is a gas gauge?
4. How do you size a Kanban, that is, what is the Kanban formula to figure out how many to put in a bin?
5. What are the rules of a Kanban system?
6. Can you explain the different types of Kanban systems?
7. How are JIT and Kanbans related?
8. What is the simplest way to size a Kanban?
9. What is a two-bin Kanban system?
10. What are some of the failure modes for Kanban?
11. Excess inventory is always the sign of a problem. What problem do Kanbans hide?
12. How should Kanban bins be labeled? What is the difference between the front and rear labels?
13. Where did the name water spider come from? What does the water spider do?
14. What is the difference between lineside inventory bins and material warehouse inventory?
15. What did you learn from this chapter?

Notes

1. http://dict.regex.info Japanese to English dictionary; http://www.saiga-jp.com Kanji to English.
2. Yasuhiro Monden, The Toyota Production System (Norcross Georgia: IISE Press), 2012.
3. Toyota's website http://www.toyota-global.com/company/vision_philosophy/toyota_production_system/just-in-time.html
4. Kanban Just In Time at Toyota, Japanese Management Association (Atlanta, USA: New York Productivity Press, 1986); Monden, Toyota Production System (Engineering & Management Press, 1993); Shigeo Shingo, Toyota Production System—Nonstock Production (Atlanta, USA: New York Productivity Press, 2006).—
5. The EDD concept replacing FIFO was communicated in personal correspondence to Charlie Protzman from Professor Matthias Thurer on December 18, 2014. In his words, "This has nothing to do with FIFO. FIFO is the worst of so-called time-based rules. I would prefer Earliest Due Date which transfers into FIFO if the lead time is standardized. What you say may happen if:

   ■ We have a rule which does notl consider urgency (as shortest processing times)
   ■ Workers cherry-pick. But with reduced inventory levels this shouldn't happen anyway.
   ■ FIFO is just a nice rule for scientists since it renders some problems mathematically tractable. I would never recommend it in practice."

6. CV is computed by dividing the standard deviation of the usage by the usage mean. One can also look at the standard deviation of lead time to the mean. Other more complicated factors that can be considered are throughput velocity, machine utilization, and autocorrelation processing time.
7. http://en.wikipedia.org/wiki/Coefficient_of_variation—In probability theory and statistics, the CV is a normalized measure of dispersion of a probability distribution. It is defined as the ratio of the standard deviation σ to the mean μ: $C_v = \sigma/\mu$. This is only defined for nonzero mean and is most useful for variables that are always positive. It is also known as unitized risk. The CV should only be computed for data measured on a ratio scale. As an example, if a group of temperatures are analyzed, the standard deviation does not depend on whether the Kelvin or Celsius scale is used. However, the mean temperature of the data set would differ in each scale, and thus, the CV would differ. So, the CV does not have any meaning for data on an interval scale.
8. http://www.informaworld.com/smpp/content~db=all~content=a773184565. An investigation of the factors influencing the number of Kanbans required in the implementation of the JIT technique with Kanbans. Published in International Journal of Production Research, Volume 25, Issue 3 March 1987, pages 457–472.
9. Top Chef: Texas ©2012 Final Six.
10. Mike Basler, Materials Manager.
11. Contributed by Dean C. Newswanger, Former ITT Executive Director, Lean Enterprise via personal correspondence January 19, 2015.

Additional Readings

Baldwin, C., Clark, K., Magretta, J., and Dyer, J. 2000. Managing the Value Chain. Boston, MA: Harvard Business Review.
Cimorelli, S.C. 2005. Kanban for the Supply Chain. New York: Productivity Press.
Gross, J.M. and McInnis, K.R. 2003. Kanban Made Simple. New York: Amacom.
Harris, R. 2006. Making Materials Flow. Brookline, MA: Lean Enterprise Institute.
Iyer, A.V., Seshadri, S., and Vasher, R. 2009. Toyota Supply Chain Management. New York: McGraw Hill.
Louis, R.S. 1997. Integrating Kanban with MRP II. New York: Productivity Press.
Louis, R.S. 2006. Custom Kanban. New York: Productivity Press.

Lu, D.J. and Kyokai, N.N. 1989. Kanban Just-in-Time at Toyota Japan Management Association. Cambridge, MA: Productivity Press.

Taylor, D.H. 2004. Lean Supply Chain (Practices & Cases). New York: Productivity Press.

Taylor, D.H. and Brunt, D. 2001. Manufacturing Operations and Supply Chain Management. London: Thomson Learning.

Vatalaro, J.C. and Taylor, R.E. 2003. Implementing Mixed Model Kanban. New York: Productivity Press.

Wincel, J.P. 2004. Lean Supply Chain Management. New York: Productivity Press.

Chapter 3

Line Balancing: Station Balancing versus Baton Zone Balancing (Bumping)

There is no way in hell you can do a job in 4 hours as expensively as you can do it in 9 months.

Tom Peters[1]

How to Balance the Work

If we have a process in which there are 30 minutes of total labor time (TLT) per unit and six people working on the line, how much work should be done by each person?

The answer is 30 minutes ÷ 6 people which equals 5 minutes per person

This requires each person to be given the same amount (5 minutes of work) and each person, in turn, must do their fair share of the 5 minutes' worth of work. To accomplish this, we need to consider the skill set of the operators or staff performing the tasks or activities. This works well if everyone in the line can do the same work and at the same speed.

It is important that each person has the appropriate cross-training to enable flexibility among tasks, processes, and equipment. A new layout and workstation setup, along with the benefits of the new system must be outlined to staff ahead of time, so that clear expectations are set and they have a clear understanding of how they are going to work in the new process. Operators and team leaders should have all been an integral part in redesigning the new process using the transport-inspect-process-delay (TIPS) and workflow analysis (WFA) tools to identify waste and create the new standard work. This participation is critical to a successful implementation and buy-in of the new line. If we do not leverage each person's knowledge in the analysis and redesign, we will not obtain the best results. As stated earlier, everyone (and especially the supervisor) needs a full

DOI: 10.4324/9781003185802-3

understanding of what is being done, why it is being done, what is in it for the company, and, above all, what is in it for them if they go along with the changes.

Batching Progression in Manufacturing

Batch-Style Manufacturing

Traditional manufacturing used to be set up in functional areas where all similar equipment was located together (see Figure 3.1). Each area was called a department, and each department was noted on a work order where labor was attached and tracked. Large batches of material would flow from one department to another. Operators would process the entire quantity of a work order through their operation before passing the batch off to the operator at the next department who was going to carry out the next required process.

For example, milling would be done in one area, turning in another, mechanical assembly in another, and painting in yet another. Many factories also had an inspection operation that needed to be carried out in a separate inspection department between each of these operations.

When you think about it, manufacturing is simply taking an order and converting raw materials (information, components, or product) into a product, which is sold for cash. This is defined as the order entry to cash cycle. There is a cost to converting the raw material to finished goods. The longer material takes to move through the business delivery system, the more cash is tied up in work in process (WIP) and the more cost is involved. This is often referred to as conversion cost. Functional layouts and batching cause operators and materials to travel long distances, which equates to increased material handling costs, additional space for all the WIP, and investments in computer systems and material requirement planning software to control and track the WIP. This batch-style manufacturing created large piles of WIP at each operation and in queues between operations. Not only does it tie up a lot of money in partially completed products (WIP), but it also requires planners and expediters to keep track of it and creates the potential to cause large amounts of scrap and rework costs if a step near the beginning of the manufacturing process was skipped or performed incorrectly.

Figure 3.1 Functional batch layout. (Courtesy of Ancon Gear.)

Focus Factories

As we got smarter, we started to transition from multi building or functional departments divided by walls to a concept called focus factories. Focus factory meant that everything we needed to build the product was contained within the four walls of the area or building. It did not necessarily mean it was laid out in a Lean fashion. Everyone used the definition differently, but everyone then seemed to have focus factories. Typically, batch-style manufacturing was still prevalent in this environment.

Cellular Layouts

The next move was to cellular layouts where all the different equipment needed to produce a product or family of similar products were grouped into cells. This cellular-type manufacturing lined up all the process steps in the order they needed to be performed, eliminated most of the travel, and shortened the queues required to manufacture the product. Some companies would create virtual cells. These were cells that supposedly operated Lean, but the equipment was not moved.

Batch-style manufacturing was still used in the early cell environments, but as already stated, much of the waste associated with transporting the product from area to area was reduced. The areas still contained other wastes, that is, mura and muri, which accompany the batch-style production techniques. Most operators were still trained to do only one operation or task so they would take the next work order in the schedule, process the entire group through their task, and then push it forward to the next sequential operation/operator for them to do the same.

These cells were many times converted to U-shapes in accordance with Lean teachings and looked good, but upon closer inspection (see Figure 3.2) were still sit-down and contained all

Figure 3.2 U-shaped sit down batch cell. (From Big Archives.)

the WIP but just spread it out among the new cells that were set up. With this type of new layout, the operators in the new cells are still just performing the same tasks they always have, the only difference being it was now being performed in a U-shaped cell. Customers not familiar with Lean would think this was a Lean cell. This system still causes an imbalance of labor because the tasks/operations almost never contain the same amount of labor and are sit-down operations. The area the operator worked in within the cell was called a station. Being the stations had uneven amounts of work, operators would end up being either overloaded or underloaded and that is the waste of mura.

Operators whose process or group of tasks contained less labor than the operator before them in the cell would have to sit idle for much of the time waiting for the product to get to his or her station. Companies essentially ended up paying the operators to sit idle much of the time. Conversely, if an operator's process or group of tasks contained less labor than the operator after them in the cell, they would essentially bury the downstream operator with WIP inventory. The buried operator would be rushed and overworked, which can be a significant cause of mistakes and stress. Scrap and rework are increased due to mistakes, and because of the large amount of work in process in the cells, many finished goods units would be negatively affected.

HP Model, Station Balancing, and In-Process Kanbans (WIP Caps)

Today the cellular models we see date back to 1983 when Hewlett Packard created an instructional road show video demonstrating stockless production or how to move from batch to small lot flow to one-piece flow manufacturing. The video also showed the pilot line at HP in Greeley, Colorado (see Figure 3.3), which the video was modeled after. The video was powerful in demonstrating the advantages of moving from a push system of six units at a time (batch production, see Figures 3.4) to a pull 3 (producing three units at a time, see Figure 3.5) and to a pull 1 (making one unit at a time). The idea behind the pull 3 system in the video is that there is a square

Figure 3.3 Doug McCord and the Model Line at HP which video was modeled after. Notice it is a sit down cell with Kanban squares between each worker. (From 1983 HP Stockless Production Video --public domain.)

Figure 3.4 Simulating batch to pull 3 then pull 1 production. (From 1983 HP stockless production video—public domain.)

in between each operator (Kanban) which must be filled with three units prior to the next operator removing any pieces from it. In addition, once the previous operator reaches the WIP cap of three units, they are supposed to stop producing until the pieces are removed from the square by the next operator in line. In the video, the facilitator makes an interesting comment: "Now we are going to convert from pull 3 to pull 1. This is the ideal that theoretically you never get to but are always striving to get to." Note that it was a sit-down line with Kanban squares between each operator. At the time, this was a revolutionary concept for most American manufacturing.

It has one day's worth of inventory that bypassed the stockroom and was located next to the cell. The video emphasized the need for participative management and quality control (QC) circles where the employees help to fix problems on their lines.

Many companies we have visited, knowingly or unknowingly, have this model or variations of this model in place. However, as we continued to learn about Lean, we found some basic problems in the video teachings. Companies that have implemented this model probably got great results after converting to a pull system with a WIP cap, but they are not getting anywhere near the results possible with a truly synchronized and balanced one-piece flow line. Our experience shows that companies which utilize this type of manufacturing can still increase productivity 10%–50% or more!

Some companies teach the concept of WIP caps in their Lean master classes, however, with bumping, we eliminate this need for WIP caps. The WIP cap calculation computes the number of parts allowed in the Kanban square between operators. It is based on the belief that the operations are balanced based on theoretical cycle time, while ignoring the variation inherent

- Total WIP in the system = 9
- One piece at each station and three pieces between each station

Figure 3.5 Pull 3 example. The 3 pieces in between each operator are called WIP caps. This means the WIP should be no more than three. It is really a push system (BIG archives)

to the operators themselves. While operator variation is unavoidable, it is often ignored during station balancing simulations. Eliminating operator variation is impossible, and the problem is amplified in station balancing. The good news is that operator variation can be handled in a positive fashion, where operators help each other or flex. This enables lines with naturally fast operators to increase output. Overproducers to boost throughput.

We call the "pull 3 or pull 1 or any system with WIP caps" the lazy man's balance (see Figure 3.6). In effect, the line is being balanced by the WIP present between the operators. Remember, excess inventory and idle time hide problems. With this Kanban square system, we encounter both idle time (when we fill up the square to the WIP cap quantity) and the fact that the inventory in the Kanban is excess. The excess materials in the Kanban squares hide the fact that the line is imbalanced (if you have not learned how to "read the WIP"). The other problem we have witnessed is that even if the WIP caps are labeled with the max amount allowed in the squares (which in many cases are bins or trays), the operators that don't have enough work will inevitably fill them with more than the max and in many cases as much as will physically fit in the area.

Lines that utilize this model have the following characteristics:

■ They are sit-down lines.
■ They were originally balanced based on a station approach with the goal of equal work at each station.
■ There are spaces or Kanban squares (WIP) in between each operator. These spaces tell the operators when they can produce and have varying quantities based on the number of parts someone has calculated as the max number of units the square can contain (WIP cap) before one is to stop working.

We have seen that the number of units in the Kanban squares which is supposed to be capped will vary, but ranges from one, as demonstrated in the HP tape, to as many as one can fit into the designated space when it is totally out of control, as it is in most cases. Some companies

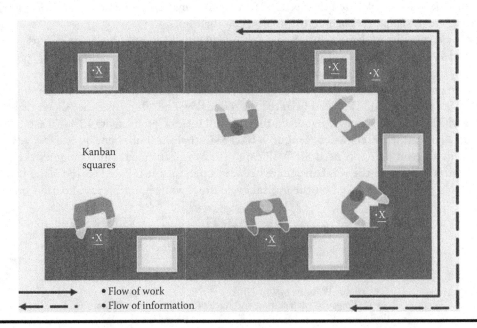

Kanban squares

• Flow of work
• Flow of information

Figure 3.6   Kanban squares between operators—lazy man's balance.

inappropriately designate this truly excess inventory as standard work-in-process or SWIP. The result of this video, and teachings based on this video, was the suggestion of an influence of station balancing as the preferred Lean line implementation method, which is what we see in place throughout most of the Lean world today.

Waste in Lean Lines

Many of the forms of waste mentioned throughout this chapter can be and usually are still present in most Lean manufacturing environments. We call these lines Lean lite! If you aren't running true single-piece flow, you essentially build many of these wastes into the manufacturing process because they are part of the batch system. When you think about it, a Kanban square (WIP cap) in the line is still a push system with the illusion of a pull system. The operators are still pushing product into the Kanban squares, so it is not a true pull system. It can only be a true pull system if there is no excess WIP in between the operators.

All the manufacturing techniques mentioned earlier force operators to produce multiple units (WIP), travel excessive distances, leave the line to get parts, put parts down, pick parts up, and either they or the product sits idle. If one were to list every step used to manufacture one part (or sandwich) on an assembly line, how many of them would truly be value added or necessary? The goal of an assembly line should be to do only the steps necessary to complete a product once it is started on the assembly line.

Lesson Learned: If you watch the line very closely, you will see each instance of where you are losing fractions of parts each cycle or during a setup.

Muda, Mura, and Muri Wastes

1. Muda refers to the seven wastes credited to Taiichi Ohno (Figure 3.7).
2. Mura refers to inconsistent or uneven use of a person or machine based on variation in the loading of operations or processes not defined by the customer. Mura results when operators or machines have a high level of work and then end up doing nothing. We see this in

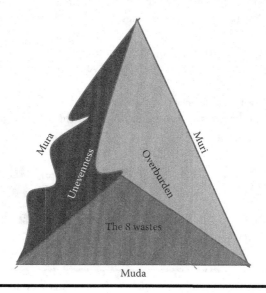

Figure 3.7 Muda, muri, mura.

machine shops all the time. We also see this in factories where parts may come back from plating in late afternoon, and the company rushes to get them assembled and shipped by 5 p.m. In addition, mura can mean uneven pace, variation in flow, inconsistency or fluctuation of quality, material consumption, production output, energy use, cost, orders, as well as manpower and machine requirements previously mentioned.

3. Muri refers to the overburden on equipment, facilities, or operators. Muri is pushing a machine or person beyond their normal capabilities. This results in safety and quality problems, machine breakdowns, and defects. We see this at airports when people bring heavy baggage, and the agents must physically strain to move the luggage. It would also include constantly having to bend over and pick up heavy items or repeating wristy intensive operations, which are ergonomically unsafe and can result in tendonitis or carpal tunnel syndrome. In addition, muri can mean beyond current capacity or difficult to do, see, hear, learn, train, teach, reach, lift, or process, or excessive workload.

Mura and muri are the two wastes that are the most prevalent in our next discussion. The key to continuous synchronized flow and reducing or eliminating these wastes on a machining or assembly line is implementing baton handoff style between line operators and implementing level loading scheduling techniques.

Station Balancing Is Like Swimming Relay Handoffs

The next progression in cellular manufacturing was what we call station balancing. The goal here was to move from batching to one-piece flow or the pull 1 in the HP video (see Figure 3.8). Station balancing consists of simply trying to divide [the total labor required to build one product produced by the cell] by [the number of operators in the cells].

Taiichi Ohno described the material handoffs in the pull 1 HP type of assembly Kanban system as swimming relay handoffs.[2] In a swimming relay, the swimmer cannot leave the starting block until the prior swimmer has touched the wall. In a cell, the next operator cannot start an operation until the prior operator completes the work at their station and moves their part(s) into the Kanban square. The Kanban squares have rules:

1. The rule is that you can't start working on a part unless there is one in your Kanban square.
2. You must stop working on it once you have filled your downstream Kanban square.

This approach, with Kanbans in between stations, is still a push system. This is because each operator is pushing to a Kanban square versus pulling from the previous operator.

- Total WIP in the system = 5
- One piece at each station and one piece between each station

Figure 3.8 One piece in process Kanban—push system with ceiling of one, i.e. WIP cap = One piece – Lazy man's balance.

Station Balance Example

Most Lean companies implemented station balanced lines some time ago, and the process has normally never been updated. To set up a station balanced line, one must determine the total labor content to build one unit from start to finish. In our example, it takes 3 minutes of TLT, and the cell has three operators (see Figure 3.9). To station balance the line, we would attempt to divide the cell into stations that contained exactly one minute of labor each.

In this type of setup, the operators are assigned and trained to work at one station. The operators complete the processes assigned to them at their station and pass the product down the line when it is completed. To set up this line, the product flow for the part may be changed or parts or equipment moved to other operators to balance the flow.

Problems with Station Balancing

■ The major problem with this approach is that people are not robots, and we all work at different rates. If someone is having a bad day, is tired, or if there is a new operator working on the line, the labor at the stations will vary from the one-minute labor target. Even if all the operators were able to perform the work at the stations consistently at the one-minute target, which is impossible, one could never divide the labor into exactly one-minute stations. Even the best-balanced line will incur problems because as one operator becomes more efficient, they will speed up and create an imbalance. Sometimes the one-minute increment point in the labor content may fall right in the middle of a task, which can't be split. For example, the operator may be in the middle of threading a fastener. In this case, you would not have them stop when the screw was half in and push it to the next station. So, the next operator will sit there idle.

■ If the line needs to run more than one model or style of product, it would also be difficult to keep the labor balanced. One model may have close to one minute of labor at one of the stations, but the next model being run may require only 30 seconds of labor to complete the operations/steps contained in the same station. Special options for products (like an extra piece of hardware) that require assembly of selected units at a station may also create an imbalance since it is done only occasionally.

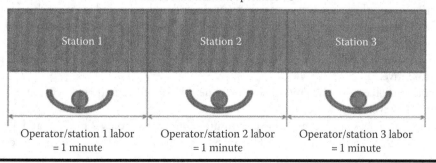

Figure 3.9   Station balancing example.

■ Because station balancing was designed based on a set number of operators, if an operator is missing, it creates problems. The line becomes batched up by station with operators completing the parts on the station prior to moving the parts to the next station. This will significantly lower the output of the line. Thus, the operators batch the production from one step to the next.

Author's Note: We see this station balancing paradigm in our classes whenever we ask the class to design a new layout. The first question they ask is how many operators are we going to have? Just by asking this question we know the line will end up being station balanced.

■ Most station balanced lines are sit-down lines. The problem with sit-down lines is that the product flow is normally lost. This is because the station was balanced based on a certain labor content, and there was no real thought given to how the product flows. For example, if a process utilizes an arbor press three times, then the operator changes the fixturing and uses the same arbor press to do different operations for the same or different subassemblies.

■ Sit-down stations are 10%–30% less efficient than stand-up and walking lines. This is because the operators are trapped at their stations, many times with equipment surrounding them, which prohibits any type of true flexing on the line. Let's face it, if we are all sitting, what are the chances we are going to get up out of our chair and come help you out? And if we did, for some reason, decide to help you out, would we be able to help you out? The answer is probably no since the persons in front and behind you are sitting at stations as well. Therefore, any batching we do is an invested yet deferred labor cost since we are working on a future and not the current unit. This goes back to the saying "if you are working on what you don't need, you can't be working on what you do need."

■ Sit-down stations have health and safety considerations. Aside from the obvious health benefits of standing and walking versus sitting, there are also safety issues related to sitting and twisting, and sitting and reaching.

■ The next problem with this type of system is when the operators dry out the line going from one product to another. In this case, each operator must sit and wait until enough inventory is in the line to start working again (we call this wetting the line). If there is a large amount of labor in a unit, two hours, for example, some operators near the end of the line may sit idle for hours.

■ Yet another problem with this system is if an operator is out sick or on vacation. Since the line above was balanced for three people, when someone is out, the remaining operators don't know how to run the line or, in some cases, can't do the operation at the station where the person is out because they are not cross-trained. Where they are cross-trained, we normally see them work at stations 1 and 2 for most of the day and batch up all the parts prior to station 3, and then they move to station 3 at the end of the day and try to work off the batch.

■ If we have a fast worker in a station balanced line, he/she will finish the work and sit idle. Since they are not working at all, our direct labor costs are inflated, and the cost of making our product becomes more expensive (assuming we even track it), which makes us less competitive.

■ Another problem we encounter is where a line is balanced to takt time (customer demand) instead of cycle time.

■ For example, let's say the takt time is 3 minutes, but we have only 2 minutes and 40 seconds worth of TLT. 160 seconds divided by 3 = 53.3 seconds. But our takt time is 60 seconds. So, we will have to put 60 seconds worth of work at stations 1 and 2, and 40 seconds at station 3. So, every cycle, station 3 is idle for 20 seconds.

■ Another issue is when the total labor changes due to a different product or even sometimes a slower operator. We find the engineer, or team leader will either continue to run it the same way creating more variation and WIP in the process or they may try to rebalance the line. To rebalance the line, they will literally move tools, material, and equipment to different stations. In many cases, the process flow (PFA) is lost, and the product will start to travel backward which is a blatant violation of Lean flow. First in, first out (FIFO) is also lost.

Because of these problems, we end up with either idle time, WIP inventory between stations, or both. Remember, extra WIP or idle time is always the sign of a problem. The idle time is the result of the variation in the speed of the operators or the lack of being able to split the labor evenly. In either case, you always end up with an operator either waiting or being rushed by the operator before them. Since idle time causes batching, the operator before them will generally not like being idle and will many times continue to complete their portion of the labor on additional units. This will bury the person after them, which will compound the stress on that person. Station balancing is more productive than batching but not as efficient as true one-piece flow. It is also not as effective as one-piece flow because if defects are found, there can still be quite a bit of bad inventory in the system.

Station Balancing Examples in Restaurants and Fast Food

We see station balancing in fast food restaurants all the time. At this fast food restaurant (see Figure 3.10), they have one-piece flow lines with the cashier at the end. They are set up to flex because the ovens and microwaves are behind them. However, they don't normally flex because they are station balanced. There is a cashier, the meat builder, and then the fixings person. Their biggest problem is the system they use, because variation is constantly introduced by people having to make up their mind and waiting to instruct the person behind the counter what to put on their sandwich. So, in the best case, they are one-piece flow but not balanced. What generally happens is the meat builder will build up several sandwiches between them and the fixings person and then start to help the fixings person if they are able. The register person sometimes flexes, but again it requires putting on and removing gloves, so they normally are idle watching the others at work.

Figure 3.10 Station balancing at a popular fast food sandwich shop. (From BIG training materials.)

Company Y restaurants fixed the order problem by having people decide what they want ahead of time and enter it into a computer or mark it on a bag. The cashier here is at the front of the line (I guess this was put in place to make sure people are stuck waiting and can't leave without paying when there is a rush). Normally, only two people (the cashier and the sandwich maker) run this line.

At yet another sandwich restaurant, the operators are divided up into cashier, sandwich maker, and a final assembly person who puts on the extras, bags the sandwich, and calls out the customer's name. The sandwich maker and final person have an oven in between them. This system is always hopelessly out of balance because the cashier, who has the least amount of work, is idle most of the time and again can't touch the food because they would have to put gloves on. The sandwich maker has less labor than the final person, so the final person is always behind. In addition, the sandwich maker will start batching the sandwiches because they have all the tickets stacked up in front of them (Figure 3.11).

So, the final person will be idle while they are batching and then gets hit with a bunch of sandwiches all at once from the oven. Since the oven is in between them, they can't flex and help each other out. The next problem is encountered when the team leader sees where one of the stations is behind. So naturally they come in to help. What does this do to the line balancing?

Let's say we had a 1-minute cycle time at station 1. Since the team leader comes in to help, the cycle time is now cut to around 30–40 seconds. It is not exactly 30 seconds because the station is not set up for two people, so they get in each other's way, which slows them down. Now the final person on the end gets really backed up. You also lose FIFO on the sandwiches because the person coming in to help will pick the easiest sandwiches or ones that have the meat they can reach and push those ahead before the others. This then makes the customers who have already paid really upset!

But since the customer have already paid, who really cares? Bottom line is none of the workers or team leaders for that matter are at fault here. This is the system that was designed by management for them! They are doing the best they can do with the knowledge and tools provided. We see the same examples in factories all over the world.

Figure 3.11   Sandwich restaurant where sandwich maker is buried by the cashier.

Station Balancing: Operator Load Balancing Charts

When we are line balancing, we must allow enough time for the operators to perform each task. An industry standard taught in every Lean class is to create man loading or station charts (see Figure 3.12). The left-hand graph shows the workloads for each person. Operator 1 has 40 seconds, 2 has 45 seconds, 3 has 30 seconds, and 4 has 65 seconds. Based on this simple load diagram, we can determine that work is accumulating between operators 1 and 2. Operator 3 immediately performs any work received and proceeds to really back up operator 4, who is the bottleneck. We can predict that the cycle time, based on the theory of constraints (TOC),[3] is going to be 65 seconds. This means that operator 1, if forced to wait for operator 4, would have 25 seconds of idle time, operator 2 would have 20 seconds of idle time, and operator 3 would have 35 seconds of idle time each cycle. But instead of being idle, they will almost always continue to work (batch) so the inventory will pile up. Remember, idle time is one of the things that can force us to batch. As before, we can predict how much work will pile up and where. Since operator 2 is the next slowest operator who is 20 seconds faster than operator 1, then for every four pieces, we will back up a full piece prior to operator 4.

The line in each graph in Figure 3.12 shows the 60 seconds takt time (customer demand rate). If we divide 180 seconds of total work (40 + 45 + 30 + 65) or labor time by the takt time of 60 seconds, it shows we only need three operators. We can then rebalance the work across the three operators to meet the takt time and free up a person. What do we do with the person we free up? It is very important that we never lay anyone off due to continuous improvement activities, and there is a proactive plan in place to retrain and redeploy workers to other jobs or areas as this occurs. This last statement is critical to communicate to the operators (team members) and is a good starting point as an organization's Lean journey begins.

The problem with operator load charts is that they are symptomatic of station balanced lines and seldom drive waste elimination. Many times, kaizen teams will go out with stop watches and time each operator and record their times. Then they go back to the war room and (without the

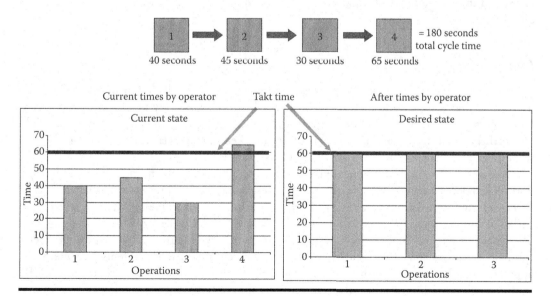

Figure 3.12 Traditional station balancing loading chart. (From BIG training materials.)

operators) restructure their work and processes to get everyone rebalanced. As stated before, they will shift work, parts, and sometimes tooling and equipment around in the layout to get everyone balanced. However, the work itself is not analyzed or targeted for waste elimination. The work is just rebalanced. The problem with this methodology is by shifting work, parts, and tooling around many times, we lose the product flow. This type of balancing has been taught as part of kaizens going back to the 1980s, but it is our opinion this is misguided thinking. If one utilizes baton zone balancing, we never have to change the layout and thus do not disrupt the product flow or incur the other wastes associated with station balancing.

Baton Zone Balancing versus Lean Line versus Station Balancing

How to Read Your Lean Line: Is Your Lean Line Balanced?

The true test of Lean is found by examining and looking for two items on your lines or in the office process. These are excess inventory and idle time.

Excess Inventory

Is there anywhere in the line that has extra WIP inventory, WIP caps, Kanbans between operators, or any other excess inventory in the line or informational process? If there is excess inventory, it means either the line is not balanced or there is a piece of batch equipment or equipment which is not functioning properly (downtime), has a lot of variation, or is not process capable. People should never be the reason for imbalance if the line is set up with baton zone balancing. The only reason people would be imbalanced is due to the workstation design where an operator is tied to a station, which means an operator cannot bump them out of that station, the line is station balanced and the operators are sitting down, or the operators are not cross-trained forcing people to bump around them.

Idle Time

Does anyone in the line have idle time? It is important to look closely and be objective. It is not unusual to find team members (workers) busy batching a subassembly or making unnecessary movements to look busy, which hides the idle time. Idle time appears when: the line is station balanced, there are sit-down stations where operators can't flex, operators lack cross-training, they are waiting on a machine, or in a few cases they are just plain lazy.

Excess inventory and idle time are the two main signs of a problem in any line. However, not all problems necessarily manifest themselves as excess inventory or idle time. Excess inventory always covers up some type of problem. This is an example of what we referred to earlier as hidden waste. We need to question why any excess inventory is found in a process. Therefore, the analogy of lowering water level (inventory) (see Figure 3.13) to expose the rocks (problems) was created. Our goal is to lower the inventory so the problems become more apparent, and we can deal with them. This means that wherever there is inventory or SWIP inventory in place, it should be reviewed to make sure only the minimum amount necessary is utilized.

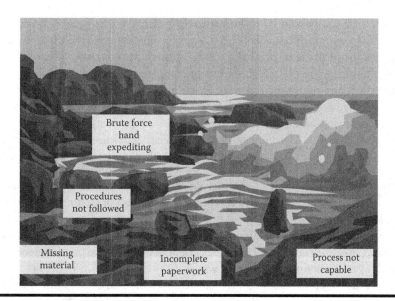

Figure 3.13 Reducing the water level exposes the rocks below the surface. Excess inventory always hides problems.

SWIP (Standard WIP)

SWIP is a calculated buffer based on replenishment times utilized to link processes together. Therefore, we implement Kanbans (SWIP) that are inventory buffers, but we consider them inherently bad because excess inventory is evil; however, Kanbans may be needed to keep non sequential lines linked together and the processes flowing. Lean is not about getting rid of all inventories as then we would not be able to produce a product. Some inventory is always necessary. The goal is to minimize the inventory, have the right amount of inventory to meet the cycle time and to maintain continuous flow, and fix problems so they don't come back.

Bumping to the WIP

Another problem we incur when first setting up the line is that want to bump to the WIP, not each other. If you don't stay on the line for 3–4 weeks, they will revert to this behavior.

One-Piece Balanced Synchronized Flow

To obtain one-piece balanced synchronized flow, one must change the paradigms and systems that exist in sit-down station balanced lines and be open minded enough to agree to develop a new approach. This approach means we set up the line and standard work to follow the flow of the product regardless of the times at each station. This sounds easy but is difficult to do. We create stations based on what makes sense for the product, not what makes sense to balance the operator's time at each station! There is an important distinction. In the earlier example, we would set up the line to flow from station 1 to station 4 since this is the product flow. We eliminate the Kanban squares and balance the operators into work zones across the stations. We tell the operators: you no longer have stations, and the work zones are guidelines only! The rule is you must continue to build until the operator at the station after yours pulls the part from you. In some cases, a subassembly may have to be set down on a square, but this is different from the in-process Kanbans discussed earlier. The goal would be to immediately attach the subassembly or build the subassembly into the final assembly, but this is not always possible especially if there are several subassemblies, which must be made in parallel to make up the final assembly. When the last operator (closest to the end of the line, i.e., pack and ship) completes a unit, they then walk back to the operator before them and bump that operator by taking their part from them wherever they may be in the process. The bumped operator then goes and bumps the operator before them and so on until the first operator in line starts a new part.

This system is based on a baton zone relay handoff versus a swimming relay handoff. It requires the operators to flex. Some of the major differences with this approach are as follows:

■ Additional pieces of equipment, tooling, or parts may be needed. Some or all equipment may have to be duplicated to break up multiple process steps performed on the same piece of equipment.
■ Operators must stand, move, and bump as required to maintain continuous flow.
■ The stations must be stand up height and redesigned with the parts sequenced in the order of assembly (the basis for true standard work).
■ Operators must be cross-trained on the entire line. This also enables the operators to rotate on the line from position to position.
■ Major variation should be removed (but many times can be handled with flexing).
■ Day-by-hour charts must be in place, so operators and team leaders catch problems as they occur.
■ Operators must follow the guidelines for running the cell (see Figure 3.14).
■ First person only drops their piece of WIP and bumps if they can't advance or if the other person will bump on top of them.
■ Standard work must be defined, and all operators must abide by the standard work (i.e., do it the same way every time). If a worker(s) is out, it is very difficult to run station balancing. With bumping, it is easy to run the line with less or more operators and they can move in and out on the fly without messing up the line.

Guidelines for Running the Cell

• Have QDIP meeting once a day
• Record day by hour chart and month by day chart
• Do not run orders if they are short ANY parts
• Operators should never wait for a machine! Do not stand at machines while they are running. Bump and take the part from the person in front of you.
• Do not bump to the WIP bump to the person
• You may rotate positions any time
• Run the line one piece flow
• Need batch of 20 to wash, batch of 20 cooling and batch of 20 working from between both sides – standard WIP
• Do not run 2 small orders in a row unless they use the same parts fill
• Check all orders for today and lookout next two days for parts shortages
• Rework on line for quick fixes and take off line for major tear downs or test failures
• Cell lead must support line first before working on reworking or repairing units
• Parts should not go on back shelf unless they are washed and ready
• Test should pace the line. The goal should be to keep the tester running as much as possible (this will be based on takt time)

Figure 3.14 Guidelines for running the cell example.

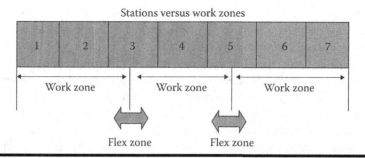

Figure 3.15 Flex zones.

The Bumping Process Explained in More Detail[4]

To facilitate work balancing, we utilize a concept Taiichi Ohno referred to as Baton zones, or flex zones, which are areas where handoffs occur between operators (Figure 3.15). The layout must be designed with short, easily shared steps around the zone. Long operations should be split into smaller steps.

In this system, the operators or assemblers are spread out on the line to work just like runners in a relay race. Like the baton handoff in the relay race, the operators hand off the product to the operator after them and then bump them to the operator before them until the first operator is reached who goes to the beginning of the line and starts a new part. The main difference from station balancing is all the operators in this type of line are not waiting for the person before them to hand them the product (or the baton) like in a push-type station balanced system. Instead, they are literally pulling the part from that operator even if they have not finished their station's work.

The entire baton handoff cycle is triggered by the completion of a product at the end of the line. Hence a true pull system. (Note: there are variations to the trigger depending on the type of products, subassemblies present, and equipment utilized in the line.) When the operator at the end of the line (let's call them operator 3) completes the product and places it in a bin, tray, or hopefully the shipping box, then operator 3 moves back down the line to the operator immediately prior to them (operator 2) and takes their product from them regardless of where they are in the process. It is very difficult to get operators to hand off their parts initially. They want to finish their work at the station first, which will cause operator 3 to be idle until they (operator 2) hands it off. When the product is given to operator 3, operator 2 then moves down to take the part from operator 1, this is considered a handoff or what we call bumping. This bumping down the line causes a baton handoff and bump by each subsequent operator on the assembly line until the operator closest to the beginning of the assembly line no longer has a product to work on. This first operator (in our example, operator 1) will then start another product at the beginning of the line. The rule is that the operators on the line must continue to work on the product in their hands until they are bumped or complete a product (if they are the operator at the end of the line).

Batching versus Station Balancing versus Bumping

Batching

Let's start with an exercise. You will need a minimum of three people to complete this exercise.

Person 1	Person 2	Person 3
First person	Second person	Last person

Batching exercise: This exercise is very simple. Cut out about 50 strips of paper about 2 in. × 6 in. if three people are participating (proportionally increase the number of strips for larger groups). Run the exercise for 4–5 minutes.

First have each person print their first and last names on the strips of paper in 10-piece batches. After the first 10 are completed, they are passed to the next person and then the first person starts on the next 10. Continue the batching exercise until the time is up.

Results: Once the time is up, record on a flip chart when the first piece was completed, how many strips of paper were completed, how much WIP was in the system, and if there were any defects, that is, names unreadable or spelled wrong, etc., and how many strips of paper would have had to be checked and maybe scrapped if a defect was found in the first batch.

Station Balancing (Swimming Relay)

Then run the exercise again implementing one-piece flow. Each person now fills in their name on a strip and immediately passes it to the next person. In some cases, WIP will build up between participants. This is normal. Compare the same results information at the end. What did you discover? You should have seen a significant improvement in output but probably found while there was much less WIP there was still some in between the players and some people had some idle time. The WIP would have built up between someone with a short name versus someone with a longer name. The idle time would have been witnessed with the person after a longer name that had a shorter name. This is the problem with station balancing. One cannot capture the time lost between stations with different labor times.

Bumping (Baton Zone Balancing)

Next, run the exercise and put the slowest person first, the second slowest person second, and the fastest person last. As soon as the fastest person is done filling in their name, they pull from number two regardless of how much of their name number two has completed. Number two then pulls from number one. Number three then finishes number two's work and adds their work and sets it down and pulls the next one from number two, again regardless of how much number two has done. Sometimes number two may not have anything done and sometimes number one's work might not be done in which case number three finishes number one's work, number two's work, and their own work and sets it down. Number two may have to finish number one's work after they pull. This means the last person will normally end up writing their own name and then part or all the second person's name and the second person will end up writing part of the first person's name.

Each person continues to work until the strip of paper is pulled from them. This means that in some cases, number two might do some or all of number three's work in which case they set it down and then pull from number one. Now tally the results again and compare to the first two trials. Normally you will see a big increase from batch to one-piece flow and then a much smaller increase with bumping, normally 2–10 additional strips depending on the variation of the size of the names. This normally represents 5–20% increases in productivity. One can now see with bumping our output increases and the WIP is limited to 2 or 3 pieces in the flow if done properly.

The simple exercise described above was created in Holland by Bert Overweg and Leontine Van Buren[5] to demonstrate the advantages of batch versus flow,[6] I then modified it to show the impact of bumping on productivity versus station balancing. You can cut out strips of paper or use yellow stickies, index cards, etc. We now use a pen exercise to demonstrate this exercise.

We had three people participate and gave them 4 minutes to do the exercise. When we did batch, our output was 20 pieces, with one-piece flow 29 pieces, and with bumping 35 pieces. This was because two of the names were much shorter than the third person, so they had a lot of idle time before bumping (i.e., just like station balancing).

Anyone can set this exercise up to be very repeatable by having each person write something specific on the cards and creating the bottleneck. You can also move the bottleneck around to show people what happens if you don't have the fastest person at the end for instance.

For a baton handoff style line to work, the following points must be considered when setting up the line:

- All the equipment, tools, and components must be laid out in sequence according to the PFA in the order they are needed. In some cases, equipment or parts may have to be duplicated on the line for this system to work.
- There must be standard work in place on the line; otherwise, errors will be made, and people will not know what step to continue once the part is handed off.
- Everyone must be cross-trained for at least one operation before and after them.
- Avoid staff using their hands as fixtures because operator flexing will be constrained.
- When there is a significant mismatch between the planned balance points where service is being transitioned, the team should investigate to find a root cause and generate a corrective action.
- There cannot be any one step that is longer than the takt time or required cycle time to complete.
- The line must be a standing walking line. However, we can make exceptions when designing a line for physically challenged or disabled.

The main difference between a station balanced and bumping line is the presence of idle time and wasted labor time in station balanced lines. These are eliminated on a baton handoff line because the operators don't stop after completing the steps assigned to them.

With Bumping Pull Should Start from the Last Station[7]

Sam Mitchel explains:

> What I was trying to show in the pictures is, if you have a true pull system on your Lean lines and the line is balanced, the pull should be decided on when the last station completes their work due to variation in product, materials, consumables, etc. Dividing-and-distributing the work is good and may need to be done several times during a new implementation, then afterward go into a true pull system and then rebalance when noticeable changes take place.
>
> The top graph is showing a 5-minute pull (see Figure 3.16). If you set your line up to pull every 5 minutes (station balancing—swimming relay), you will never do any better than 5 minutes pulls, which means you can do only worse. Your average time of the pulls will always be higher due to setting your target minutes at 5. For example, if your minimum pull is set at 5 minutes, your average pull time for the day may end up being 7 minutes due to variation and then you are never doing pulls faster than 5 minutes. With 420 minutes of work time and averaging of 7 minutes pulls, it will give you 60 pulls in 420 minutes.

Figure 3.16   Sam Mitchell describing a 5-minute pull (period batch) to the team members.

The bottom graph (see Figure 3.17) is showing what will happen if the Lean line pulls when the last station completes their work (bumping—baton zone balancing). For example, if the line pulls when the last station completes their work, the line may be pulling in 5, 7, 3 minutes, etc., depending on the product, material, consumables, etc. So, in this scenario the line's average pull time was 5 minutes, so for 420 minutes, the line would make 84 pulls instead of 60 parts.

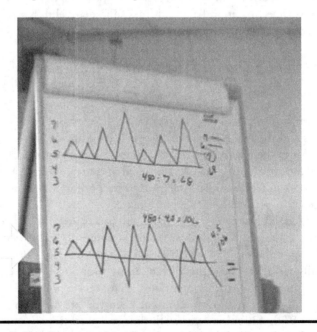

Figure 3.17   Sam Mitchell describes one-piece flow bumping to the team members.

Figure 3.18   Sam Mitchell explaining bumping pull system to the team members.

With a pull system and with the control point being at the end of the line and pulling when the last station completes their work instead of having a set time to pull the line ends up compensating for the variation and reduces cycle time average (see Figure 3.18).

Extreme Bumping Conditions

Although the flex zone usually encompasses a small area that will account for the normal variation in the rates at which different operators work (since we are not robots), in some unusual cases, this flex zone can completely overlap the operators' work zones both before and after each operator. This condition happens when there is a problem such as an assembly error somewhere on the line or there is a batch washer or oven in the flow that must be unloaded and loaded. If an operator notices that they improperly assembled something, they now can take some extra time to fix the error. The error is then recorded on the day-by-hour chart, which starts the 5 whys, plan-do-check-act (PDCA) and root cause corrective action (RCCA) process.

The operator before the former operator who encountered the problem will need to continue up the line and may reach operations they don't usually encounter under normal running conditions. If the error takes too long to fix, an operator may catch up to the operator working on the error and be forced to stop, and this does create idle time (waste). For this reason, there needs to be cell guidelines, and the supervisor or team leader must be trained on how to handle this situation. The line needs to develop ahead of time a policy for handling these situations. The option in this case, which is best to take, will depend on the type of line, the operations included in the line, and on how well the operators on the line are cross-trained. If the problem is not severe (i.e., within a takt time or cycle time of the line), some options are as follows:

■ Having the operator hand off the problem unit to a team leader to fix the problem off the line. In this case, the operator hands off the unit and goes up the line to bump (take the unit) from the person prior to them. This would allow the line to go back to running normally.

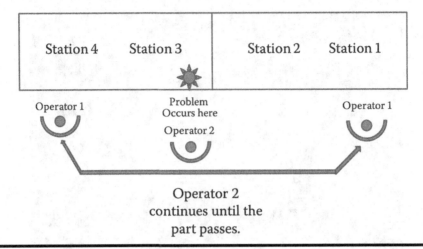

Figure 3.19 Operator 1 catches operator 2. Operator 1 passes operator 2, then instead of bumping on return they continue back to the beginning of the line where they should be. (From BIG training materials.)

■ Have the operator who catches up to the person having the problem pass them and continue with their unit up the line. Depending on the step and the labor at the step where the problem occurred, the person with the problem unit may have to stop to allow the person passing them to use a tool, machine, or work area to pass. Hopefully, the problem will be fixed before the next time an operator comes back down the line to bump, which will allow the line to begin running normally again.

■ Have operator 1 who catches up to operator 2, who is having the problem, hand off their unit (the good unit) to operator 2 and then operator 1 takes the unit with the problem which operator 2 was having and continues to work on it (Figure 3.19). This will allow operator 2 who previously had the problem unit to continue down the line. This way operator 1 gets a fresh set of eyes on the problem. Hopefully, the problem will be fixed before the next time operator 2 comes back down the line to bump operator 1, which will allow the line to begin running normally again (see Figure 3.20).

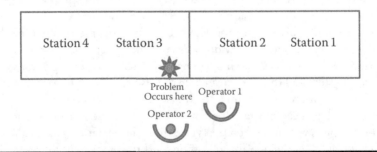

Figure 3.20 Operator 1 catches operator 2 . Operator 2 stops their operation on part 1 and waits while operator 1 takes their part 2 and completes the operation which was a problem for part 1. Once part 2 passes (completes) the problem operation for part 1, operator 1 hands off his (good) unit to operator 2 and then continues to work on part 1 until the unit is completed (normally this is a testing operation and trial and error fixes are part of the process). (From BIG training materials.)

■ Stop the line completely and fix the problem or take a temporary countermeasure. Obviously, this is the least popular (because operators want to keep working) but best action to take if the problem is severe (longer than a takt time). The entire team can focus on working on the problem and generate ideas to prevent the problem from happening again. After the problem is solved, the entire line can restart and run normally again.

We have had plant managers undo the baton zone system below because somewhere in their past they had been told by their Japanese sensei that this is not what Ohno intended, and if the person at the end of the line doesn't have as much work as the cycle time, we should keep it that way to expose the waste! That is, line imbalances should stick out and be visible, so we have a reason to get rid of them. Ironically, it was Ohno that proposed baton zone balancing.

We told the plant manager that their sensei may have been right based on their level of Lean knowledge at the time but because of the analysis we conduct using the BASICS® approach, we already know where the splits (theoretical handoff/bumping points) are supposed to be and whether operators are bumping where they should be. When we design the line, we plan out each station and the times for each step to the second within each station. In this case, the operators overlap stations and continue to produce until they are bumped. All operators become very visible in this system as there is nowhere for them to hide. The variation in the pace of different operators is smoothed out with the bumping.

However, the plant manager's line had so much idle time that he was losing one part for every three produced. Over the course of the day, while the line was still more productive than the old batch line, it was still not very efficient. So, bottom line, we don't agree with his sensei's premise that this operator should be idle every cycle and don't believe Mr. Ohno would have tolerated so much waste. We believe Mr. Ohno really did intend for us to use Baton Zone Balancing just for that reason.

Line Balancing Rules—Requirements for Bumping

1. Line must be designed for stand-up and walking.
2. Everyone must be cross-trained.
3. May have to duplicate tools, fixtures, or materials.
4. If rework is a big problem, some extra stations may have to be added to handle the repair or allow extra time to rework the units. Obviously, the goal is to eliminate the rework but in the real world this does not always happen.
5. SWIP must be labeled and always maintained.
6. On mixed model lines, since several orders could be running down the line at the same time, one must figure out how to handle the paperwork. Normally, the paperwork travels with the first unit.
7. Operators should rotate several times a day.
8. Eventually with some experimenting, you will learn how to introduce people to the line and remove them from the line and keep the line running. In some cases, if people must be added you may have to add stations. The goal is to have people moving and walking, not standing in one place on the line.
9. It is better to bump down time versus having the last person move to the first position (this is called rabbit chase).
10. The line tends to work best when the fastest person is last as they create the pull. However, this should not be an excuse for slow people not to have to speed up.
11. Do not bump to the SWIP; you must bump to the person.
12. Operators should never have to wait on a machine. WIP the machine, and it takes the machine out of the equation (as long as the machine time is not more than the TLT [less idle time]).

13. When balancing the cell, start with the bottleneck. Assuming there is demand, the bottleneck should never be idle. You can only go as fast as your slowest machine. The bottleneck should never be a person, only a machine.
14. There should be a training progression path for each line and within lines across the plant.
15. Don't tie workers to a station (i.e., with a piece of test equipment) with long cycle times.

Bumping Considerations

Work imbalance occurs typically because an operator did not follow the standard work, may not be flexing to assist a coworker, or a stop-the-line strategy was not initiated so the problem could be addressed. People should understand that they now need to work as a team and flex/bump as required. We are still requiring them to think and do the appropriate activities to get the job done.

Standing/moving operations promote operator/staff flexibility and health. A staff member who sits is more likely to either build inventory or to wait (adding seconds or minutes to a process), as it takes more effort to get up from a chair rather than the ability to move around when standing and walking. You will find staff members who are used to sitting for tasks may initially resist (sometimes strongly) the suggestion of standing and walking and vice versa. From an ergonomic viewpoint, sitting is bad for you. Sitting all day (being sedentary) leads to back problems and obesity, which can eventually lead to the possibility of early mortality. You will need to transition from sitting to standing by adjusting workbench heights to the proper height for standing. This will make the transition easier, as staff will find the task or activity, they are performing easier to do if they stand. A general guideline for allowing stand-up chairs on the line is for operations or tasks where a person would have to stand in one place with no movement for 10–15 minutes at a time.

Advantages of Bumping

Aside from the obvious elimination or reduction of some of the wastes mentioned earlier in this chapter, there are more obvious advantages of the baton handoff style line. In general, bumping is an extremely adaptable, resilient system for balancing the line especially when compared to station balancing and batching. Some of the advantages are following:

■ Maximizing team member's efficiency and promotes teamwork
■ People are visible and must work their fair share
■ Bumping can easily handle significant amounts of variation in product labor content, cycle times and product which have many options, etc.
■ It is easy to assess the progression of the assembly work i.e., how much work has been completed and how much time remains
■ Maximizing output of the line by using the fastest person to create the pull
■ Minimizing the effect of absenteeism
■ The line does not have to be U shape
■ Drives cross-training
■ Ability to easily measure output
■ Quality improvements and mistake proofing opportunities surface from breaking the operations into small steps
■ Incorporation of subassemblies or other operations being performed off-line
■ Eliminates idle time (assuming SWIP is in place)
■ Line is not dried out each shift or after each product model change

- Variation with options or mixed model is easy to handle
- It is easy for operators to rotate in and out of the line
- It is easy for operators to rotate to a different position in the line

How to Set up a Baton Handoff Style Manufacturing Line?

- Film the current state line.
- Conduct the TIPS analysis (PFA) with the operators.
- Conduct the WFA with the operators.
- Do the block diagram for the major products that run on the line. Question the order of each step. We generally find that we change the order of the steps when we really understand the product flow. Sometimes different models have a different sequence of operations only because two different engineers developed the routings.
- Label the block diagram with tools and equipment required at each station. If the line is a mixed model, update the model with different color steps to show where those steps are encountered. This means that some steps may be skipped from the first model. Then label the block diagram with utilities required and any special quality requirements.
- Next label the block diagram with the labor times for each station.
- Calculate the total throughput time.
- Calculate the TLT.
- Calculate the daily demand, takt time and cycle time, and capacity.
- If it is a simple line with low TLT, we can normally set up the line without a formal layout computer-aided design (CAD) drawing. If the line is complicated with high labor times, then we will create a CAD layout and design each workstation prior to implementing the line.
- Train the operators on Lean, baton/flex zones, and bumping.
- Cross-train the operators where possible prior to implementing.
- Implement the line.
- Run the line with each operator individually first.
- Then run it with two operators and then three, etc., and teach them how to bump on the real line.
- Teach them how to rotate. Generally, we allow and encourage them to rotate throughout the shift.
- Develop hourly output targets (day-by-hour targets) for each model run on the line.

What will happen on the baton zone line in the earlier case where we talked about the line with 160 seconds worth of work earlier in the chapter? If the takt time is 60 seconds, our cycle time will be around 53–54 seconds. Therefore, we will be running faster than takt time and will overproduce. We generally stop the line when they hit the daily output number required so that we don't overproduce (the number one waste).

If there are problems in the line, it will be obvious when watching the line (assuming the standard work has been created with the splits and it is available at the cell). Problems will also show up in the day-by-hour chart if the operators don't make their output number. It is important that these problems are addressed in real time and are not waiting until the end of the shift or the next day's huddle meeting.

Failure Modes of Baton Handoff Lines

1. Most people want to bump to the SWIP, not the person.
2. They are not cross-trained and cannot bump.
3. Equipment is off the line requiring operators to leave the line disrupting the flow.

4. Line is not stand-up and walking.
5. Team leader or supervisor doesn't understand how to run the line.
6. SWIP is dried up or not maintained in the line.
7. All components for the product being built are not available when the order is released.

Examples of How to Balance One-Piece Flow Lines with Variation

There are two types of bumping scenarios. One is as described above where the operators do the bumping i.e., bump the person. The other is where the operators remain at their stations and the part moves to them i.e., bump the part. This means they must have all the tools and materials at every station necessary to complete the product. This type of line lends itself to certain types of processes i.e., cleaning and finishing. This next example is this second type of process. In the example (see Figure 3.21), operators were chipping and grinding casting parts coming from the foundry. These parts were then used as part of a final assembly operation. The parts weighed about 30 pounds each. The work content in each part varied from approximately 5 minutes up to 12 minutes depending on the type of part and molds utilized. Not only was there variation from part to part (i.e., different part numbers) but also the same variation existed between parts within the same lot.

Note: The correct approach would have been to fix the problem at the source in the foundry. However, we all know that the correct approach is not always the route taken for a variety of reasons, so in the meantime we are forced to deal with the situation as it presents itself while the upfront problems are being studied and hopefully resolved. The inherent risk of working around the foundry problem is once one figures out a way to deal with the variation; it now takes the pressure off fixing the foundry problem! As discussed earlier, the balancing approach we are about to describe was designed by Taiichi Ohno to handle small minor variations in operator cycle time. However, we are now going to be using this approach to handle large variations in cycle time. Therefore, one could argue the bumping will be hiding all the variation which exists.

To balance this line, we converted from a purely batch process where each operator was given a daily quota of castings to produce. They would typically work on up to 10–20 castings at a time doing one side at a time (there were 4 sides). For example, they would start with all the castings on side 1 and chip and grind each one and then turn all 20 over to side 2, etc. We first tried setting up a line where we had each operator work on two pieces at a time with a two-piece buffer (designed to handle the variation). The parts were put on a conveyor to make them easily movable by hand from one operator to the next. The productivity increased significantly over the batching process and was in place for several months.

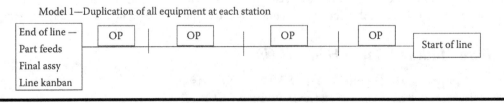

Figure 3.21 Model 1 duplication of work at each station. (From BIG training materials.)

We then implemented true one-piece flow and gave each operator one piece to work on at a time. To accomplish this, we started with operator 1 and had him work on the casting for one and a half minutes and then introduced operator 2. Operator 2 started on the first casting while operator number one grabbed the next casting. After a minute or so, we then introduced operator number three and he started working on the first casting, operator 2 took the part from operator 1, and operator 1 took a new casting from the bin and started on it. Finally, we introduced operator 4, and he took the first casting from operator 3, 3 took the second casting from 2, 2 took the third casting from 1, and 1 grabbed a new casting from the bin. This is called wetting the line. Now each operator has one piece. The way the line flows is as follows: every operator will continue to work on their casting until the casting is pulled from them by the next operator in line. So, when operator 4 is done, he pulls from 3, 3 pulls from 2, 2 pulls from 1, and 1 grabs a new piece. We call the operator piece of this bumping. Each operator bumps the operator preceding them and takes their piece, no matter where they are in the chipping and grinding process.

For this technique to work properly, again there must be some cell guidelines or bumping rules in place:

- First, there must be a finishing quality standard. There must be well-defined quality characteristics and checks so that each operator knows they are making good parts. In this case, there was a go/no-go gauge to run on each side to make sure it was finished correctly. In addition, once we linked it up to the next cell, we had only a small amount of WIP prior to discovering any mistakes. In the past, there could be several months' worth of WIP, which made it impossible to find the root cause of any problems discovered in the final assembly operation.
- We must have a work standard in place. This means that we have defined the steps and the order in which we are going to carry out the steps for each operation. Every operator must follow the work standard so that when the piece is handed off, it is easy to determine what has been done and what has yet to be completed. If a work standard is not in place or is in place but not followed, quality problems will result.

  Author's Note: We cannot have true standard work in this situation because of all the variation in the castings and the corresponding variations in cycle times. Therefore, we can have work standards which contain two of the three components of standard work (sequence of operations and SWIP)
- Each operator must be cross-trained in every operation. In other words, each operator must be able to complete apart from start to finish on their own.
- The last person (i.e., operator 4) is responsible to inspect the part and make sure that it meets all quality requirements prior to placing the unit in the Kanban. Our rule was don't put it in the Kanban for final assembly until you know it is good.
- Each person needs to stop immediately (not finish up what they started) when the bumping or pull occurs. If the person does not handoff the part immediately, the operator that is bumping will be idle and lost output will result.
- You should never be idle or standing waiting.
- All tools and materials need to be located at or easily accessible to each station. In this case, we needed all the finishing tools at EACH station. Gages had to be shared across the stations (this sometimes slowed the process down, but the gages were very expensive).
- There must be a Kanban of finished parts prior to final assembly to cover the variation problems within the chipping and finishing process. The Kanban cannot be eliminated until we are able to eliminate the variation or produce the parts, even with the variation, within the takt time of the final assembly process.

Results: The WIP was initially reduced in this case from several months to several hours. The Kanban at the end of the line cannot be eliminated until we are able to eliminate the variation or produce the parts, even with the variation, within the takt time of the final assembly process.

Detailed Scenarios

Scenario 1—No Variation in Finishing Times

If there was no variation in the castings and each operator had the same amount of work, we could have true standard work because it would be a repeatable process. We then need to have the exact tools and materials at each station to carry out the standard work. This means that:

- Each operator follows the sequence of operations (steps) exactly in order
- Each operator hits the exact cycle time for each step
- SWIP is in place where necessary to safely meet the cycle time

Note: We are differentiating cycle time from takt time here because takt time is based on the customer requirement, whereas the required cycle time is the time dictated by the factory demand and the number of operators available and working on the line. For example, our takt time might be 2 minutes per part. However, our labor content is 5 minutes per part. This means that we need to run with either two or three operators. If we run with two operators, each operator will have 2.5 minutes worth of work and will be running 2.5 minutes cycle times, which does not meet the 2 minutes takt time. We would have to work overtime to meet the customer demand or find a way to reduce the waste. With three operators, we will be running to 1.66-minute cycle times or 100 seconds. This means that we will be overproducing units since our cycle time is quicker than the takt time. In this case, we should stop the line early and redeploy the operators to another area or work on kaizen.

Scenario 2—Variation at the Last Station

If operator 4 has less work in his piece at his station, as compared to the other operators, then he will complete the piece quicker and bump and pull the part from operator 3. For example, if the average work at each station is 2 minutes and operator 4 finishes his up in 1 minute, each of the other operators will have worked on their piece only for 1 minute. Once he pulls from operator 3, the part he receives from operator 3 will have been worked on at that station only for 1 minute. So, theoretically, operator 4 will now have an extra minute's worth of work on that piece. If that is the case then it leads to scenario 3.

Scenario 3—Variation Continued

If operator 4 has more work in their piece, the other operators must continue to work on their pieces until such time as the bump occurs. This means that when the piece gets to the end, then less work will be required. In these cases, the cycle time per part will always be different depending on total labor content; however, the overall output will average out based on the average total labor content across the overall lot of parts. Keep in mind, the bumping is covering up the problem of the variation, but it eliminates any idle time that would normally be generated in a station balancing-type scenario. If the line was station balanced, each person would only do the side they were responsible for and then would wait, sitting idle, to pass it off when the next operator was ready.

This is a very difficult concept for operators to understand especially in union environments (which this was). We have trained people, for so long, to do only the work required for that station, that they feel when they do more work on a part, they are working harder, or should get paid more, for the additional work they are doing on the part. Our response to this is that we are paying you by the hour for an hour's worth of work regardless of the type or number of stations worth of work you are performing. This really comes to a head when one operator is not pulling their weight and the other operators must make up for that person. This needs to be discussed, and HR needs to be involved to determine how the company will deal with this situation when it comes up. This can be an additional benefit to OPBSF because it brings greater visibility to this type of situation.

Scenario 4—Variation Continued

This scenario is a continuation of scenario 3. In this scenario, operator 4 has just gotten a piece that requires 3 minutes worth of work and operator 3's piece requires only 2 minutes worth of work. In this case, operator 3 continues to work on the piece. Operator 3 will complete his piece before operator 4 completes theirs. What do we do in this case? Operator 3 will push his completed piece in between him and operator 4 (assuming there is room). Operator 3 will then bump back to operator 2 and pull his piece and so on down the line. Once operator 4 is done, say a minute or two later, operator 4 will put their piece and the already completed piece from operator 3 in the finished goods Kanban and then bump back to operator 3. In some cases, operator 3 may have only just started on that piece. This is fine because the line will always balance itself out.

Exceptions

In some cases, it does not make sense to wait until the operator (operator 3) at the end is completed to bump. Once the operators see the bumping in action, they will be self-balancing and figuring out when to bump. If I am operator 2 and moving faster than operator 3, I may have them set the piece down early and bump operator 1. This prevents us from being on top of each other and bumping back to the same spot at the same time. In the same way, if operator 2 bumps back the same time as operator 1 and there are subassemblies at the beginning of the line, operator 2 can bump to the second subassembly versus bumping on top of the first operator.

Results: By implementing bumping, we increase the output and corresponding productivity by 60% (see Table 3.1.)

Job Rotation

An important part of line balancing is to make sure that people are rotated within the cell for cross-training but eventually outside the cell as well. The more flexible the workforce is, the more flexible the company can be to its customers. Job rotating (see Figure 3.22) can be done each hour, after breaks, or after lunch, based on whatever makes sense for the business. Job rotation also gives the workers a sense of accomplishment, and by learning new skills, they become more marketable. Additionally, it can break down silos and provide a better understanding of the whole process.

Table 3.1 At Company X We Were Able to Implement Baton Zone Balancing and Increase the Output 60%

Baseline Metrics—2-Piece Flow	
Operators	4
Units per hour	26
DL mins per unit	9.2
Throughput time (minutes)	33
Cycle time (est. batch minutes)	2.3
Space	
Demonstrated Lean after metrics OPF	
Operators	2 −50%
Units per hour	32.5 +20%
DL mins per unit	3.75 −60%
Throughput time (minutes)	3.75 −94%
Cycle time (minutes)	1.875 −18%
Space	Freed up 2/3 of conveyor

Source: BIG Archives.

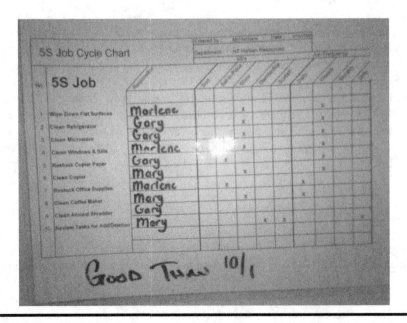

Figure 3.22   Job rotation chart.

Perceptions: People Think You Want Them to Work Faster

Whenever we are training staff in the new or revised standard work, they almost always think we want them to rush. This is not the case. Staff should be coached not to rush, because if activities/tasks are rushed, mistakes and defects will occur. If we rush, quality will suffer, processes will need to be reworked, and any time you might have saved in elimination of waste will be lost in reworking defects. In addition, rework creates a financial burden that is not tracked by finance and will lead to decreased customer satisfaction. The saying we recommend posting in each new Lean system implementation is "Quality first; the speed will come" (see Figure 3.23). The other challenge we often face is while the workflow may be revised, the actual work is not, and staff become so concerned with following the new process, they forget to do what is normally required as part of the job which, in fact, did not change. When this occurs, it can inadvertently lead to unjustified misgivings about Lean. As staff are cross-trained in new workflows, revised work, new work, and standard work, role clarity is extremely important to ensure that this does not occur.

Performing Lean implementations and applying Lean tools will enable us to become knowledgeable about how long tasks take to perform and enable reasonable targets to be established. An increase in productivity occurs when the process is redesigned with work in the proper sequence and balanced across the staff with the right tools, at the right time, in the right place to eliminate waste in the process.

Figure 3.23 Quality first the speed will come. Graphic design by Dave Morrison and Barry Rodgers. (From BIG Archives.)

There are some situations that cause cycle-to-cycle imbalances, such as defective materials, higher labor content products, and unanticipated distractions. All these will impact the balance of work and flow of the process. The staff in each line must be flexible and empowered to overcome these imbalances.

How to Read the WIP

This is a very important section. The assembly, machining lines and even the office lines can talk to you. But you must be able to understand the language. You must be able to see what the line is trying to tell you. It is the WIP in the line, or sometimes lack of, that does the talking. This section will discuss how to interpret what the WIP is trying to tell us. The work in process within a line will speak to you if you know how to read it. For instance, the following examples are assuming one-piece flow lines that are station balanced or with bumping but not running correctly, or we have elected to station balance a machine within the bumping. In this case, there are two machines and two operators.

Case 1: See Figure 3.24 reading the WIP.

1. If there is no WIP in between and the operators are handing off and no one is waiting, the line is balanced perfectly and synchronized, and the operators should be bumping.

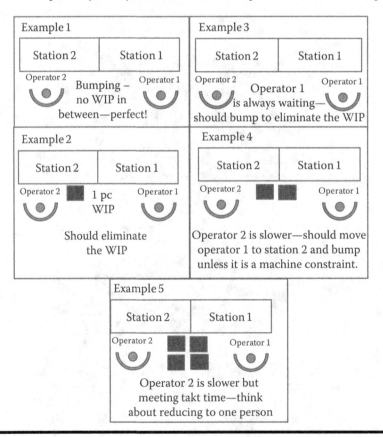

Figure 3.24 Examples—what if scenarios for stations with or without machines. (From BIG training materials.)

2. If there is one piece of WIP always in between each machine, they are balanced and probably could be handing off from operator 1 to operator 2 to eliminate the WIP.
3. If there is no WIP and operator 1 is always waiting, operator 1 has less work than operator 2. This could be fixed by bumping or, if station balanced, moving work from operator 1 to operator 2 (not a Lean solution).
4. If there is more than one piece of WIP in between, it means operator 2 is running slower than operator 1. This could be fixed by bumping or if station balance, by moving work from operator 2 to operator 1 (not a Lean solution). If the machine time is the constraint, but still meets the TT, then we either need to balance the machine times by speeding one up or slowing one down.
5. If there is significant WIP in between the machines and we are still hitting takt time or our required cycle time, it means that we can think about reducing to one person instead of two.

Case 2: Do I need one or two machines?

There are two machines doing the same operation. We were watching the operation run originally with two operators. Operator 1 was batching four pieces at a time. The other was in training doing one piece at a time and averaging 35 seconds cycle times. Operator 1 was known to be the fastest person on that machine; but could not keep up with the required cycle time of 23 seconds. Doing the four-piece batch, he was averaging 32 seconds per piece.

This is an example of converting external to Internal Time (where it is not a traditional setup): the first problem we found was that much of the work was being done on internal time versus external. For example, the machine would stop and then the operator would get the next part versus getting the part while the machine was running, and he was standing there idle. (Note: we see this at every Lean company.) We then worked with the operator to get the standard work running correctly. The machine time was 10 seconds. To load and unload, the machine took 7 seconds. The first trial involved running both machines correctly. The operator averaged 34 seconds cycles for both machines and 17 second cycles; we were getting two parts during each 34 second cycle. When he ran one machine, he was averaging 20 seconds cycles. At first, we could not figure out why. Then we discovered he was waiting for the machine to finish welding. Since it only took him 7 seconds from starting the machine and putting the completed part in the bin and then grabbing the next two parts to be assembled, he was now waiting 3 seconds for the machine to complete its 10 second cycle. Therefore, if you want to run on 23 second cycles, he will have 6 seconds extra each cycle in which to bump or do another operation. So, it turned out, we only needed one machine. In the event the cycle time was longer on the machine, let's say 25 seconds, then we would need the second machine and we would unload, load, and start the alternating machine each cycle.

Result: We were able to free up one machine, reduce the back end from three operators to two operators, and move the extra machine to another line which enabled that line to do one-piece flow. (Before this the team leader for the other line had to bring his parts over to this line to weld them, forcing them to batch.) Because the operator had not been trained on internal versus external time, he was averaging 32 seconds per part, and everyone thought he was a hero. The fastest guy. But when we put the microscope on the process, we found we could reduce that 32 seconds to 17 or a 47% improvement!

Rabbit Chase Pros and Cons

The rabbit chase line balancing methodology has each operator make their own parts by working around the entire cell every cycle. So instead of one operator bumping back to another, each operator is continuously circling the cell working on making a complete product from start to finish. There are pros and cons to this approach:

Pros

- Promotes cross-training because everyone must be able to run the entire cell.
- Each worker owns their piece.
- The most experienced can lead the changeover and create one cycle or one-shot changeover.
- Easy to insert new workers into the line (just as easy as bumping).
- The slower assemblers will stand out.
- One person (most experienced) can be responsible for changing cell over.
- Full cross-training is required.
- Each person is accountable for the piece they built giving them ownership (but you still may not know which ones they built).
- Can spread out fatigue if a particular operation on the line is very tiring.

Cons

- It is more difficult to trace who made an error and to work with them to root cause it.
- Tends to be much slower and less productive due to the additional walking required for each person especially if the cell is not in a U shape.
- No successive checks are possible.
- You can only go as fast as the slowest person (Herbie principle[13]).
- Lose teamwork—there is no pressure exerted to keep pace with the other team member.
- The rabbit chase is generally less productive. You lose the time pressure that exists when working on a team and bumping.
- If they are not cross-trained, they slow down the line.
- It is easier to learn the line when starting with the part of the line in bumping versus having to run the entire line right away.
- Some people start to batch or say, "I like doing this operation, just go around me."
- The rabbit chase hides the line problems, that is, parts or tools out of order.
- There is more walking than with baton zones, which can be a problem when working with heavy parts or operator fatigue is a consideration.
- The faster worker will always lap the slower worker, causing them to wait every cycle or to interrupt the other operator to pass them each cycle like a foursome playing through in golf.
- If someone gets lapped, they must either give their part to the faster person or wait behind the slower person (idle time) while they finish the part at the workstation where they are passing them. If the slower person does hand off their part, they will be idle until the faster person finishes the operation at the point where they caught them. We had one operator just stay at one station in rabbit chase because he liked it. So, everyone would drop off their part to him and pick up the one he had completed.
- It is always less productive than bumping. The pace is not driven by the fastest person.

Station Balancing Oxymoron

Whenever we conduct Lean training, we present the class with a layout exercise. We tell the class the following:

There are three operators.

There are six operations with these times:

Station 1—10 seconds
Station 2—25 seconds
Station 3—15 seconds
Station 4—20 seconds
Station 5—30 seconds
Station 6—20 seconds

For some reason, maybe it is in our DNA, the first question we get from the class is can we change the order of the stations? We respond yes, but "Why do you need to change the order?" We don't get an answer.

The participants determine that the TLT is 120 seconds. The next step is to divide it by three operators. They naturally come up with 40 seconds per operator. This means putting stations 1 and 5 together, 4 and 6 together, and 2 and 3 together. How many of you would agree with this approach? The next step we are told by the class is to calculate the WIP cap or in-process Kanban size between each operator and then we would schedule the line to 80% efficiency in case the operator has to leave the line or gets fatigued doing light-to-medium assembly-type work. These responses are generally coming from Lean Masters!

If we implement the suggested solutions from the class, the problem we have now is we have lost our product flow. Why is this important? There are three basic steps to creating a Lean line. The first is studying and deciding how the product should flow. The second is identifying and removing the waste from the operators, which build the product. Finally, the third is reducing setup times which force us to run large batches.

So, we let the class move the stations around, station balance the line and tell us what the inventory quantity should be in the Kanbans. We then point out that the product no longer flows in the correct order. The class responds: "You told us we could move them." We state: "Yes, but we also said you shouldn't have to move them!" The class is now perplexed. The next question we ask them is "Now that you have moved the stations around and the line is balanced, if we have to run it with two operators, what would you do?" Well, they would now combine stations 1, 5, and 6 and 2, 3, and 4. So we respond: "Are you going to change the layout of your line and move the stations around every time the number of operators changes? What if one person must run the line or five or six people need to run the line to get the required output? What are you going to do now?" This question is normally greeted by silence. This silence is conducive to what we see on the factory floor because the bottom line is no one knows how to run it!

The other problem is once you try to balance different people or even the same person, are they going to consistently hit the same cycle time repeatedly? Our experience is people normally hit to within a second or two for each step in an operation; however, as people get more familiar with the line (learning curve—log-log chart), we find people improve at different rates. It is not unusual to

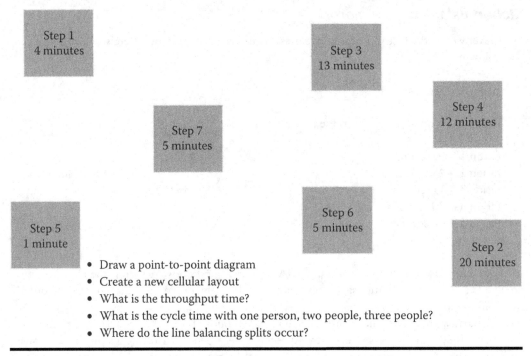

- Draw a point-to-point diagram
- Create a new cellular layout
- What is the throughput time?
- What is the cycle time with one person, two people, three people?
- Where do the line balancing splits occur?

Figure 3.25 Layout exercise.

come back to a station balanced line and find the operators asking to be rebalanced because the line is all out of whack.

In addition, people are not robots. Occasionally, we are going to run into some type of problem. This problem may be from picking up a part, to having to rework a part in the line multiple times due to a supplier component problem or poor engineering design.

Again, we call this type of in-process Kanban line which the class usually comes up with, the lazy man's balance. This is because the true work necessary to maintain the product flow and balance the operators is replaced with a Kanban square of material placed between the operators that hides the line imbalance. Remember, excess material is always the sign of a problem, and in this case, the excess material is inherent in the in-process Kanban. Anyone can design a line with a Kanban square.

Layout Exercise: Try the layout exercise (see Figure 3.25). The answer is in Figure 3.26.

Layout Design

Layouts, that is, workstations need to be developed based on what makes sense for the PFA. The layout should never change. The layouts are not based on how much work each operator will need. Our layouts can run with one person or 10 people (assuming that there is enough labor content and room in the line). This is the most difficult concept for people to get in Lean training. They always want to move the product steps around to balance the labor at each station.

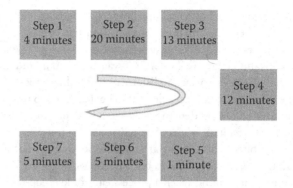

Answers

1. The product goes from 1 to 7 in order of the steps
2. Create a U shaped layout, could have been also a straight line
3. Throughput time is 60 minutes
4. Cycle time with 1 person is 60 minutes, 2 people is 30 minutes, 3 people is 20 minutes
5. The split with two people is 6 minutes into step 3
6. The splits with three people is 2nd person starts 16 minutes into step 2 and 3rd person starts 3 minutes into step 4

Step	Time	Cumulative Time	2 People	3 People
Step 1	4	4		
Step 2	20	24		20
Step 3	13	37	30	
Step 4	12	49		40
Step 5	1	50		
Step 6	5	55		
Step 7	5	60		

Figure 3.26   Layout exercise answers.

Monuments and Line Balancing

In some cases, there may be no choice but to work around a monument. For instance, at a company in upstate NY, we had a wash step in the middle of the process. The parts and operators' hands were oily prior to the wash operation so the operators couldn't move down the line past the wash point and work on the clean parts with oily hands. In this case, SWIP was set up in wash racks with the correct quantity to cover the wash process time. This line was then run like two separate Lean lines: one line ran up to the wash operation and the second from the wash operation to the end of the line. Because the two lines will never be equally balanced (equal labor), the SWIP is used as a visual indicator of when to flex a person from one line to the other. When the first line is running faster than the second, extra WIP will build up at the wash operation. Once one extra rack is created, a person from the first line cleans their hands and moves to the second line. Now the second line is running faster than the first. After the material on the extra rack is burned off, the person who moved to the second line moves back to the first. This solves the issue of having to wipe or wash oily hands every cycle to move down the line, but you carry extra WIP and the output is more erratic, that is, low in some hours and high in others. Keep in mind that even though the SWIP allows us to work around this monument (wash operation), it is still covering up a problem. The better solution would be to figure out how to keep the parts and the operator's hands from getting oily in the first place.

TOC: Theory of Constraints and Lean[8]

Jeff Smith states:

> When I came up through the ranks, the prevailing operations footprint was to have "like" machines gathered in one area, called departments, with their own supporting workers. This

resulted in predictable bottlenecking, inventory builds, quality problems, etc. At the time, I was working in a textile mill that processed hundreds of thousands of yards of fabric a week.

The director of the division recognized this was a problem and brought in a firm to teach us Eliyahu Goldratt's TOC. As it was taught to us and implemented, the key focus was to establish flow. To accomplish this, the product process had to be mapped out and machinery and resources reconfigured to be dedicated to the production of similar products and sized to market demand (takt rate). Redeploying these assets in the classic U- or L-shaped cells resulted. Within the cells, the constraint in the process had to be identified and exploited. Constraints are bottlenecks that cannot meet customer demand. A constraint is always a bottleneck, but a bottleneck may not always be a constraint.

A constraint is found when a process cannot keep up with the preceding process. It is only a bottleneck if it is the slowest process in the line. However, not every bottleneck is a true constraint if we can still meet the takt time. A true constraint is a phenomenon where the performance or capacity of an entire system is limited by a single or limited number of components or resources. With station balancing many times, we find more than one physical constraint, but only one of those constraints is the bottleneck. In Lean, we don't schedule around the constraint; we schedule based on customer demand.

Exploiting a constraint entails buffering either with inventory or labor to ensure the constraint never goes idle for lack of resources or material from upstream processes. This was so important that temporary downstream resource issues were not allowed to impede constraint output—it was run into inventory for later retrieval and processing. Additionally, the importance of maximizing output often resulted in assigning the most experienced operators to the constraint until it was broken.

Because there would always be a constraint somewhere in the process, the training encouraged picking or assigning the constraint for best advantage and control rather than continually chasing the next constraint. There were exercises to illustrate the difficulty of achieving a balanced line. The lesson was that a balanced line sized to the market demand will not achieve total expected output because there is no way to recover from lost time at any of the now balanced process steps. The more complex and the more the number of steps, the greater the likelihood of cumulative lost capacity across the entire process (rolling throughput yield). This loss could be predicted statistically. The poker chip dice game provides a crude illustration. Ordinary dice are given to four operators.

The dice are all the same and thus represent the balance in the line. The numbers 1–6 represent inherent variability at each operation due to operator fatigue, skill, tool wear, etc. Each operator starts with a buffer of six chips in the upstream section to the operator's station. At the beginning of each round, the operator begins by moving the inventory quantity into his workstation, rolls the dice, and places (produces) a quantity of chips equal to the number on the dice in the downstream space between the two operators. The balance, if any remains, goes in the cell. In the second and following rounds, output potential is determined by the dice and available material. If you roll a six but only three are available, that is all your station can produce into the next process step. This is repeated for five cycles with WIP, and final output measured after each round. While there is consistent flow, it is not predictable, and the classic hunt for the constraint ensues by observing the inventory build and alternatively the lack of inventory at workstations across the process.

Lesson Learned: Identify the constraint and ensure that both the upstream and downstream process steps had excess capacity. In other words, an unbalanced line was desirable.

Jeff goes on to say:

"The locations marked A and B in Figure 3.27 shows the process times for each process step. This is a typical approach to identify the constraint operation and determine the size of the buffer needed in front of the process. In this example, the constraint is at operation step TEST (283 seconds). Our now obsolete training would establish a buffer of units in front of the test, and output from the test would trigger gateway production of the same amount to keep the buffer stable. As you can see, there is plenty of excess capacity upstream of the constraint. While the constraint at test was being

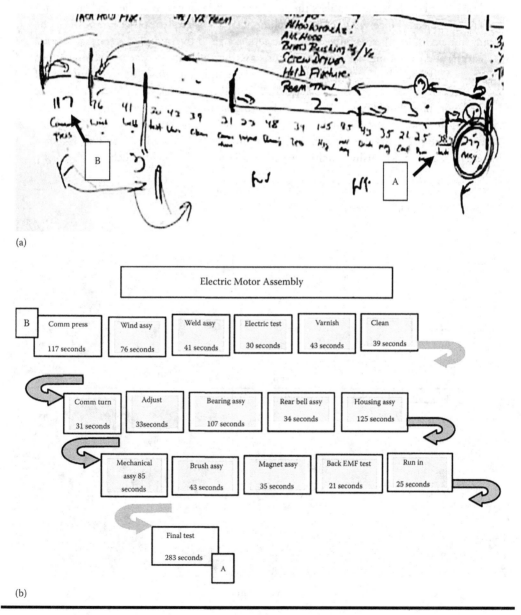

(a)

(b)

Figure 3.27 (a and b) Theory of constraints vs. bumping.

broken, upstream manning would float back and forth between upstream workstations filling KB squares sized to maintain the buffer in front of test.

In the Lean baton zone balancing approach, I recently learned from Charlie, the constraints are identified up front via video and analysis of each step of the operation. The PFA will identify machine bottlenecks while the operator analysis will show processes that contain high labor content. However, in Lean, operators should never be considered bottlenecks as we can always add more. It may be necessary to lengthen a station or add an extra machine or tooling. In addition, we use bumping or flexing to average out the labor per person across the stations on the assembly line. Machines should not be a bottleneck unless the machine time is longer than the total labor content in the cell. Once we WIP the machine (i.e., always have a piece of SWIP in the machine), it takes the machine out of the equation, and the bumping steps just include loading and unloading the machine versus standing and waiting for the machine. Once we identify the labor content and the takt time and determine the total number of operators required (i.e., divide TLT by the planned cycle time), we know exactly where the labor splits should occur. We then use bumping to absorb any idle time that might exist if the line was previously station balanced (swimming relay handoffs). The results (see Figure 3.28) we experienced with bumping increased productivity by 61% over batching and 35% by using batching versus the TOC method with much less inventory.

2″ and 3″ motor line 10-18-10

Baseline metrics (not including shafts or pack)		Baseline product flow
Operators	5	
Cell lead	1	
Units per day	40	
Paid minutes per unit includes OT	79.2	
Thru-put time (Working days)	4.42	
Cycle time (min-Est.Batch)	10.13	
Overtime #hrs /day	4.8	
Space (sq. ft)	5167	
Travel distance (ft)	813	
WIP #	528	

Actual Lean metrics November 2010 data			After Lean flow
Operators (eliminated 2nd shift)	5	0%	
Cell lead	1	0%	
Units per day	80	100%	
Paid minutes per unit	30.8	61%	
Thru-put time (Working days)	.93	79%	
Cycle time (min)	5.03	50.03%	
Overtime #hrs	0	100%	
Space (sq. ft)	1640	68.3%	
Travel distance (ft)	318.5	60.8%	
WIP # (until UV cure is enacted)	75	85.8%	

61% increase in productivity

Figure 3.28 Examples—what if scenarios for stations with or without machines. (From BIG training materials.)

Variation Is the Enemy of Lean but Can Be Tamed

In our many years of Lean implementation, we have never run into lines where there is always the same amount of work in each unit or each unit is produced as planned. Most lines are mixed model, small lots with high variation and normally engineering issues, like trial-and-error building, tweaking, tuning, etc. Therefore, we have had to learn to cope and compensate for the variation. There are some inherent dangers in this approach. For example, once you compensate for the variation, the underlying cause of the variation still exists but is covered up now because of the line balancing approach and may never get fixed. In addition, any time lost due to the variation is still lost time, but it is not as obvious although it is obvious to the trained eye.

People Resisting Change

There is a saying that the problem isn't that people resist change. The problem is that the change hasn't been presented in enough of a positive way (what's in it for me) for the employee to agree to the change. Our experience goes back to the change equation. Unless there is a compelling need to change, people will resist change no matter how positive the change is framed. People will initially resist this approach even after Lean training and implementation on the line. We normally ask the operators to give the change two to three months to work and by then they have normally adjusted to the change. New hires have no problem adjusting to the changes because they never knew the old way of doing it.

Quick Response Team

Be prepared for all the problems that batching has hidden to immediately show up as soon as you implement Lean. This is a lesson that no matter how much it is preached still leaves companies woefully unprepared. The main reason is that most companies think they are doing a pretty good job right now. However, all that material is hiding problems just waiting to bite you. We suggest that the Lean team helping to implement the line stays with the line for several weeks, until the operators have adjusted, and the major problems can be resolved. This time frame varies depending on the complexity of the line. Maintenance, engineering, and quality all need to be on call to fix problems on the spot. If problems aren't dealt with quickly, you run the risk of having the line quickly revert to the old non lean ways.

Idle Time

Idle time can only be observed! This means you can't see it if you are sitting in your office or simply walking by the line or walking through an office area. Sometimes the idle time is hidden by the operator. This occurs when the operator builds excess inventory or the operator works hard to look busy. Anyone walking by would think that they are busy when they are doing busy work. Don't confuse looking busy with value added work. Idle time is difficult to remove in station balanced lines as it requires moving work from one station to another to balance the line. This is not always practical. Idle time can also be driven by poorly designed test equipment where the operator must stand and wait for a set of tests to complete prior to hitting the return key to move to the next test. Other times we have monuments in place. For example, a wash area where operators are forced to leave their stations, travel to the washer, then wait until the machine cycle is completed before returning with the clean parts to their cell or line. Idle time also occurs when tools break or are missing and the operator must find someone to help them prior to continuing production. We have often witnessed operators standing in line waiting to get parts or tools out of a stockroom. The company keeps these big inventory or tool storage rooms because they are afraid someone will steal the inventory. We now end up losing many hours of manufacturing time just to make sure no one steals the tools or materials. Idle time occurs in machine shops during changeovers, where an operator watches the setup team do the changeover. It also occurs when operators stand and watch their machines "just in case the machine were to break down or do something unexpected," they could be there to stop it.

We must work first to go on the floor and see this idle time and then work to eliminate it. This is where key concepts of jidoka, 5S, standard work, and line balancing interconnect.

Mixed Model Lines

Why Batching Appears to Be Better than Fixing the Variation

Many companies, after trying one-piece flow, go back to batching because they feel one-piece flow improvement is not getting the promised results. This problem is most often found on high-mix/low-volume lines. With lines containing high variation, batching appears to be the only option; however, with determination and perseverance, we have yet to find a line where we had to return to batching. The lines may not initially perform as well as they did with batching. And normally what we find is an initial drop in productivity or an increase in productivity but a decrease in output. The most difficult problem is exacerbated because generally companies do not have good baseline metrics, so it is almost impossible to tell if Lean has improved productivity or not. On these lines, the model changeovers vary from several times a week to several times a day. This means it is virtually impossible to do before and after metrics on the same model type. Sometimes it may be days or weeks before that model type is run down the line again. Most of the variation tends to be in determining if the product is good. The variation may be as follows:

- Inconsistent testing results. The parts pass but are bad, or the parts fail but are good.
- Judgment-based inspection.
- Lack of good finishing standards.
- Tuning required with electrical circuits, etc.
- Lack of good cleaning standards.
- Design issues result in several first article builds are required, and must be tested, before building the rest of the work order can proceed.
- Tolerance stack ups.
- Poor drawing specifications or parameters that are not documented in the drawing.
- Trial and error builds.
- Issues with materials, that is, thickness tolerances on shims—material must meet some selection criteria or must be sorted.
- Measurement systems issues—the equipment is not capable of measuring to the customer spec.
- Process capability issues.

All these issues will come immediately to the surface when implementing one-piece flow. You must be prepared to deal with them. In the batching world, other WIP could be built while the investigations were pursued or for example, while waiting half an hour to an hour for first article results. In Lean, the line is now down until the problems are resolved.

The advantage to the Lean system is that it will force you to deal with these problems. However, if you don't or cannot deal with them, there will be constant pressure to return to batching to get the output perceived in the past. In our experience, if the Lean line is implemented correctly, in these situations where we have extremely high variation, we almost always do as well as batching or we see slight to moderate increases in productivity right away. As discussed in an earlier chapter, there has only been one exception in over 30 years where it took us several months to improve over the batching results. It was due to a very high learning curve on building the product. However, we eventually saw an increase of more than 50% in productivity over batching. Other cases where the results were only slightly better than batching were because the line was not run correctly by the team leader and the problems were not addressed. One must realize when you revert to batch that it takes all the pressure off fixing the problems. The question normally boils down to senior management's commitment to Lean. These types of implementations tend to show which companies are capable of sustaining Lean, and this variation is behind the reason which many companies fail. In some cases, the pressure of output wins over the desire to fix the problems.

Mixed Model Changeovers (If Required)

We must compare the batch flows to the Lean flows. Let's assume that there are six people on the line when batching. Whenever a model changes over, the rest of the line keeps running while the first station changes over. This is the same for the second station as it changes over and so on. The definition of internal setup for a line like this is from the last piece completed on the last station to the first good piece of the next lot out of the last station. An all-encompassing measure of changeover for a mixed model cell (not counting preparation) would be from last good piece at station on to first good piece at the last station.

When changing over a one-piece flow line, we must dry up the line each time. During the initial changeovers, no one knows what to do. The first station changes over and then the other five team members must wait for the other stations to change over. This time adds up and reduces line capacity and output.

The changeover time per station is still the same whether it is batch or flow. The problem is when each station is done, they stand around waiting for the last station. Normally, for mixed model lines, the first piece is used as a trial-and-error piece and must be used to set up each piece of equipment. This standing around steals capacity from the line just like in a machining cell that has long setups is wasting capacity.

The key here is to focus on quick changeovers for the Lean cell. Remember, for an assembly line, the changeover time should be zero. The setup should be videoed and reviewed with all the operators and look for opportunities to externalize as many tasks as possible just like we would in a machine setup. Each person should have standard work for the remaining internal setup tasks. The ideal setup would not require a piece to trial and error but have the settings preset or pre marked so the piece is not required.

Mixed Model Matrix

This figure shows what we call a mixed model matrix. On the left side are all the different operations the product might see (see Figure 3.29). On top (x axis) is each of the model types. Then in

	Station	Operation Description (What They Do)	Model 1	Model 2	Model 3	Model 4	Model 5	Model 6
1	Operation 1	11.0	11.0	11.0				
2	Operation 2	16.0	16.0	16.0				
3	Operation 3	40.0	40.0	40.0	54.0	42.0	54.0	42.0
4	Operation 4	33.0	33.0	33.0	29.0	29.0	29.0	29.0
5	Operation 5	25.0	25.0	25.0	31.0	31.0	31.0	31.0
6	Operation 6	60.0	60.0	60.0	33.0	32.0	33.0	32.0
7	Operation 7	50.0	50.0	50.0				
8	Operation 8	5.0	5.0	5.0	7.0	7.0	7.0	7.0
9	Operation 9		14.0	14.0		14.0	14.0	
10	Operation 10	12.0	12.0	12.0	10.0	10.0	10.0	10.0
11	Operation 11	19.0	19.0	29.0	9.0	9.0	9.0	9.0
12	Operation 12	19.0	19.0	19.0	19.0	19.0	19.0	19.0
	TLT seconds	290.0	304.0	314.0	192.0	193.0	206.0	179.0
	TLT minutes	4.8	5.1	5.2	3.2	3.2	3.4	3.0
	Units per hour 1 person	12.4	12.4	12.4	12.4	12.4	12.4	12.4
	Units per day	93.1	93.1	93.1	93.1	93.1	93.1	93.1
	Units per hour 2 persons	24.8	23.7	22.9	37.5	37.3	35.0	40.2
	Units per day	186.2	177.6	172.0	281.3	279.8	262.1	301.7
	Units per hour 3 person	37.2	35.5	34.4	56.3	56.0	52.4	60.3
	Units per day	279.3	266.4	258.0	421.9	419.7	393.2	452.5
	Units per hour 4 person	49.7	47.4	45.9	75.0	74.6	69.9	80.4
	Units per day	372.4	355.3	343.9	562.5	559.6	524.3	603.4
	Units per hour 5 person	62.1	59.2	57.3	93.8	93.3	87.4	100.6
	Units per day	465.5	444.1	429.9	703.1	699.5	655.3	754.2

Figure 3.29   Mixed model matrix.

each box is the cycle time per model per operation. When the operations are summed up for each model, it yields the TLT. This can then be divided by the number of operators to figure out the average cycle time and output per hour and per day.

Problems When Running the Line

The first problem we must generally overcome when running the line is testing. Many times, mixed model lines have different run times depending on the model. In addition, many times the tester may require several retests to pass the part. This means that whenever the test time is longer than the cycle time of the line, then the rest of the line is down until the part passes. This plays havoc with trying to balance the line. Over time, we need to determine the cycle time of each part at each station. Many times, the labor time is the same across most models, but some models may hit different stations than others. In this case, over time, we build this matrix shown above.

The day-by-hour chart quantities per hour must be adjusted to include the time lost due to setups, first piece, etc. and consider the model being built. In the example in Figure 3.30, we show the impact of the test cycle and the output capacity of the line. This is a good news/bad news story. The bad news is we are losing capacity; the good news is we know what we are losing and why we are losing it. The bottom line is that if the tester is the bottleneck machine in the process (remember, people can't be true bottlenecks), we still can't go any faster than the tester whether we are building batch or one-piece flow. To calculate the labor for this type of cell, one must take the TLT divided by the time it takes to unload, load, and test the part (assumes someone is dedicated to the test equipment).

Other problems exist in machines that don't produce a good part every cycle. In some cases, we must batch these machines and have them always run one order ahead to have good parts for the line.

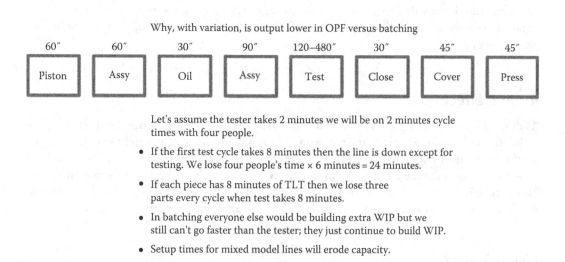

Why, with variation, is output lower in OPF versus batching

60″	60″	30″	90″	120–480″	30″	45″	45″
Piston	Assy	Oil	Assy	Test	Close	Cover	Press

Let's assume the tester takes 2 minutes we will be on 2 minutes cycle times with four people.

- If the first test cycle takes 8 minutes then the line is down except for testing. We lose four people's time × 6 minutes = 24 minutes.

- If each piece has 8 minutes of TLT then we lose three parts every cycle when test takes 8 minutes.

- In batching everyone else would be building extra WIP but we still can't go faster than the tester; they just continue to build WIP.

- Setup times for mixed model lines will erode capacity.

- Rework time will erode capacity.

Figure 3.30 Shows the impact of the test cycle and the output capacity of the line. (From BIG Archives.)

How to Fix the Problems with Variation

It is important to revisit the eight things that force us to batch. The setup times can be fixed by studying the cell and externalizing as much work as possible. Sometimes it means adding a water spider to the line or an external setup team to make sure the materials and tooling are always ready for the next order prior to changing over the line. The first-piece trial and error need to be addressed by engineering. Many times, engineering will refuse to fix the problem. It may require requalification of the parts and extraordinary costs. In this case, we need to work to decrease the variation as much as possible. Many times, these cases should become perfect Six-Sigma black belt projects. As far as the testing issues, again we need to work with engineering to fix the test sets or to loosen the tolerances (assuming they are still within the customer spec). We have found many times that the test specs are the result of advances in testing technology. In the past, a part might have passed the test if it was within a tenth of the tolerance. Now we have test sets that can measure thousands. Engineering decides to set the tolerance to five one-hundredths. Now the parts fail every time. Engineering uses this information via trial and error to set the tolerance for each part. With normal common cause variation in production, the tolerance for one lot may not work for the next. This means that engineering must be called again. Basically, this is since engineering is not really understanding the performance tolerance of the parts. So, they become lazy engineers and let production figure it out. This greatly slows down production, and there are no engineering measures to hold them accountable. Hence, only production suffers. The other by-product of this situation is rework. Until engineering adjusts the tolerance or the parts are adjusted or the test set augmented to pass the parts, the cell creates a bunch of rework. Again, this problem still exists in batch but is covered up by all the WIP being built at the other stations. However, the person at test is normally blamed for not getting their output.

To resolve these problems, we either must get with engineering, and sometimes sales to fix these problems or live with them on the line and adjust the staffing on the line to reflect the cycle time for test.

Lesson Learned: Keep in mind, the main reason to implement one-piece flow is to expose the problems; and that it will. In this case, especially on mixed model lines, every problem regardless of how long it has existed will come to the surface and then often be blamed on the Lean implementation or team.

Iceberg Effect

As discussed earlier, we are all familiar with the example of lowering the water level exposing the rocks. This doesn't quite apply to the problems in mixed model lines. It is better to use the analogy for this case which Davide Barbon calls the iceberg effect.[9] By lowering the water level, we don't expose rocks but an entire iceberg. We must chip away at the iceberg little by little to eliminate it. This iceberg is the compilation of many barriers most of which are not only technical and process related but cultural as well. In some cases, it may take years of effort to eliminate the iceberg.

Union Impact

Lean is typically more difficult to implement within union environments. The first place we implemented this approach was in a union factory. The biggest hurdle is getting the union workers to work as a team. One must get over the thought process, "If I flex, I am doing someone else's work." The idea is to work as a team and realize that any work is all our work. However, with some unions, "team" is a bad word. The more we flex, the more we produce. This means better job security, and at many plants where it was implemented, it meant a bonus check at the end of the month.

At ETG, based on simple changes and zero capital dollars, the increase in output resulted in over $2,000 a year to each union's person's paycheck. The other hurdle is work rules and cross-training. We normally must negotiate with the union to combine job descriptions to flex and cross-train. It is never a problem to flex to a lower labor position because we are already paying them more than the lower classification job rate. However, flexing up is a problem because now they are due more pay. That said, we have never had a union environment where we were not able to implement Lean. Ninety-nine percent of the time the employees love it. The resistance comes mainly from union middle management which is somewhat of an oxymoron.

100% Efficiency with Humans

We close out the chapter with a notion discussed in an earlier chapter. Looking at it from a very analytical Lean or motion study purest point of view, an operator who uses both hands and feet at the same time is 100% efficient (a piano player or drummer is a good example). How close can we get to this in manufacturing? Normally, we look at the use of both hands simultaneously as 100% efficient, but technically, it is only 50% efficient since we are not using our feet unless we are standing and walking. Even then walking is transportation, which is waste. People who use one hand as a fixture to hold something while the other hand is working on it are only 25% efficient and using a hand as a fixture is also a common reason that operations cannot be split between two persons. Watch the work being performed. Can a fixture be made to hold the part for the person and free up the other hand? (Table 3.2). As the TLT gets under 10 minutes, moving to finer and finer increments of time become necessary to continue to drive improvement. This is where motion study comes into play.

Table 3.2 Motion Study Form

Motion Analysis of Operators					
					Observer
	Time Analysis Starts			**Time Analysis Ends**	
Date	Description	Code	Apply # of Tick Marks Observed	Computer Time and Motion Analysis	Code	Apply # of Tick Marks Observed
Class 1 — The Essence of an Operation (Highest Value)					
1	Assemble	A		Setup paperwork	SP
2	Disassemble	DA		Remove paperwork	RP
3	Use	U		Typing	T
Class 2 — Preparatory or Follow-Up Motions	Description	Code		Description	Code
4	Transport empty	TE			
5	Grasp	G		Grasp mouse	GM
6	Transport loaded	TL			
7	Release load	RL			
Class 3 — Incidental Motions	Description	Code		Description	Code
8	Search	S		Application transfer	AT
9	Find	F		Screen switch	SS
10	Select	Se			
11	Inspect	I		Inspect screen	I
12	Pre-position or re-position	Pos			
13	Hold	H			
14	Prepare	Pre			
Class 4 — These Should Be Eliminated If Possible	Description	Code		Description	Code
15	Think or plan	TP		Think or plan	TP
16	Rest for overcoming fatigue	ROF		Unnecessary typing	UT
17	Unavoidable delay	UD		Screen delay	SD
18	Avoidable delay	AD		Oper. influenced delay	OD

Gilbreth 18 fundamental motions

Source: Unknown.

Chapter Questions

1. What are two reasons station balancing does not work well?
2. What hides problems on manufacturing lines?
3. What two things will point to a problem on a manufacturing line?
4. What is a baton zone?
5. What are three failure modes of baton handoff lines?
6. What are three advantages of baton handoff manufacturing lines?
7. What are in-process Kanbans? Are they the same as SWIP?
8. Describe bumping.
9. What is a mixed model matrix?
10. What is rabbit chase?
11. What is meant by the Lazy Man's Balance?
12. What are five-line balancing rules?

Discussion Question

Should we balance lines by station balancing first and then bumping or go to bumping right away? What are some pros and cons of each approach?

Exercise

Set up a line with bumping. How did the results compare with station balancing?

Notes

1. Speed Is Life, Tom Peters, a co-production of Video Publishing House and KERA ©1991.
2. Taiichi Ohno, Kanban JIT at Toyota (New York: Productivity Press), ©1986, p. 115.
3. Eliyahu Goldratt, The Goal (MA: North River Press), ©1992.
4. Taiichi Ohno, Kanban JIT at Toyota (New York: Productivity Press), ©1986, p. 115.
5. When I asked Bert, who is from Holland, if I could use his name in the book, he said the following: "It would be an honor. But it is more important people benefit from the exercise." Based on personal correspondence dated March 19, 2015.
6. Batch versus Flow exercise created by Leontine Buren and Bert Overweg.
7. Content from Sam Mitchell, a past Steel Foundry Operations Executive, now has his own machine shop SLS Machining.
8. This content was supplied by Jeffrey A. Smith, CPIM, Plant Manager, Consolidated Container Co. via personal correspondence on January 24, 2013.
9. Davide Barbon, Executive at ITT Industries.

Chapter 4

Lean and Machine Shops and Job Shops

It is not necessary to change. Survival is not mandatory.

W. Edwards Deming[1]

What We Find

Machine shops vary as much as the work they handle. Some machine shops have fairly steady demand products, but most are job shop-type environments where lot sizes can run from one piece to hundreds. Most feel Lean doesn't or can't apply to them, and with rare exception they would be wrong. We have yet to find a machine shop where no Lean principles could be applied. In a worst-case scenario, one could still apply 5S, total productive maintenance (TPM), setup reduction, visual controls, and material flow (i.e., Kanban, CONWIP, COBACABANA, heijunka)[2] to most machine shop environments. Even job shops in most instances can set up cells. Will some parts cross cells? Depending on the equipment available, the answer is normally yes. There are always some parts that never fit. We call these misfit parts.

Where to Start? Group Tech Matrix

In most machine shops, the best place to start is with a group tech matrix (Table 4.1). The group tech matrix will work regardless of the number of parts or lot sizes involved. The goal of the group tech matrix is to determine what, if any, families exist and to what extent of the parts they will cover. We have created group techs with 30 parts and some with thousands of parts. The first step is to determine if most of the parts follow the same process steps or use the same equipment or are subjected to the same operations in a similar order. Some parts may skip certain machines but they can still work in the cell. Most shops can set up at least one and normally more cells. Parts that don't fit any cells or simply will not flow one piece or small lot are relegated to what we call the misfit or model shop cell.

DOI: 10.4324/9781003185802-4

Table 4.1 Group Tech Matrix with Xs

Part/Machine	Machine 1	Machine 2	Machine 3	Machine 4	Machine 5	Machine 6	Machine 7	Machine 8	Machine 9	Machine 10	Machine 11	Machine 12	Machine 13	Machine 14	Machine 15	Machine 16	Machine 17	Machine 18	Machine 19	Machine 20	Machine 21	Machine 22	Machine 23	Machine 24
Part 1	X			X	X	X		X		X			X		X				X					X
Part 2				X	X	X		X		X						X	X		X			X		
Part 3				X	X	X		X		X						X	X		X			X		X
Part 4				X	X	X		X		X			X		X		X		X					X
Part 5				X	X	X		X		X						X			X					X
Part 6				X	X	X		X		X						X	X		X					X
Part 7				X	X	X	X	X		X						X	X		X			X		
Part 8				X	X	X	X		X	X					X				X					X
Part 9				X	X	X	X		X	X					X				X					X
Part 10				X	X	X	X		X	X					X				X					X
Part 11				X	X	X	X		X	X					X				X					X
Part 12				X	X	X	X		X	X					X				X					X
Part 13				X	X	X	X		X	X					X				X					X
Part 14				X	X	X	X		X	X					X				X					X
Part 15				X	X	X	X		X	X					X				X					X
Part 16				X	X	X	X		X	X					X				X					X
Part 17				X	X	X	X		X	X					X				X					X
Part 18				X	X	X	X		X	X					X				X					X
Part 19				X	X	X	X		X	X					X				X					X
Part 20			X		X	X	X	X		X			X		X				X	X				X
Part 21				X	X	X	X	X		X			X		X				X					X

Most shops don't believe us when we tell them Lean applies to them. Machinists resistance to change on the degree of difficulty scale is *level 3*, which is very high for Lean implementations.

4D Group Tech Matrix

The group tech may start with Xs where a part runs across a machine or operation (see Table 4.1).

We can then turn the Xs into machine run cycle times for each part (Table 4.2).

If you multiply these times and the average daily demand, it will immediately provide a capacity analysis with the loading hours on each machine. As the project progresses, the same matrix can be used to develop the Kanban lot sizing for each part (Table 4.3).

Upon completion, we can see the Machining Analysis from Group Tech Matrix where we start looking for families (Table 4.4).

Master Layouts and Functional Batch Areas

Company X was working on their master layout and had the group tech matrix pictured (Table 4.5). We ran the data through a pivot table and then sorted it multiple ways to see if we could find a family of parts. Some families did pop out as well as some questions. What questions would you ask? The first one we asked was the difference between polish and hard tumbling. We were told the parts could go to either. This immediately freed up the polish machine. We asked what the difference was between the grinders. We were told one machines a larger diameter. Cutoff was essentially a manual operation. Why does part 14 not hit in either grinder? We were told that the supplier grinds them to size. So, we came up with the following potential families:

1. Grinder 2, furnace, cutoff, round, tumble
2. Grinder 1, furnace, cutoff, round
3. Grinders 1 and 2, furnace, cutoff

The People Doing the Job Know Best ... Sometimes

There is a term called warusa kagen, which refers to things not yet problems, but are still not quite right. They are often the starting point of improvement activities because if left unattended they may develop into serious problems. Many times, we hear the saying, the people doing the job know best how to do it. It is usually the operators who first notice warusa kagen and who therefore are on the front line of improvement.[3] While this saying is mostly accurate, there are exceptions. For instance, some machinists know how to do the job on their machine but don't really understand everything the machine (or the programing) can do. They can run their parts in their sleep, but when it comes to improving the job, many times they haven't been trained on how to use the machine, how the machine works, or the various options available on the machine.

At one company, we found the operators were very experienced in their jobs and had been doing those jobs sometimes for over 20 years but had never experimented with speeds and feeds. Since we weren't part of their paradigm, a day's worth of experimenting found we could run the parts almost twice as fast and get better quality. Yet, the operator, when told and shown the results, refused to run the parts that fast because he or she didn't feel comfortable with it. Many times,

Table 4.2 Same Group Tech Matrix with Average Daily Demand Multiplied by the Machine Run Time with the Total Hours per Day Required to Run the Parts (without Setups)

Work Center	99722	99723	99721	99720	96201	99017	24600	91630	91620	533A1	533B1	533C1	533A1	533B1	533C1	53519	53514	53925	53924	91640	54231	24802	26412	26501
Part/Machine	Machine 1	Machine 2	Machine 3	Machine 4	Machine 5	Machine 6	Machine 7	Machine 8	Machine 9	Machine 10	Machine 11	Machine 12	Machine 13	Machine 14	Machine 15	Machine 16	Machine 17	Machine 18	Machine 19	Machine 20	Machine 21	Machine 22	Machine 23	Machine 24
Part 1				.012	.004	.033	.047	.039		.024			.024			.031		.031			.004			
Part 2				.188	.107	.499	1.289	.613		.492			.492						.159	1.022	.112			.424
Part 3				.000	.000	.000		.000	.032	.000			.000						.000	.000	.000			.000
Part 4				.244	.102	.681		.823	1.494	.527			.630			.761		.761	.000	1.396	.107			
Part 5				.064	.018	.186		.219	.035	.104			.104						.030		.019			
Part 6				.012	.004	.033		.039	.073	.024			0.24						.007	.067	.004			
Part 7				.000	.000	.000		.000		.000			.000						.000	.000	.000			.000
Part 8				.020	.008	.056			.103	.044			.055					.063			.009			
Part 9				.549	.231	1.531			2.837	1.199			1.511					1.728			.243			
Part 10				.006	.003	.017	.015			.014			.017					.020			.003			
Part 11				.008	.002	.023	.017		.042	.014			.019					.017			.002			
Part 12				.283	.082	.822	.602			.484			.689					.616			.086			
Part 13				.007	.002	.019	.014			.011			.016					0.14			.002			
Part 14				.014	.005	.040	.032			.029			.039					0.39			.006			
Part 15				.632	.237	1.789	1.433		3.299	1.302			1.765					1.769			.254			
Part 16				.015	.006	.042	.033		.077	.030			.041					.041			.006			
Part 17				.001	.000	.002	.002		.004	.002			.003					.002			.000			
Part 18				.000	.000	.000	.000		.000	.000			.000					.000			.000			
Part 19			.001	.000	.000	.000	.000		.000	.000			.000					.000			.000			
Part 20					.000	.002	.001	.002		.001			.001			.002		.002			.000	.002		
Part 21				.007	.003	.021	.017	.025		.012			.012			.020		.020			.002			
Part 22			1.650		.689	4.603		5.561		3.571			4.258			5.152		5.152		9.436	.689			
Part 23				.091	.035	.256		.309		.186			.237			.263		.263		.524	.037			
Part 24			.001		.000	.002	.002	.002		.001			.001					.002			.000			
Part 25				.235	.079	.671		.793		.469			.469			.591		.591			.086			.521
	13.22	6.87	5.95	6.32	5.30	34.07	8.79	42.24	11.02	34.86	24.19	0.32	51.02	24.06	0.32	68.53	0.89	68.02	3.48	51.19	12.27	1.37	7.47	15.38

Table 4.3 Same Chart with Kanban Analysis

				Work Center				
Part/ Machine	*Greenstock #*	*Base Number*	*Total Parts per Run*	*Kanban Qty (Parts per Tub)*	*# Tubs*	*Tubs in Process (on Hand)*	*Number of Weeks between Setups*	*Working Days Worth of Parts per Tub*
Part 1	1172057	1118548	1,010.92	3,661.80	0.28		7.2	36.2
Part 2		1118835	15,330.65	2,365.05	6.48		2.0	1.5
Part 3		1118835		2,365.05				
Part 4		1118861	20,944.94	3,509.98	5.97		2.0	1.7
Part 5		1119051	5,731.91	4,771.05	1.20		2.0	8.3
Part 6		1119064	1,004.46	3,719.73	0.27		7.4	37.0
Part 7		1119065		4,339.06				
Part 8		1122090	1,709.37	3,322.36	0.51		3.9	19.4
Part 9		1122090	47,091.85	3,321.72	14.18		2.0	0.7
Part 10		1122090	535.75	3,321.09	0.16		12.4	62.0
Part 11		1122110	706.48	4,675.56	0.15		13.2	66.2
Part 12		1122110	25,262.22	4,674.59	5.40		2.0	1.9
Part 13		1122110	590.21	4,673.60	0.13		15.8	79.2
Part 14		1122120	1,222.59	3,849.07	0.32		6.3	31.5
Part 15		1122120	55,001.30	3,848.30	14.29		2.0	0.7
Part 16		1122120	1,283.79	3,847.52	0.33		6.0	30.0
Part 17		1122130	62.24	3,133.11	0.02		100.7	503.4
Part 18		1122130		3,133.11				
Part 19		1122130		3,133.11				
Part 20	1172054	1123110	50.65	3,855.89	0.01		152.3	761.3
Part 21	1172057	1123520	644.92	4,330.89	0.15		13.4	67.2
Part 22		1123600	141,543.95	3,351.12	42.24		2.0	0.2
Part 23		1123605	7,866.10	3,479.89	2.26		2.0	4.4
Part 24	1172051	1127000	56.18	4,069.20	0.01		144.9	724.4
Part 25		1130180	20,647.67	4,190.53	4.93		2.0	2.0
			2,075,449.91		60.00			0.00

Table 4.4 We Ran the Data through a Pivot Table and Then Sorted It Multiple Ways to See If We Could Find a Family of Parts

Part Number	Centerless Grind 1	Centerless Grind 2	Furnace	Cut Off	Polish	Round	Hard Tumbling
Part 15		X	X	X		X	X
Part 16		X	X	X		X	X
Part 17		X	X	X		X	X
Part 22		X	X	X		X	X
Part 54		X	X	X		X	X
Part 59		X	X	X		X	X
Part 65		X	X	X		X	X
Part 70		X	X	X	X	X	
Part 71		X	X	X	X	X	
Part 14			X			X	X
Part 7	X		X	X		X	
Part 10	X		X	X		X	
Part 11	X		X	X		X	
Part 27	X		X	X		X	
Part 8	X		X	X		X	
Part 9	X		X	X		X	
Part 60	X		X	X			
Part 61	X		X	X			
Part 62	X		X	X			
Part 63	X		X	X			
Part 64	X		X	X			
Part 38	X			X			
Part 39	X			X			
Part 40	X			X			
Part 41	X			X			
Part 42	X			X			
Part 43	X			X			
Part 44	X			X			
Part 45	X			X			
Part 32	X	X	X	X			
Part 33	X	X	X	X			
Part 34	X	X	X	X			
Part 35	X	X	X	X			

Note: Some families did pop out as well as some questions. What questions would you ask?

Table 4.5   Machining Analysis from Group Tech Matrix

Available Time	16.50	16.50	16.50	16.50	16.50
Takt time (TT) per machine minute	5.45	2.86	11.21	4.30	3.24
Avg. run cycle time per machine (minute)	3.00	1.75	3.00	3.00	3.00
Demand on the machine (hour/day)	9.08	10.08	4.41	11.51	15.29
Setups 3/week (avg. hours per day)	1.20	1.20	1.20	1.20	1.20
Total demand per day run time + setups	10.28	11.28	5.61	12.71	16.49
Lost time due to inspections (internal time)					
Grand total demand on machines	10.28	11.28	5.61	12.71	16.49
Capacity available	6.22	5.22	10.89	3.79	.01
% at capacity based on hours	62.3	68.4	34.0	77.0	100.0
No. of parts per day	181.52	345.68	88.29	230.21	305.89
# of parts available capacity per day	306.00	524.57	306.00	306.00	306.00
% at capacity based on # parts	59	66	29	75	100
Available time less setups and inspect downtime	180.32	344.48	87.09	229.01	304.69
Additional parts that could be produced per day per machine	3,424.95	11,465.15	1,653.43	4,349.92	5,787.89

we have found that a simple call to the machine manufacturer (if they are still around) can provide solutions or options that no one knew existed. In general, people will do the best job they can with the tools and training you give them. How often have you seen an operator take a screwdriver or some other tool and use it in a dangerous fashion because it was all they had available?

Process Flow Analysis

Once we do a group tech matrix and determine a cell can be created, we do a process flow analysis (PFA) on the part(s) in the cell to make sure we have the steps in the correct order (Tables 4.6 and 4.7). Many times, routers will have steps in a different order for similar parts. We have found that this is normally due to different engineers designing the routers. Most times the steps can be changed on routers to put them in the same order. A PFA and point-to-point diagram (cell layout with point-to-point part travel paths drawn on it) are the best tools to double-check that you have the right equipment/machines in the cell and they are in the right order.

Table 4.6 PFA with Omits

No. of Steps	Omit (X)	Description of Product Step	Baseline Time (s)	Post Lean Estimate Time	Distance (in ft)	Distance Post (with Omits)	Machine	Person Who Touches It (Job Class)
1	X	Parts sit as bar stock	14,400	0		0		
2		Mori	125	125		0	Mori	Eric
3	X	Sits in parts tray in mori	16	0		0		
4		Move to hand to inspect	3	3	1	1		
5		Inspect part	19	19		0		
6		Lathe	80	80	5	5	Lathe	
7	x	Sits on lathe— lost first in, first out (FIFO)	1,260	0	2	0		
8		To gear cutter	3	3		0	Gear cutter	
9		Gear cut	300	300		0		
10		Sits on gear cutter	29	29		0		Joe
11		Inspect gear cut	11	11		0		
12	x	Sits in egg carton	300	0	1	0		
13		Sand	51	51	8	8		John
14		Lathe deburr	45	45	1	1	Lathe	
15		Mill	22	22	5	5	Mill	
16	x	Sits in egg carton	11,520	0	2	0		
						0		
						0		

Table 4.7 PFA Results

Summary	Baseline	Post Lean Projected	Reduction	Reduction (%)
Total steps	16.0	11.0	5.00	31
Original sec.	28,184	688	27,496	98
Minutes	469.7	11.5	458.27	98
Hours	7.8	.2	7.64	98
Days	1.1	.0	1.05	98
Weeks	.2	.0	.2	98
Distance	20.0	20.0	—	0
# of people	3.0	1.0	2.00	67
# of machines	5.0	5.0	—	0
VA (%)	1.8699	76.60	−74.73	
NVA (%)	.34	13.95	−13.61	
Storage (%)	97.66	4.22	93.45	
Inspect (%)	.11	4.36	−4.25	
Transport (%)	.02	.87	−.85	

Workflow Analysis

Just like when we analyze assembly operators, we can use the same tools (including video) for analyzing machine operators. We record each step the operator performs (with the operator present) and then look for ideas for improvement (Tables 4.8 and 4.9).

Table 4.8 Work Flow Analysis (WFA)

OP Step	Omit (X)	Description	Key Points Quality and Safety	Analysis Codes Enter Either VA, RW, PW, MH, UW, R T I	Current Time (Seconds)	Estimated Time
1		Open door Mori	Mori	RW	1	1
2	X	Press button		RW	2	0
3		Pick up pliers		RW	3	3
4		Pull out bar		RW	2	2
5		Close door Mori		RW	2	2
6		Press start/cycle machine		RW	1	1

(Continued)

Table 4.8 *(Continued)* **Work Flow Analysis (WFA)**

OP Step	Omit (X)	Description	Key Points Quality and Safety	Analysis Codes Enter Either VA, RW, PW, MH, UW, R T I	Current Time (Seconds)	Estimated Time
7		Open part catch		RW	1	1
8		Take out part		RW	4	1
9	X	Grab mic		RW	2	0
10	X	Inspect		RW	2	0
11	X	Put down mic		RW	1	0
12	X	Pick up mic		RW	1	0
13	X	Inspect		RW	13	0
14	X	Put down mic		RW	1	0
15		Move to lathe	Lathe	RW	2	2
16		Remove from chuck		RW	1	1
17		Reach for hose		RW	1	1
18		Blow off		RW	3	1
19		Put down hose		RW	1	1
20		Reach for deburr		RW	1	1

Source: Ancon Gear.

Table 4.9 **Example of a WFA for an Operator and Machine**

PFA Step	WFA Step	Step Description	Improvement Ideas	Cycle Time
1	1	Wait on part		8
	2	Got part		2
	3	Walk to inspection		2
	4	Inspect part	Need better location for print	148
	5	Walk to end		4
	6	Put parts in tray		12
	7	Check		5
	8	Inspect part		127

Source: BIG Archives.

Workflow Analysis Example

At Company X, we were filming the operator running two machines. In most factories, this would be considered great. While we were filming, we noticed the operator had a significant amount of idle time. At first, he did his full quality check. This was done every 25 or 30 parts. Then he waited. The machine was bar fed so all he had to do was remove the parts from each machine, dip them in a bucket to wash off the coolant, and then put them in a bin. The rest of his time was spent waiting for the machine for about 130 seconds on average not including every 25th cycle inspection. Pretty soon on the video, you see, let's call him Billy, starting to Windex the machine glass. The next cycle, he swept the entire cell. The next cycle, he started wiping down the machines. During the analysis, we asked if this was normal, but of course we knew it wasn't. Billy was trying to look busy since he was being filmed. But was the idle time his fault? No, of course not, it was management's fault. They are the ones who created the layout that drove all this waste. When we were done with the improvements to the cell (see bottom picture of Figure 4.1), Billy was not only running the machines but also washing, marking, and packing the parts. In the course of transitioning the rest of the machine shop to this process, we were able to eliminate what used to be separate, functional washing, marking, and packing departments. Billy, after a month or so when he learned the processes and felt comfortable with them, actually liked the new way better. He said the days were really long before when you had nothing to do but stare at the machine and now the day flies by. No one was laid off but the people who were marking, washing, and packing were retrained for other positions. One operator was thrilled that she was finally able to cross-train on the machines instead of washing parts all day long. Now she is a team leader (supervisor) for a cell. The former supervisor was promoted to lead their Environmental, Health and Safety (EHS) effort.

Homework: Can you think of any examples from your current or previous work experiences?

Step No.	Description	Comments/key points	Ideas	Cycle time min Cycle time secs	3.25 195	2.77 166	2.87 172	2.90 174.00	2.75 165.00	Max 253.0	Min 187.0	Avg 233.6	Std dev 12.1
4	Inspect part and put in bin			Split time	9					9	9	9	
5	Idle time	Add pack and ship		Alt. start time (optional)		000315	000601	000853	001147	134	81	121	22
				Cum	000235	000523	000815	001105	001355				
				Split time	81	128	134	132	128				
6	Pick up parts from machine and washes			Alt. start time (optional)						17	13	16	2
				Cum	000248	000540	000831	001122	001412				
				Split time	13	17	16	17	17				
7	Walk to other machine			Alt. start time (optional)						7	4	5	1
				Cum	000255	000544	000835	001126	001417				
				Split time	7	4	4	4	5				
8	Pick up part and wash and dry			Alt. start time (optional)						21	15	18	2
				Cum	000315	000601	000853	001147	001432				
				Split time	20	17	18	21	15				

Analysis revealed significant idle time for machining operator.

After results:

Parts now washed, marked, packed by machine operators and sent to shipping kanban location. Transferred solution to several machining cells. Freed up functional marking, and packing departments and supervisor. Estimated savings $600K annually. Also, improved on time delivery and reduced WIP inventory, and freed up space and cash do to the decrease in throughput time.

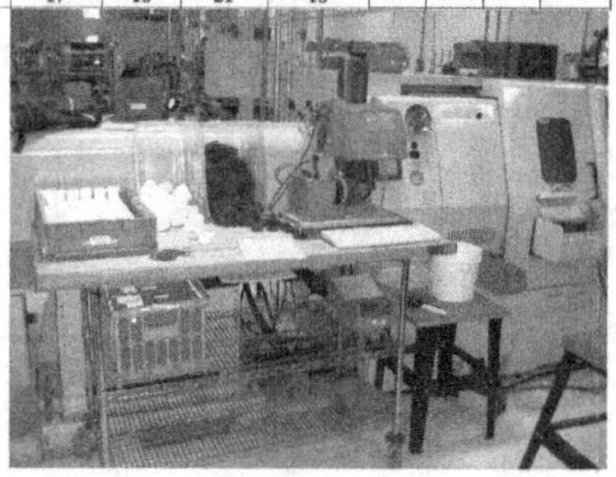

Figure 4.1   Improvements made to machining cell using ten-cycle analysis.

Results: In another area of the same factory, parts were made that were used to feed a different cell. We were able to have one operator run six machines, freeing up two operators. After implementing several kaizen activities, where the washing, marking, and packing departments were eliminated, and with attrition (which is when people leave or retire), the company went from losing money to making money over the course of 2 months.

Ten-Cycle Analysis for a Machining Cell

While one can use the workflow analysis (WFA) for a machining cell, we generally use the ten-cycle analysis tool (Figure 4.2); but we don't always do all ten cycles. Sometimes we do less and sometimes more. This is because most of the time where people are interacting with machines we are unloading, loading, and then cycling the machine. There may be a deburring step or quality check after the machining but in most cases the machines do the work. The other advantage with analyzing machines is that the operators normally have short cycle times where they interact with the machine. For instance, loading, unloading, and then cycling (starting) the machine can take less than 30 seconds and sometimes just a few minutes. This is very short compared to many assembly operations that can take hours. The other advantage this tool gives us is the ability to see if there is any variation between cycles. It is not unusual to find activities the operator does on every fifth part, like a quality check, or where the machine is cleaned out, etc. Since this time is man versus machine time, we need to take the labor into account to determine the total labor time (TLT). In the following example (Figure 4.3), what do you notice?

There is a significant amount of wait time (around 40 seconds on average) for machine 1 (step 18) and a large variation in the wait time for machine 2 (step 13). Notice the variability in some of the other operations.

Step No.	Description		Cycle Time Min	4.53	5.63	5.82	Max	Min	Avg	Std Dev	Std Dev	Cum Time	1	2	3	4	5
			Cycle Time Secs	272	338	349	401.0	255.0	319.7	41.6							
1	Mori	Alt. Start Time (optional)	0				28	21	24	4	15.0%	24	1.00	1.00	1.00	1.00	1.00
		Cum	23	601	1146												
		Split Time	23	21	28												
2	Lathe	Alt. Start Time (optional)					62	16	33	25	78.0%	57	1.00	1.00	1.00	1.00	1.00
		Cum	43	703	1202												
		Split Time	20	62	16												
3	Wait	Alt. Start Time (optional)					70	11	39	30	76.7%	95	1.00	1.00	1.00	2.00	2.00
		Cum	54	738	1312												
		Split Time	11	35	70												
4	Gear Cut	Alt. Start Time (optional)					58	53	55	3	5.3%	150	1.00	1.00	2.00	2.00	3.00
		Cum	152	831	1405												
		Split Time	58	53	53												
5	Inspection	Alt. Start Time (optional)	300				24	14	19	5	26.0%	169	1.00	2.00	2.00	3.00	3.00
		Cum	314	851	1429												
		Split Time	14	20	24												
6	Lathe & Sand Deburr	Alt. Start Time (optional)					90	78	84	6	7.1%	253	1.00	2.00	3.00	4.00	4.00
		Cum	438	1009	1559												
		Split Time	84	78	90												
7	Mill	Alt. Start Time (optional)					69	62	66	4	5.7%	320	1.00	2.00	3.00	4.00	5.00
		Cum	540	1118	1707												
		Split Time	62	69	68												

Figure 4.2   Ten-cycle analysis tool example. (Ancon Gear.)

Step No.	Description	Comments	Ideas		Cycle 1	Cycle 2	Cycle 3	Cycle 4
Part No:	Core							
Description:								
					operator 1		operator 2	
				Cycle Time	92	94	93	104
1	walk to machine 1			Alt. Start Time (optional)	10:39:14		10:27:25	10:28:58
				Cum	10:39:16	10:40:37	10:27:26	10:28:59
				Split Time	2	1	1	1
2	set core on conveyor			Cum	10:39:18	10:40:40	10:27:30	10:29:01
				Split Time	2	3	4	2
3	get tool and clean out machine	Sprayed core release - 7 sec		Cum	10:39:20	10:40:44	10:27:33	10:29:07
				Split Time	2	4	3	6
4	Cycle Machine 1	machine time = 76 sec		Alt. Start Time (optional)			10:27:40	
				Cum	10:39:21	10:40:45	10:27:41	10:29:08
				Split Time	1	1	1	1
5	walk to machine 3	Some wait included		Cum	10:39:25	10:40:47	10:27:50	10:29:28
				Split Time	4	2	9	20
6	set core on conveyor			Cum	10:39:28	10:40:50	10:27:54	10:29:35
				Split Time	3	3	4	7
7	get tool and clean out machine	Greased machine - 9 sec		Cum	10:39:32	10:40:54	10:28:01	10:29:39
				Split Time	4	4	7	4
8	cycle machine 3	machine time = 72 sec		Alt. Start Time (optional)			10:28:11	
				Cum	10:39:33	10:40:55	10:28:12	10:29:40
				Split Time	1	1	1	1
9	walk to machine 4			Alt. Start Time (optional)			10:28:21	
				Cum	10:39:34	10:40:56	10:28:25	10:29:41
				Split Time	1	1	4	1
10	unload machine 4 and clean out 1 step			Alt. Start Time (optional)			10:28:27	10:29:45
				Cum	10:39:36	10:40:59	10:28:31	10:29:49
				Split Time	2	3	4	4
11	cycle machine 4	machine time = 79		Alt. Start Time (optional)				10:29:49
				Cum	10:39:37	10:41:00	10:28:32	10:29:51
				Split Time	1	1	1	2
12	set core on conveyor			Alt. Start Time (optional)			10:28:25	10:29:41
				Cum	10:39:39	10:41:02	10:28:27	10:29:45
				Split Time	2	2	2	4
13	wait for machine 2			Cum	10:39:44	10:41:05		
				Split Time	5	3	16	
13	walk to machine 2			Alt. Start Time (optional)			10:28:12	10:29:51
				Cum	10:39:46	10:41:07	10:28:14	10:29:53
				Split Time	7	5	2	2
14	unload machine 2 and set on conveyor			Cum	10:39:48	10:41:09	10:28:17	10:29:56
				Split Time	2	2	3	3
15	get tool and clean out machine			Cum	10:39:52	10:41:14	10:28:20	10:29:59
				Split Time	4	5	3	3
16	cycle machine 2	machine time = 74 sec		Cum	10:39:53	10:41:15	10:28:21	10:30:01
				Split Time	1	1	1	2
17	wait for machine 1			Alt. Start Time (optional)			10:28:31	
				Cum	10:40:36	10:42:01	10:28:58	10:30:37
				Split Time	48	52	27	41

Figure 4.3   Ten-cycle Analysis Example Courtesy Ancon Gear.

Note: **What do you notice?**

Job Step	Process Step	Labor Value Added (sec)	Labor Non Value Added (sec)	Machine Non Value Added (sec)	Machine Value Added (sec)	Complete Time (sec)	Standard Wiip	Bottle Neck	Prod Cap (units/day)
	Cumulative Times:	0	0	0	45	45			
	Percent:	0.0%	0.0%	0.0%	100.0%	100.0%	5		
1	Press	0.0	0.0	0	4.000	4.00	0.41		13,320.00
2	Former 1	0.0	0.0	0	9.200	9.20	0.93		5,791.30
3	Former 2	0.0	0.0	0	9.900	9.90	1.00	X	5,381.82
4	Pin Shear	0.0	0.0	0	5.647	5.65	0.57		9,435.10
5	Assembly machine	0.0	0.0	0	5.647	5.65	0.57		9,435.10
6	Assembly machine 2	0.0	0.0	0	5.236	5.24	0.53		10,175.71
7	Loader	0.0	0.0	0	5.236	5.24	0.53		10,175.71

Figure 4.4 Ten-cycle analysis results converted to PPCS - part production Capacity Sheet example. (Authors.)

Lesson Learned: The ten-cycle analysis tool will expose variation and nonstandard work immediately and will show if the process is stable. Here is a PPCS for a totally automated line (Figure 4.4). Note that there is no labor time.

Ten-Cycle Analysis and Variation

In Figure 4.5, we see medium to high variation across each step. The first questions we ask are:

- Have the operators been trained properly in the standard work and are they proficient in the standard work or still learning?
- If they are trained and proficient—are they following the standard work? A review of the video analysis compared to the standard work will reveal this.
- If they are trained, proficient, and following the standard work then the standard deviation is a result of some other problem in the process. It could be man, method, machines, or materials.

In the short term, we will use bumping to offset the variation where possible. If the layout does not allow bumping for some reason and these become pure station balanced operations and/ or isolated islands. We would then have to add work in process (WIP) in between the operators to buffer the process until the variation can be addressed. Line balancing is always managed using

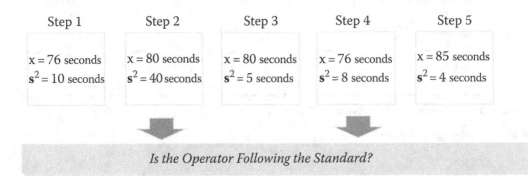

Step 1	Step 2	Step 3	Step 4	Step 5
$x = 76$ seconds $s^2 = 10$ seconds	$x = 80$ seconds $s^2 = 40$ seconds	$x = 80$ seconds $s^2 = 5$ seconds	$x = 76$ seconds $s^2 = 8$ seconds	$x = 85$ seconds $s^2 = 4$ seconds

Is the Operator Following the Standard?

Figure 4.5 Ten-cycle analysis and variation.

some percentage of people and/or materials (WIP). In the long term, we work to eliminate variation through use of black belt tools (design of experiments (DOE), measurement systems evaluation (MSE), Failure modes effects (FMEA), black belt process mapping) and mistake proofing.

Utilizing Variation Analysis to Assure Production Linearity and to Determine Black Belt Projects

When implementing Lean in machining or assembly, the first thing that pops out is variation … normally everywhere! The ten-cycle tool highlights this variation immediately as one is analyzing the video. The first thing one discovers is that they can't fill in the form in order on every cycle. In addition, there may be variation within cycles for the same step with the same or different persons. These steps are now candidates for fixing and improving with our Six Sigma tools.

Part Production Capacity Sheet

Once we have the PFA and WFA or ten-cycle analysis complete, we can create a part production capacity sheet (PPCS). We reviewed this tool in an earlier chapter. This, along with the setup times and lot size, will give us the capacity for each machine and the overall process for the particular part we are following. In some cases, we will need a PPCS for each part, part type or family of parts. The PPCS along with standard work is a tool for the supervisor to use to manage their line (Figure 4.6). Very quickly one can ascertain:

- The TT
- The cycle time
- The capacity information for each operation
- The value-added (VA) and non-value-added (NVA) people versus machine times
- The location of the bottleneck
- The number of operators required to meet the TT
- Whether or not we have the ability to meet TT

Yamazumi Board

The Yamazumi board has different uses and varies by company. In general, it visually displays the load on each machine or machining center compared to the available time (Figure 4.7). Sometimes it is used to compare cycle times for operations to the TT. This board breaks down process steps in time slices indicating VA, NVA, periodic work, setup/change over time, etc.

Resistance to Lean

In manufacturing, we have found that machinists tend to fight Lean the most. They are very independent and typically start out not wanting any part of standard work. At Ancon Gear, they actually found that it was easier to hire new machinists out of trade school for their

Annotations (arrows): **Number of operators** · **Capacity for the cell** · **Capacity for each operation**

Summary / header block

Part Number	Electrodes	AWT (Hours/Day)	Seconds/Day:	Customer Demand	Takt Time	Total Labor Time	Number of Operators Required	Factory Demand	Factory Cycle Time	Variance to Takt Time	Number of Operators Required	Head Count:	1	2	3	4
Part Name	Various Mixed Model	16.50	59400	1151	51.61	121.00	2.34	1151.00	51.61	0	2.3446	Cycle Time: s	121.00	60.50	40.33	30.25
	Hours per Shift	7.50								Total # Operators Required	5.158	Cycle Time: m	2.02	1.01	0.67	0.50
												Hourly Output:	29.75	59.50	89.26	119.01
												Production Capacity (zero Setups)	490.91	981.82	1472.73	1963.64

Process detail block (Time Distribution / Tool Exchange)

Order of Process	Description of Process (PPF Steps)	Station Name/Number	Labor NVA Time (seconds)	Labor VA Time (seconds)	Machine NVA Time (seconds)	Machine VA Time (seconds)	Complete Time (seconds)	Bottle Neck	Tool Exchange Units	Tool Exchange s	Time Allocated (Setups)	Daily Capacity	Hourly Capacity
Totals			0	121	0	916							
1	L25-3			4		180	208				24	285.76	17.32
2	STAR			8		180	180				19	330.00	20.00
3	TSUG2			8		180	188				14	315.96	19.15
4	L20			5		105	105				12	565.71	34.29
5	L25-2			4		180	180				49	330.00	20.00
6	TSUG1					20	20					2970.00	180.00
7	B12					20	20					2970.00	180.00
8	Rhoff			26		4	30					1953.95	118.42
9	Rhoff			20		2	22					2724.77	165.14
10	Stuff inserts			5		0	5					11880.00	720.00
11	Riviter			2		0	2					29700.00	1800.00
12	Riviter			2		0	2					29700.00	1800.00
13	Doosan			8		16	46				22	1285.10	77.88
14	Takamaz			9		27	45				9	1318.23	79.89
15	Robo drill												
16	Laser marker			3		2	5					11880.00	720.00
17	Pack/assembly			17		0	17					3494.12	211.76

Figure 4.6 PPCS Machining.

Figure 4.7   Yamazumi board showing loading on machines or operations. Sometimes used for station balancing operations. (Courtesy of MarquipWardUnited, a division of Berry-Wehmiller, Inc.)

Lean system and teach them gear machining versus trying to get their current machinists to accept Lean.

Lesson Learned: While some managers truly embrace Lean and some actually drive the changes, most tend to initially resist or downright fight the changes. Change takes us outside our comfort zone where there is perceived risk. One must become comfortable managing this risk. When they see the positive impact of Lean, they eventually come around. This brings up a point that most Lean consulting is sold through the shop floor side of the companies, while the real need is to sell Lean through the board of directors and office of the CEO.

At Company X, we were piloting our new Lean system approach. The employees involved with our team were part of and embraced the changes. The area finance director, however, would not get involved with the team and totally disagreed with our changes. He refused to speak directly with the team and purposely distorted our very positive results during a budget presentation to the CEO. This set the team back several months. After much coaching from his peers and finally witnessing firsthand the changes, he reversed his position with the CEO, but by then the damage was done.

Setup Reduction

Once again, we don't know of any machine shop that cannot benefit from setup reduction. Many times, the group tech matrix will help us reduce and sometimes eliminate setups, due to the families of parts we are able to put together. By creating families of parts, we can many times then load all of the tools in the carousel for that family, thus eliminating the need for changeover. The best place to start in any machine shop is with the most challenging setup or the most frequent type of setup you perform daily or weekly. We hear from companies that if they have extra capacity they should not worry about reducing setups. How would you answer this question? Our answer is that wasted labor time is still being expended on a longer than necessary setup. The reduced times result in flexibility in supplying your customer, enabling them to reduce their lead times and the benefit of reducing WIP and freeing up cash. Most important is it shows the ongoing drive against complacency.

Cross-Training

The next major obstacle we run into is cross-training. Too often, people are trained and are specialized in one machine or one area or type of machine. When we put the machines together, we need machinists who can run every machine. They don't necessarily have to be able to set up or program each machine but they have to be able to run them and be able to program tool offsets if required.

Scheduling to Minimize Setups

This involves lining up the jobs (work orders) in the best order to minimize the setup changes. Most shops do this already because it seems like common sense. However, many times it is not followed and most of the time it is due to external forces. For instance, management wants a part stopped and another part started because of a hot customer request. This unexpected, yet many times common, type of interruption can result in very large changeover times. The other difficulty is when we start reducing lot sizes, we increase the number of setups. Remember, the lesson learned was not to reduce your lot sizes until you have reduced your setup times.

Moving Operations in Line

When possible, we should move any operations performed off-line (in another area) into the machining (or assembly) line. Some good examples of these types of operations are painting or welding (Figure 4.8). We would normally use a point-to-point diagram and/or a process flow diagram to determine the proper placement of the operations in the line. To do this, the equipment may need to be changed or modified to work on-line. For example, a paint system may require flexible gang-type ducting and a small self-contained booth versus the gigantic paint booth (Figure 4.9), which many times is used to paint small parts or have long conveyors in and out of the booth. In Figures 4.10 and 4.11, the company switched to a dip method of painting and created a special paint and hang dry rack for the WIP needed to accommodate the paint drying time. This new method did not require any special ventilation. Prior to this, the parts were taken halfway across the plant and waited until they were scheduled to be painted requiring much more inventory and expediting.

Figure 4.8 One-piece flow flexible cell using cutouts in paint booths and other improvements.

Figure 4.9 Before parts were batched up, scheduled, and then moved to a large centralized paint booth. (From BIG Archives.)

Figure 4.10 Parts utilizing a breakthrough method of pick and dip with standard WIP in line as part of the cell. (From BIG Archives.)

Figure 4.11   Switched from large paint booth to pick and dip method one-piece flow.

Why and How to Move Away from and Move Out Toolboxes

What is the problem with toolboxes in machining? (Figure 4.12) The same problem exists in machining as it does in assembly. Toolboxes collect stuff (Figure 4.13). By their very nature, they create waste, and with some exceptions, most are a mess. This means there is a lot of searching required to find the right tools and many times it requires a trip to someone else's

Figure 4.12   Problems with tool boxes.

toolbox to find the right tool or look around at every station to see who took your tool. The tools should be company owned. There are many reasons for this, one of which is that in some cases operators have modified the tool on their own and this information gets lost with them when they leave. Another is the toolboxes get locked up after the shift. When the next shift comes in, if a tool breaks or they need another tool, they don't have access to one and the work stops.

Figure 4.13   Toolboxes collect stuff. (From BIG Archives.)

One way to accomplish the transition is to have a meeting with all the machinists or workers who have toolboxes and tell them of the new company policy to provide tools and remove the toolboxes.

1. Leave the toolboxes in their current location until all company tools are in place.
2. Move the toolbox away from the area but in sight of the operator. This way if they need a tool, they can get it plus they can still see their toolbox (comfort level). If they need to get a tool out of their box, they should inform the supervisor who should order the tool.
3. After a month or so, move all the toolboxes into a centralized staging area. Again, if a tool is needed, they can still get it. After another month or two and no more trips are made to the toolbox area, have them take their toolboxes home.

The biggest objection we find is we are told the tools will get stolen. In reality, we have found this with rare exceptions not to be a problem. We find they normally don't get stolen but are borrowed for use in another area and never returned. If every area has the tools they need, the tools should not disappear. If the tools are walking out of the building, you have a much bigger problem that needs to be addressed with video cameras and other types of security. All tools needed to set up, adjust, load, and unload the machine should be stored right at the machine in the open, labeled, and easily accessible to the operator and presented in the right order based on machine requirements.

Place Machines Right Next to Each Other

Our goal with machines is to put them as close together as humanly possible (Figure 4.14). Why should we put the machines right next to each other? Many of you will object to this principle but hopefully you will keep reading. When we first set up a Lean line, everyone argues to put as much space in each machine as possible and to keep the aisleways large as well. They insist that the room is needed for the movement of parts or carts of parts from machine to machine. Moving machines can be expensive, especially if you have to bring in a rigger to move the equipment for you. Once the line is set up with all this space and the operators start to do a one-piece flow, and the large batches and carts full of parts go away, they suddenly realize they have to walk much more to cover the distances and space between the machines. They will immediately forget their former arguments and insist the machines be moved close together. The management will then say "We just paid all this money to move the equipment, we are not moving it again." Now the operators are stuck. The other group that will complain about moving the machines together is maintenance. They will argue they cannot get access to panels to work on the equipment. While this is true in many cases, control boxes or panels can be moved to the rear of the machine versus the side or front and many times we cut new access panels into the machine from the front or behind as necessary. The other problem with moving machines together is the chip conveyors, which are located on the side of the machine. When we visited world-class companies in Japan, all of their chip conveyors were located in the rear. Why is this not so in the United States?

> Joe and Ed Markievicz, owners of Ancon Gear tried to purchase a new gear machine from Japan back in the 1990s. Joe states, "We asked for a rear chip conveyor and the distributor told us, to their knowledge, it was never requested from one of their US customers before. They had to special order the components for the rear chip conveyor from

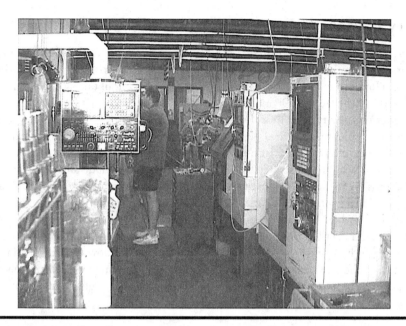

Figure 4.14 Machines literally next to each other to facilitate one-piece flow. (Courtesy of Ancon Gear.)

Japan". Interesting! The concept for the rear chip conveyor was to get the machines close enough to reduce travel/takt time from machine to machine. After many weeks of back and forth phone calls, the rep finally agreed to special order one with a rear chip conveyor.

Get Rid of Tables Wherever Possible

This is a difficult challenge for most machinists. Why? Because, we want our table! But if you keep a real open mind, do you really need it or just want it? For the current batch-type process, you may really need it; but as we convert to flow, the table will just get in the way. Tables that are not truly utilized or where space on them is not utilized, will just collect stuff and make 5S more difficult. As we remove the tables, it enables us to put the machines closer together and decrease the walking distance (one of the eight wastes).

Need for Latest Drawings and Programs

It goes without saying that we need a process to ensure we always have the latest drawings, setup sheets, or work instructions available. We also need to make sure that we update these documents as we improve methods or processes for the equipment or work product. We can't tell you how many times we have found machinists working with out-of-date documentation. With the internet and advances in technology working to the latest revision can be accomplished fairly easily by eliminating paper copies in favor of computers located at the machines with a centralized server. We also need to convert machines and drawings to metric in the United States. So, we have one international standard.

Don't Try to Move Subassemblies Out of the Line If Possible

Many times, not only non-Lean thinkers but also Lean experts feel they have to move subassemblies out of line to reduce their cycle time or improve their metrics in some way for the final assembly line. However, we argue against this. What is the benefit of taking the assembly off-line? One still has to pay the labor for it, and once it is off-line, we immediately create the need for an inventory buffer of some type to link the processes together. Often, these off-line subassemblies result in a person(s) in a separate area performing the task on an isolated island where we can no longer recoup the excess fractional labor. These off-line operations normally become batched up and overproduced! Why? Because they can! It is best to work to include all operations on the line or as many as possible to the extent it makes sense. Initially we may not have a choice. For instance, a computer numerical control (CNC) machine producing parts for multiple cells, on its own, will have to be off-line and feed a Kanban rack. The same is true for a batch-type wash process. It is the batching or centralization in some cases that creates the need for the operation to be off-line; however, we should be working to convert the batch washer to a flow washer or find a machine we can dedicate to the line versus using the CNC machine. Too often, we utilize CNC machines where they may not be necessary and we could be utilizing smaller, right sized equipment.

Avoid the Temptation to Outsource Everything

Too often, in order to be Lean, our first thought is to outsource the subassembly whether it is fabricated or assembled, but we should first ask this question: can the supplier do this better or cheaper than we can? The answer may be yes in the unlean environment, but once we implement Lean in-house, we should be cheaper than the supplier. So often we hear that we need to outsource it because it is not our core competency or we need to have a certain percent of the product outsourced to meet some corporate objective. However, once we outsource something, the following occurs:

- We lose control of the part. This means if you are not truly partnered with the supplier, we are subject to any problems, schedules, or other more preferred customers of the supplier. If it is in-house and the parts are behind schedule, we can expedite them.
- It is also more difficult to do Kanban with a supplier than it is internally (or should be).
- Buffer inventory will be needed between the outside process and the in-house line.
- It may be difficult to insource it again (i.e., if you sell or scrap, all the equipment needed to fabricate it).
- It is easy to lose the recipe or the know how to fabricate or assemble the parts.
- You are passing on your technology to the supplier (if you outsource too much, the supplier can bid against you).
- Your overheads now go up because you have less material against which to spread your overheads making this now an ongoing spiral to outsource even more. Our goal with Lean should be to work toward more vertical integration.
- You become reliant on the supplier for future price decreases or subject to their price increases (especially if you no longer can build it in-house or don't have a backup supplier).

The exceptions to these guidelines for outsourcing can be for processes that are hazardous, that is, chemicals, environmental protection agency(EPA) issues, and dangerous processes, or where the supplier has technology that is not available at your company or that can produce the parts much cheaper.

Insourcing/Reshoring Formula

How many times have you outsourced a part, maybe to another country, and found it wasn't exactly the nirvana everyone was preaching? Material managers pull their hair out when they are mandated to outsource. Now it has to spend months on a boat, they lose all flexibility and control, they have to send a person to monitor the subcontractor or hire someone to do source inspection, and then they get pounded because their inventory is too high.

Eliminating Waste from Your Process + Increasing Value Added

= Insourcing and/or Reshoring

These decisions normally start with a make/buy decision. This is where the internal costs of producing the product with all the burdens attached are compared to the cost of purchasing the parts outside. Many times, the analysis is flawed because most companies don't know the true cost of their products. In addition, the pre-Lean state can be generally more expensive. Our goal with Lean projects is to generate enough gains to make the cost cheaper than the outside supplier. Now we can get to the point where we can bring much of this work in-house. In a non-Lean accounting world, as we bring the work back in-house, traditional overheads look better because there is more work to put people on and thus more to absorb the overheads. Once the work is back in-house, we have more control over it.

Conveyors

Many lines (especially automated lines) have conveyors. The question is if the conveyor is actually conveying? This is what they should be doing. Normally they are storing inventory! See Figure 4.15. Many times, the conveyors are too long or sometimes

Figure 4.15 Conveyors normally end up storing parts (WIP) resulting in excessive inventory. (From BIG Archives.)

we have found conveyors that were too short and did not have enough room for the standard WIP.

> At company called Griffin Pipe (since sold) (in the example, see Figure 4.16, every person thought the bottleneck was in their part of the line because that is where at some point during the day it was backing up. But after doing a VSM and ten-cycle analysis on each station, we found the problem to be a piece of conveyor that was too short at the very end of the line. This short piece of conveyor proceeded to back up a number of the upstream operations depending on how well the line was running. Notice the variation in the scale operation. This was due to the conveyor bottlenecking the scale, which then backed up the rest of the line.

This is the value stream map (VSM) for a casting line (Figure 4.16). All of the red/white push arrows are potential rework lines, which means that the castings were sent back to the start of the process, melted down, and recycled. This rework was very costly since the parts had already made it through a significant amount of the process before being scrapped. The inventory in the line was either standard WIP or due to the bottleneck highlighted earlier in the ten-cycle analysis. The VSM analysis determined that a second of cycle time was in the hundreds of thousands of dollars per year assuming there was demand for the product (once we fixed the bottleneck at the end of the line).

Another good tool to analyze conveyors is the PFA. How long does the product have to travel? What is the total throughput time? Do products sit on the conveyor? Here is a PFA from a plant that connected each operation with a manual conveyor (Table 4.10). We ended up removing the conveyor to get the following results (Table 4.11). The number of steps was reduced by 52%, travel distance reduced from 812 to 65 ft (92%), and transport time reduced by 51.5% by putting each operation in line. Now VA has increased to 65% and storage is reduced by 96%. Total throughput time is reduced from 4.7 days (not including raw material or finished goods [FG] storage) to 1.9 hours.

Now the company could reduce their lead time to the customer and ship daily versus weekly. At Company X, they were able to achieve 99% on-time delivery (OTD) and capture a leadership position in the market. This led to other improvements where they were able to install customer Kanbans, which means that they managed the inventory in their customer's facility. Once you get into the customer facility, it is a huge barrier to entry for the competition. Eliminating the conveyors and excess WIP freed up over 50% of the floor space. After a couple of years, they were able to bring business back in-house that had been outsourced locally and from Mexico in order to not lay off their people. This was in a unionized environment in one of the most expensive labor states in the United States. The union absolutely loved it when we brought business back inside from other countries. Reducing throughput time and wasted TLT is the formula to insource or reshoring as it is being called now and to put your country's labor force back to work. Remember:

$$\text{Total Capacity} = \text{Output} + \text{Waste}$$

Automated Lines

The same BASICS® analysis tools, process flow, workflow, and setup analysis can all be performed on automated lines and machines (Table 4.12). For example, on a bottling line, we can follow the bottle from when it enters the fill line or even from receiving until it ships from the plant. For WFA, the operator will either be a person who is monitoring the equipment in case there is

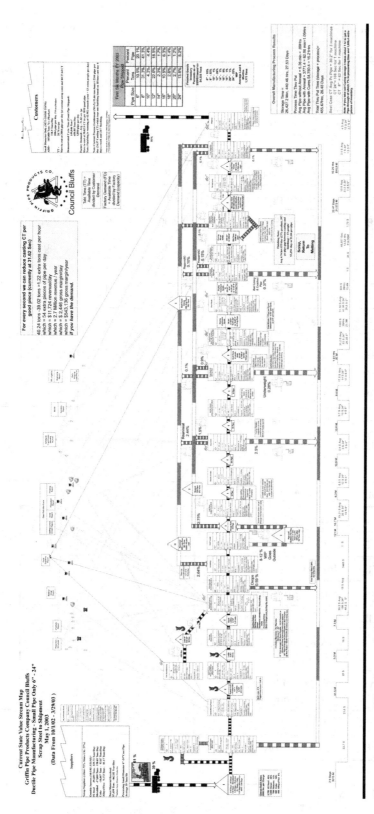

Figure 4.16 Griffin pipe Value stream mapping (VSM) analysis with cycle times based on the ten-cycle analysis—every person thought the bottleneck was in their part of the line because that is where it was backing up. But after doing a VSM and the ten-cycle analysis on each station, we found the problem to be a piece of conveyor that was too short at the very end of the line.

Table 4.10 PFA Analysis from a Plant That Connected Each Operation with a Manual Conveyor

Step	Omit (X)	Flow Code	Description	Baseline Time	Post Lean Estimate Time	Distance (in ft)	Distance Post (with Omits)
1		T	Transport to machine	120	10	20	3
2		VA	Process cut pipe	300	300		0
3	X	T	Transport to pallet	30	0	6	0
4	X	L	Storage on pallet	5,400	0		0
5	X	B	Storage on pallet	600	0		0
6	X	B	Transport to que	60	0	50	0
7	X	T	Cut pipe que	115,200	0		0
8	X	T	Move to lift table area	30	0	25	0
9	X	L	Lot delay multiple units	30	0		0
10		T	To lift table	15	15	3	3
11		VA	Install baffle	120	120		0
12	X	B	Storage	60	0		0
13		VA	Mount and tack heads	240	240		0
14		W	Paperwork	30	30		0
15		T	To cart	15	15	3	3
16	X	L	Load cart	1,920	0		0
17	X	T	Move to assy area	60	0	180	0
18	X	T	Unload cart	15	0	3	0
19	X	L	Unload remainder	60	0		0
20	X	B	Store at preweld	28,800	0		0
21	X	B	To table	15	0	3	0
22	X	VA	Tack cplgs, noz's, insert screen, p/w	840	840		0
23	X	W	Storage while operator gets screen	60	0		0
24	X	T	To floor	15	0		0
25	X	B	Store while p/w	30	0		0
26	X	T	To weld prep	30	0	45	0

(Continued)

Table 4.10 *(Continued)* PFA Analysis from a Plant That Connected Each Operation with a Manual Conveyor

Step	Omit (X)	Flow Code	Description	Baseline Time	Post Lean Estimate Time	Distance (in ft)	Distance Post (with Omits)
27	X	T	Off cart to floor	15	0		0
28	X	B	Que at pre weld	12,600	0		0
29	X	T	To middle of floor	1	0	5	0
30		VA	Mount lugs, weld cplg, clip screen	300	300		0
31	X	T	To lift table	30	0		0
32		VA	Weld inside nozzles	300	300		0
33	X	T	To pallet	15	0		0
34	X	B	Store on conveyor	9,900	0		0
35	X	T	To robot	120	0	50	0
36		B	Robot que	30	30		0
37		T	To robot	20	20	0	0
38		VA	Robot weld	900	900		0
39		T	To floor	15	15	3	3
40		NV	Remove tailstock	30	30		0
41		B	Store while get cart	30	30		0
42		T	To cart	3	3		0
43	X	T	To wall	15	0	30	0
44	X	B	Que for grind	18,000	0		0
45	X	T	To cart	3	0	3	0
46		T	To grind	10	10	15	15
47		T	To cradle	5	5	3	3
48		NV	Grind	1,200	1,200		0
49	X	T	To floor	15	0	3	0
50	X	B	To cart	60	0		0
51		T	On the cart	3	3	2	2
52	X	T	To test	60	0	90	0
53	X	B	Storage	18,000	0		0

(Continued)

Table 4.10 *(Continued)*   **PFA Analysis from a Plant That Connected Each Operation with a Manual Conveyor**

Step	Omit (X)	Flow Code	Description	Baseline Time	Post Lean Estimate Time	Distance (in ft)	Distance Post (with Omits)
54	X	T	To table	15	0	12	0
55		VA	Mount n/p bracket	60	60		0
56	X	W	Wait get the name plate	30	0		0
57		VA	Mount name plate	60	60		0
58		B	Wait get strainer/hardware/flange	180	180		0
59		VA	Insert strainer/mount flange	420	420		0
60		T	To line	60	10		0
61		NV	Fill with water	40	40		0
62	X	B	Hang unit	180	0		0
63		T	To test	25	25	3	3
64		I	Pressure test	120	120		0
65	X	T	To drain	60	0	39	0
66	X	B	Waiting for drain	600	0		0
67		NV	Drain	240	240		0
68		NV	Remove cover and fittings	300	300		0
69		T	To paint	10	10	10	10
70	X	B	Wait for paint	28,800	0		0
71		T	To paint booth	30	30	10	10
72		VA	Paint	90	90		0
73	X	T	To dry queue	180	0	72	0
74		VA	Dry	900	900		0
75	X	B	Wait for unload from paint line	25,200	0		0
76		T	To skid	10	10	4	4
77		L	Load 3 or 4 more units	30	30		0
78	X	T	To FG area	30	0	114	0

Source: BIG Archives.

Table 4.11 We Ended Up Removing the Conveyor to Get the Following Results

Summary	Baseline	Post Lean Projected	Reduction	Reduction (%)
Total Steps	79.0	38.0	41.00	52
Original sec.	273,355.0	6,961.0	266,394.00	97
Minutes	4,555.9	116.0	4,439.90	97
Hours:	75.9	1.9	74.00	97
Days	4.7	.1	4.62	97
Distance	812.0	65.0	747.00	92
Check:	273,475.0	6,971.0	266,504.00	97
VA (%)	1.66	65.08	−63.42	−38.27
NVA (%)	.67	26.43	−25.76	−38.27
Storage (%)	97.25	4.31	92.94	96
Inspect (%)	0.04	1.72	−1.68	−38.27
Transport (%)	0.42	2.60	−2.18	−51.5

Source: BIG Archives.

Note: The number of steps was reduced by 52%, travel distance reduced from 812 to 65 ft (92%), and transport time reduced by 51.5% by putting each operation in line; now value added has increased to 65% and storage is reduced by 96%; total throughput time is reduced from 4.7 days (not including raw material or FG storage) to 1.9 hours.

a problem or it breaks down or who may be making adjustments to the equipment resulting in unplanned downtime (Table 4.13). In some cases, the operator will be the robot itself. We have utilized these tools to free up robots the same way we free up people. In the following example, the ten-cycle analysis prompts several questions regarding the function of the line. Many times, the opportunity in automated lines and factories in addition to using these analysis tools is to see if opportunities exist in:

- Jidoka
- Visual management
- TPM
- Inventory reduction between lines
- Setup reduction
- Unplanned downtime tracking and reduction
- Overall equipment effectiveness (OEE)
- Standard WIP in process

Table 4.12 Simple Downtime Analysis Sheet

Machine			Press # 18					
Date	Shift	Total Unplanned Downtime Minutes	Reason Codes					Key
9-Nov	1	315	1	6	9	10	11	1. Set up
9-Nov	2	75	6	9				2. Jams
9-Nov	3							3. Part not available
12-Nov	1							4. Machine not scheduled
	2							5. Planned downtime (PMs)
12-Nov	3	90	2	8	9	10	11	6. Unplanned downtime (break down)
	1							7. Tool change
7-Nov	2	0						8. One operator/two machines
	3							9. breaks
8-Nov	1	295	1	6	8	9		10. Cleaning
8-Nov	2	70	1	7	8	9		11. Meeting
8-Nov	3	0	14					12. Waiting for a truck to be available
31-Oct	1	310	1					13. Order complete
	2							14. No operator
	3							15. No punch
5-Nov	1	330	8	14				
5-Nov	2	420	1	8	14			
	3							
6-Nov	1	120	1	8	9			
6-Nov	2	420	1	8				
6-Nov	3	345	1	8	10			

Source: BIG Archives.

Table 4.13 What Is the Paced Conveyor Doing in This Analysis?

Step No.	Description	Comments	Ideas	Avg. Cycle Time	27	42	28	28
1	Paint lance inward travel (paints inside and outside)							
				Split time	8	10	11	14
2	Paint lance outward travel (not painting)	Why go out in 8 seconds? why not 4 seconds?						
				Split time	8	8	8	8
3	Waits for conveyor chain dog							
				Split time		14	3	0
4	Loads next part	No one else does this?						
				Split time	6	6	6	6
5	Hand sprays the end	Is there a delay built in the machine, should be sprayed in parallel						
				Split time	5	4	0	0

Source: BIG Archives.

Paced Cells

This is an interesting case. We are in the machining section of the book because in this case an assembly line is running on a big machine. It is sort of a hybrid. In essence, these lines are collections of isolated islands full of fractional labor. Because the operators are stationery, they are given chairs and are surrounded by equipment, parts, and clutter (Figure 4.17). Why are these lines so popular? Well, when converting from batch to flow, these lines create huge improvements over the batch world: less space, higher productivity, less WIP, more organized workplace, etc. But when you use the Lean tools to analyze the line, you still find tremendous waste just waiting to be removed. From a Lean assessment standpoint, we look at three things:

1. They have the product piece because the line is set up in order of assembly. It may not be in the best order but it does flow (except when the operator stops the flow). We know that just getting the product piece right gets us a 20%–40% improvement in productivity. So, we will assume limited improvement here; however, we can eliminate all this WIP.
2. The operator piece is virtually nonexistent. So, if we were working with either company, we would be able to propose another 20%–40% improvement over where they are right now.
3. As far as setups, we don't know from the pictures.

Figure 4.17 Semi-automated line gives the illusion of a paced line. It has isolated islands and any operator can stop the line to finish their task. So is it really a paced line?

The line is called a paced cell because the conveyor moves the pallets that contain the parts and the operators add parts to the products on the pallets. They may add them directly or build a subassembly, which then goes on the part. Sometimes they actually remove the part from the pallet to their workstation, assemble the subassembly to the product, and put it back on the pallet.

Many paced cells are designed and built by various companies to speed up production and increase productivity. Many of these lines have built in poka-yoke devices so quality is improved significantly. These lines however are fraught with waste and can never be balanced properly and drive batching. When doing a PFA, one will find very high storage content and in between process delays. Another interesting observation is that moving to automated lines tends to create more WIP as a buffer either between machines (due to timing) or due to anticipated breakdowns. The theory is we better add a WIP conveyor here so if part of the line breaks down the rest of the line can keep running. Since the people can't flex, they just do the same operation to each part. In essence, some of these can be considered lot delays because the lot of parts is stuck waiting to move until the parts ahead of them are completed. You see these lines set up in factories around the world today.

Even though the conveyor is moving at a certain pace, supposedly mirroring the TT, the operators have the power to stop the conveyor. This means any advantage of a paced line is gone. Since the operators can work around the pace problem, there is no sense of urgency created to fix it. The thought sometimes is that management can control and improve the output with the speed of the conveyor. Remember the I Love Lucy episode in the candy factory? Another problem is that if an operator is absent or away from the line, they have to fill the spot with someone or the line can't run.

Note: This is not a problem for bumping. It is easy to move operators in and out of the line but keep in mind it will reduce output if the line is run with less operators.

Sometimes they will add a person in an attempt to move parts quicker but all it does is add more inventory in the line. What is interesting is that the designers actually planned on this waste, which is why there is all this extra conveyor in the line. In this case, the conveyor is not conveying but storing. If it was going to be a real one-piece flow, how much space would this line need? The other wastes created are excess inventory and idle time. So, these lines fail the requirements for a true, one-piece flow synchronized, balanced line! We refer to this as fake flow or Lean lite.

How Would You Fix This Pace Line Cell?

One could analyze these lines in much less than a day. Our first suggestion would be to remove the conveyor, set up workstations based on the assembly process so the product flows down a line of benches, and then sell the paced part of the line to your competition! However, what will prevent us from doing that? You probably guessed it. These lines can run up to a million dollars or more. How willing is finance going to be to take out this line after all that capital was spent to set it up? This is where systems thinking comes into play and the concept of sunk costs becomes applicable.

> Company X, a well-known manufacturer of consumer products invited us to look at their factory where they had just installed all new conveyor lines (based on a demand flow layout) because they wanted to improve productivity and obtain a more predictable output. After a tour of the factory, they asked us what we thought. Our response was "Do you really want to know what we think?" They replied. "Oh yes, definitely." The first thing we would do is rip out all these conveyor lines. The conveyors served no purpose. There was no automation involved. It was just a way to move the products from one workstation to the next. We then witnessed a new definition for the word defensiveness. They said "You don't understand this was a major capital project for this year and has a very big return on investment (ROI) attached to it." Our response was then why did you ask us to help you improve productivity; you could have gotten an even bigger ROI by removing it and manually moving the parts between stations and bumping. Needless to say, they couldn't handle the truth, and for some reason, we were never invited back to work with them.

Lesson Learned: If you just installed conveyors in your line, at some point you may have to take them out, unless you are going to install a true paced line or a lights out line, that is, total automation.

Paced Lines Are Not Bad!

Now you may think we don't like paced lines but this is not the case. Our goal is to get to paced lines but only where it makes sense. Any assembly line that is really a paced line will generally run faster than having people manually move the products from station to station. However, it is a big investment. One also has to make sure there is no room for extra WIP in the line.

Advantages of Paced Lines

- With the help of pitch marks, you visually know if you are ahead or behind TT.
- Mistake proofing and poka yoke can be built into the product.
- You can run to a true cycle time.
- Can be set up for flexing and bumping.

Challenges

- Line balancing.
- Keeping operators from slowing down the line.
- Isolated islands are easily created.
- Don't handle rework or major line stoppages well.

Problems with Tool Cribs

Many companies experience the following problems with tools and fixture or tooling management.

- Operators don't put the tools back where they belong.
- The tools disappear (or are stolen).
- Calibration expires.
- The tools need maintenance, but the operators wait until the start of the next job to point out the problem versus sending it to be repaired at the end of the previous job.
- Operators can't find the tooling.
- Operators use the wrong tools and don't follow the standards.
- Tools occupy too much space.
- Tools are not kept clean.
- No backups of critical tooling.
- No system of tracking tooling locations.

The easy answer to which we find everyone naturally evolves is to set up a centralized tool crib (Figure 4.18). What a great idea! One person will now be responsible and accountable for all the tools and all our problems will go away. This sounds so simple but remember: centralizing is equivalent to batching, which is why we all naturally gravitate to this solution. We all like to batch! However, tool cribs are full of their own problems:

- People end up having to fill out a form to withdraw the tooling.
- Machinists end up making multiple trips to the tool crib during the setups.
- Elaborate accounting and paperwork systems are developed.
- People end up waiting in line for their tools.
- Since tools are centralized, the tooling personnel cut down the numbers of tools to save money or they forget to order them. Now the tools are not available or are being used by someone else.

Figure 4.18　Centralized tool crib.

▪ The tool crib grows and grows eventually requiring larger staff or it goes the other way and the staff is cut due to downsizing. Now the tool crib becomes a free-for-all where anyone can go in and get what they want.

So, what is the solution? The Lean solution is to keep the tools and tooling at point of use (POU) (Figure 4.19). This means you can't take the easy way out. We have to solve the root causes of the problems that drove us to the centralized tool crib to begin with. Once we set up cells and

(a)

(b)

Figure 4.19 (a) Tooling stored at POU. Tooling is managed by the team. (b) Vendor management tooling in vending machines. (From BIG Archives.)

eventually value streams, the tooling is now managed by the team and the team leaders are responsible at the beginning and end of each shift to make sure all the tooling is back where it belongs. This means the tooling has to be 5S'd (5S's) so that each tool has a labeled storage spot. We can use our daily 5S/TPM board to make sure each operator is accountable daily to ensure the tools are back where they belong, check calibration stickers, and check for damage. This will prevent tools from disappearing. If the tools are being stolen, this presents a different problem and must be dealt with by management accordingly.

Tooling Strategy

Keep the tools you use the closest to or at the machine. Generally, the Pareto rule comes into play where 20% or less of the tools you use 80% or more of the time. The balance of the tools should be somewhere in or near the cell and the ones you use the least may be further away. If there are some tools that are very large and won't fit in the cell, you may move the tools you use once a year, for instance, further away or in a centralized storage location.

Vendor Managed Tooling

There are many vendors now, especially with consumable-type tooling (i.e., drill bits, inserts) that will manage your tooling for you whether it be at POU or at a breadman or more central location (vendor managed materials). Some systems are like vending machines (Figure 4.19) where you swipe your badge and then remove the tooling. A signal is sent back to the supplier so they immediately know what tooling to replace during their next delivery or milk run.

As You Move Down the Lean Maturity Path, People Get Nervous

When we implement Lean, we start to decrease not only the inventory but also the order backlog. This starts to make the operator very nervous. Many will think Lean is going to get them laid off or the company is going to start losing money, but in fact, the opposite is true. By being more responsive to the customer and reducing costs, setup times and the customer's price, the company is in a better position to get more business. This means the sales team must be involved up front and understand the advantages Lean brings. For example, sales can now suggest that they manage the inventory for their customers by stocking our products right on their line.

Lesson Learned: Lean has proven to be a great marketing tool for many companies.

Chapter Questions

1. What is a group tech matrix?
2. Can Lean principles be applied to a machine shop with significant amounts of automated equipment?
3. When do we conduct a PFA?
4. What is a Yamazumi board? How is it used?
5. What is the PPCS?
6. What role does setup reduction play in a machine shop?

7. Should we outsource our products?
8. What is a paced line?
9. What is vendor managed tooling?

Notes

1. http://www.brainyquote.com/quotes/authors/w/w_edwards_deming.html
2. Matthias Thürer, Mark Stevenson and Charles W. Protzman, Cardbased Production Control: A Review of the Control Mechanisms Underpinning Kanban, ConWIP, POLCA and COBACABANA systems, Production Planning & Control, 2016, http://dx.doi.org/10.1080/09537287.2016.1188224, SSN: 0953-7287 (Print) 1366-5871 (Online) Journal homepage: http://www.tandfonline.com/loi/tppc20
3. http://www.qcdme.com/glossary.php

Additional Readings

Jennings, J. and Haughton, L. 2002. It's Not the Big That Eat the Small It's the Fast That Eat the Slow. New York: Harper Business.

Jordan, J.A. 2001. Lean Company Making the Right Choices. Dearborn, MI: SME.

McCormack, R. 2002. Lean Machines. Annandale, VA: Publishers & Producers.

Ohio State University. 2007. Lean Advisory Tools for Jobshops. Ohio: Zip Publishing.

SAE. 2000. Lean Enterprise Conversion, Best Practice Guide. Warrendale, PA: SAE.

Shingo, S. 1988. Non Stock Production. Cambridge, MA: Productivity Press.

Suri, R. 1998. Quick Response Manufacturing. Portland, OR: Productivity Press.

Chapter 5

Lean Applied to Transactional Settings

Most of what we call management consists of making it difficult for people to get their work done.

Peter Drucker[1]

Design Processes Lean

Let's start with an analogy; in foundries (casting companies), very hot metal is poured into a mold. Once it cools, the mold is removed. If the company has a perfect mold and a perfect pour, the casting will be virtually perfect. If it is not a good mold, or there is a problem with the pour, the company must hire people and provide equipment to repair, grind, and polish the resulting poor castings. The better the mold and the more "capable" the process, the less need for chipping, grinding, and finishing of the castings. In most cases, we spend more time trying to Lean out the grinding and finishing process versus fixing the mold issues up front. The other big problem is defining what a good, finished casting looks like is difficult because the finishing standards are very subjective.

The analogy here is that we have the greatest opportunity if we design our processes Lean from the beginning whether it is manufacturing based like the example above or transaction based as we discuss below. If companies had great engineering and informational processes up front, the waste in the factory would be greatly reduced. Many companies have a poor and cumbersome informational process that creates headaches for manufacturing and provides poor customer service on the back end. Many engineers do not understand this principle and, in fact, don't feel Lean applies to them.

Sure, we have accounts receivable days and payable days but where are the cycle time measures for the office processes? Where are the metrics for bill of materials errors? Where are the metrics for the number of Excel® spreadsheets with bad formulas? Where are the metrics for how many proposals we lost because we did not submit them on time or lost for some reason? Where are the metrics for the scrap in manufacturing encountered trying to meet specifications promised by good intentioned salespeople? Where are the metrics for all this waste our up-front processes drive? Every office process should have a safety, quality, delivery, inventory, and productivity (+QDIP) board just like the factory!

DOI: 10.4324/9781003185802-5

Transactional Supply Chain

There are two supply chains in business: the physical and the transactional. Some refer to this as the financial supply chain.[2] This involves value stream mapping (VSM) the financial information value stream from the lowest level raw materials supplier to the payment of cash by the end customer for goods and services received. This is referred by James Womack in his book Seeing the Whole.[3]

This process encompasses many processes; for example: risk management, commodities management, cash flow management, budgeting, target costing, and financial modeling to name a few. Eventually, roles in the organization may be restructured around value streams and organized under value stream managers. It is possible in large enough organizations that the value stream manager will have both physical and financial supply chain process owners reporting to them.

Transactional Process Fundamentals

Transactional processes include any information-based process. Every office process we encounter has the same or more opportunity for improvement as their sister shop floor processes with physical products. As we turn our focus on Lean transactional processes, the product piece (in transport inspect process store (TIPS)) becomes its information flow; thus, it becomes a bit challenging. For example, when we VSM an administrative process, the information process flow interacts with the information systems (IS) boxes at the top whether they be manual or electronic. It is very easy to get confused when mapping information flows while linking them to IS.

Raw information (i.e., data or packages of data) is to the transactional process as raw materials are to manufacturing processes. This information may start as a manual log and turn into an Excel spreadsheet or Access® database. If data packages start with one line of data, or historical data dumps, they always continue to grow as information is added to them or as new columns or new data tables are created. It is not long until these data packages can be broken into smaller separate packages (subsets of data), like subassemblies. Data packages are recombined, checked, or inspected and are used to print out countless historical reports that progress through approval loops. We find with many reports repeat the same information and/or end up creating manual rework systems along the way.

The data packages move through the transactional process just like in a manufacturing line; however, it is difficult to see this transactional line. The movement of the transactional line is via paper, files, e-mail, texts, scanners, computer reports, workflow[4] tools, in and out of database management and other types of storage systems. The product almost always morphs (changes from one type of form to another) as it travels through the process. There is a clear direction over recent years to move to paperless systems; yet it still seems we generate a lot of paper for some reason.

What We Find

Many office personnel, including executives, are convinced Lean is only for manufacturing and will not work or simply does not apply in the office environment. In their minds, Lean is fine if it is not in their backyard! However, we find transactional processes many times tend to be more inefficient than manufacturing and no one measures them. No one can tell you why they do what they do, only that that is the way it has always been done. We see much more over-processing waste in offices than in manufacturing. If you have any doubts, check out the signature loops required for capital requests, engineering drawings or changes, purchasing requisitions, etc.

Many changes to the transactional process are via mandate, corporate, or legal requirements. New computer systems require people to follow screen inputs that enforce the changes but don't necessarily mistake proof the inputs. It is difficult to install visual controls as they do not normally lend themselves to physical change. This means individuals must fully buy into the changes, to achieve maximum results. But it is so much easier for staff to revert to the old way to do business as it is difficult to enforce the changes. In many cases, the staff is quite frustrated with the process. They realize the process is not effective or efficient and there is nothing they can do about it.

There are many times where procedural definition and roles and responsibilities are unclear. Most newly implemented computer systems originally budgeted significant training dollars that were then cut to feed the bonus of someone higher up. Countless hours are lost as employees try to learn and use the new systems. As with the manufacturing floor, we find each office person performs various steps in their own way, and the variation within the process leads to constant rework and follow-up. Frustration with simple tasks being more difficult than needed and taking longer than they should is coupled with a sense of hopelessness as they feel there is no way to improve the situation. This leads to the workarounds and the creation of the informal system where people learn to work around the system. This adds even more variation into the process.

It is not unusual to find manufacturing processes designed around or dictated by the transactional system, that is, the enterprise resource planning (ERP) or material requirement planning (MRP) systems. Every transactional kaizen contains stories from team members of how easy the job was before the MRP system. Now they are constantly told by the information technology (IT) department what can't be done (even though sometimes they can show it has been done). Sometimes it was so bad at my company, we (operations) hired our own computer programmer because we could never get high enough on the priority ticket system to get any changes made by the IT department. Another problem is the perceived need to standardize computer platforms and transactions across business units, which may be in completely different businesses.

> At Company X, we had to wait for MRP, which only runs the data entry program three times a day because it slows the whole system down across several plants. This adds 5 to 6 hours of queue time to all orders entered or new part numbers created in the system. So, an order received for a new part at 3:30 in the afternoon cannot possibly ship the same day because the new one won't even show up until the next day. We must wait yet, another day until the order is entered, because that program only runs overnight! It takes a minimum of 2 days before the order even shows up in customer service at which point it then must be turned into a work order before it is released to the manufacturing floor or stockroom to be picked. If your competitor can ship the same day, you have lost that business forever. The worst part is that customer service must tell the customer they can't even enter their order for 2 days. How embarrassing is this? Yet this is all hidden waste. Where does this show up in the accounting metrics? There is no entry on the profit and loss statement (P&L) or entry in the chart of accounts for orders lost due to our impotent computer systems.

In Tom Peters Speed is Life video, he discusses the 0.05–5 rule,[5] which says: "most products and many services are receiving value for 0.05%–5% of the time they are in the value delivery system of their company. Translated into plain English, 99.5%–99.95% of the time, you are working on something, nothing's happening. They (the authors of the book Competing Against Time) give an example of an insurance company that takes 22 days to process a new application." Peters goes on to say, "In the course of those 22 days there is a good solid 17 minutes of work done! …. This is the world's greatest good news bad news story. The good news is, what an awesome opportunity, if your 99.95% screwed up and you just start looking at the thing you might get better; the bad news is if someone else starts looking at it before you do; you can get your hide nailed to the wall. The issue is Get Fast or Go Broke!"

Later in the same video, Mr. Peters interviews John Simpson, the then new general manager of Tight Flex Hoses. Peters says, "It was taking 3 or 4 weeks just to enter new orders. Top management looked around and found most of their customers were mad at them because they couldn't deliver their hoses on time." John Simpson talks about instances where Boeing couldn't ship a 747 because they were missing a simple (couple of hundred dollars) hose. Peters goes on to say, "They (Tight Flex) had a hot list which was really angry customers, the luke hot list with more or less angry customers, and the end of the month list which was an attempt to get something out the door on the 30th …." Simpson goes on to say, "I called in at lunch time to the operations director of one of the industrial divisions and found out the computer was broken and we could not ship product. That one was an immediate trigger I could go do something. And what I told him was probably not so kind but I told him, Ernie, I want you to get in your car, go down to the Five and Dime and buy a box of crayons and bring them back and write the customer's name on the box and ship the product. People loved it because like any good company there was a desire to serve the customer." Peters concludes by saying "the great crayon caper … sent a clear message to five hundred Tight Flex people. Do whatever you have to do to serve the customer."

The challenge with transactional processes is the constant barriers to change from "this is the way it has always been done" and all the "sacred cows" embedded in the delivery system.

At some companies, we have gone back to the old manual systems because we were able to prove the computer systems that replaced them were so cumbersome, they were three to four times slower than the old way with no value added (VA). We then worked to streamline the process and then bring back the computer system; only this time, it was tailored to the process we created and not the other way around. The best way to conquer these processes is to create the pull from the top for change and assemble cross-functional teams to run through the BASICS® model with a Lean practitioner and/or a good facilitator. The toughest processes to change are the reactive changes made to systems and put in place by the functional leader who in many cases may also now be the champion or person presiding over the kaizen.

Office Layouts

The physical office changes brought on by Lean may not be initially popular with your staff. For example, most offices are full of 5- or 6-ft partitions, which were sold as efficiency improvements; but in the end, block line of sight and reduce or eliminate crucial communication flow. They essentially create isolated islands for all your employees. Lean offices have no or low partitions (Figure 5.1). In addition, many people find themselves moving to the shop floor to be co-located with their value stream team or focus factory. This speeds up communication and accelerates the problem-solving process when the floor has problems. Lean office layouts end up containing cross-functional teams with all the different disciplines needed to run the daily business for a product line or lines. These cross-functional teams are usually called value stream teams. People are comfortable sitting with people in their same discipline (i.e., engineers sitting with only other engineers); however, this limits communication critical to the daily needs of a value stream team.

Figure 5.1 Lean office design—low partition, see through offices and one non-see-through walled conference room for private conversations or meetings. (BIG Archives.)

Overhead

Within most companies, the transactional costs are often hidden and not well understood. They are all included in the ambiguous term overhead. In many cases, there is no knowledge of current transactional capacity or current performance against that capacity. For most firms, the costs are embedded in many locations on the traditional P&L statement. For example, in the General and Administrative (G&A) section of the P&L statement, we often find costs for contracts, central accounting, legal, marketing, and the executive staff. The typical G&A costs can be large and are thought of as fixed. The reality is the consumer considering a new car purchase would not want to pay for an option on the window sticker entitled G&A costs; however, the costs are real and are concealed in every car made by every manufacturer. We find it is natural for more emphasis to be placed on producing the product and less on the transactional or administrative components because they appear to be more nebulous. However, most of what occurs in transactions within a company is driven by their systems, which are made up of processes that contain waste. Remember, if it is a process, we can improve it using lean principles.

- When we think of examples of transactional processes, some of the most frustrating encounters between customers and companies are found in processes. For example:
  - The customer trying to place or follow up on an order
  - The customer receives a product or service that is not per their expectations or is not performing properly (i.e., cable or wireless service is not working)
  - Dealing with the billing process trying to correct or make a payment

How often do we receive bills with inaccuracies? We can all think of times where we spent hours on the phone with representatives, who do not have the information they need to assist us and, worst case, will "just make up" information to get rid of us or because the timer on their phone says they have already spent too much time talking with us. We as consumers then get transferred from department to department in the ongoing but sometimes futile pursuit of a satisfactory result. Every business has transactional processes, while some businesses are virtually all transactional processes (i.e., banking and insurance). Every business, healthcare institution, financial services, and governmental agency can apply Lean, streamline the process, and eliminate waste.

Non-Value Added but Necessary Required Work

Almost all transactional processes fall into the category of non-value-added (NVA) but necessary steps. This is a key component to emphasize here, as we explore the transactional process opportunities. Financial, human resource, and sales and marketing processes are not activities a customer wants to pay for; but they are required to keep a business viable and effective. These processes supply companies with the data necessary to make the strategic decisions required to stay in business and provide the customer with better products and services at a lower cost. Indirectly, the customer may care although it is not necessarily related to providing the product in a timely manner.

One of the challenges in many organizations is that the office environment is considered a sacred ground, protected by the senior executives. Barriers are also raised by the interpretation of government regulations such as Sarbanes Oxley, Occupational Safety and Health Administration (OSHA) and ISO 9000. There are specific rules that must be followed for publicly held firms generally accepted accounting principles (GAAP[6]). We have found any process which generates or manages information can always be improved with Lean principles and tools within the bounds of full compliance of all these rules. These rules tend to become excuses for accounting and other departments as to why they cannot implement Lean. Ironically, many of the large accounting firms have or had branches that consult in implementing Lean principles. We have found it best, when a team uses a regulation as a barrier to request a copy of the regulation to first see if it exists (which many times it does not) and second to see what it really states. Ninety percent or more of the time, we have found these objections to be groundless.

We have seen Lean applied to landscaping, education, oil drilling, customer service centers, retail shops, and everything in between. The Lean process to address the transactional processes is like the manufacturing floor. However, again, the product in transactional processes is mostly data. In health care, much of the patient experience is paced not only by physical but also transactional processes. For instance, during rounding, the physician enters an order for a patient on their chart. Historically a physician would batch their orders, a clerk would process the orders in a batch, and the result would cause the first patient to wait hours for their medication. Most hospitals have migrated leveraging technology in which the physician uses a tablet or computer to enter the order directly to the pharmacy, lab or order a procedure bypassing the unit clerk, and eliminating batch processing.

As mentioned earlier, when you call customer service, your response times and responses are dictated by the level of proficiency inherent in the IS utilized by the company. How often have you been told to call back because the computer systems are down or the company representative says their computers are not awake yet? At one company, their test equipment was halted in China because their European servers were being backed up. Of course, there was no one to call due to the time difference. These are all incredible opportunities to eliminate waste, improve quality, and increase the service level for our customers. We have never found an office or service process to date that could not be significantly improved. When implementing office or administrative-type processes, we yield the same results:

- 80% reductions in throughput times (weeks to days or days to hours)
- 80% reductions in work in process (WIP) (amount of paperwork, sometimes e-mails in the process)
- 30%–50% or more increases in productivity
- 80% reductions in (non-electronic) travel distances
- 10%–20% increases in quality

Transactional Process Improvement

When implementing transactional processes, we utilize all the same tools in the BASICS® and Plan-Do-Check-Act (PDCA) models. Like other Lean initiatives, in general, people are not the problem; the system is normally the problem (see Figure 5.2). The office personnel are like other staff throughout the firm; they are always busy. The question is what are they busy doing? Most of the time, they are working on things that add no value to the customer, and there is normally significant batching in play, which reinforces the 80% reductions possible in throughput times. We need to understand where people are currently spending their time and then ascertain where they should be spending their time.

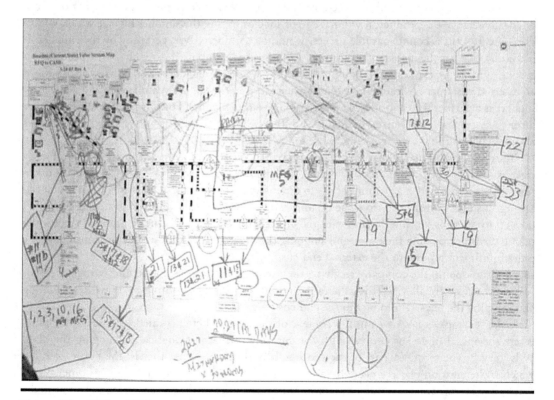

Figure 5.2   Office VSM example.

As stated throughout the book, we video the office (transactional) process and utilize the same analysis tools for information flow as we do for physical products. Tools commonly leveraged are VSM, process flow analysis (PFA), workflow analysis (WFA), deploying flow pull strategies, reduction of batch processes to decrease errors and improve quality, standard work, setup reduction (turnover), checklists, control charts, mistake-proofing (poka-yoke), visual management, right tools, right place, right time, and Kanbans. We don't always utilize every tool. We use the tools based on the problems to be solved and their complexity.

Note: There must be some accommodations made, given the realization that office transactional processes, and the professionals engaged in them, will have a different perspective given their experience with process improvement. The concept that their job is considered NVA from a Lean perspective needs to be addressed very carefully. Many of these transactional processes are led by highly educated professionals who will not react lightly to being told their job is not VA.

It is important to establish the concept of NVA but necessary (or what some companies call business VA) early on to avoid this impression. We think a better team than business VA is required work (RW). Many of these people are already working long hours, especially during peak times, such as when they are in pursuit of month-end or year-end numbers. Clearly, if you can paint a picture for them that this Lean project will help reduce their workload and the accompanying frustration, they experience you may just find you have created a motivated process improvement team.

When analyzing information flow within the context of the input and output boundaries of the transactional process, we find steps that are not VA to the external customer but strictly within the context of the process may be considered VA to the internal customer. For example, when doing an accounts payable process flow, which is NVA to our end customer, as it does not physically change the product; it will have steps such as paying the supplier invoice which within the context of the accounts payable process would be considered VA, certainly by the supplier. It physically changes the invoice, the customer (in this case the supplier) cares about the process, if it is done right the first time. Even though the supplier is not our end customer, he can be considered an external customer (or internal customer when viewing the value stream as a whole) where our supplier is a partner (i.e., considered an extension of our company). For this reason, it is important during any transactional kaizen to identify up front who the customers and internal stakeholders are and what definition we are going to use for VA.

The other important thing to keep track of is what you are following. If you are not abundantly clear as to what exactly you are following, it will result in much confusion, frustration, and lost time. For instance, when a customer calls to order a spare part for an appliance, what are you following? It starts with the call from the customer, turns into an order, and, at most companies, can take up to 85 steps or more to ship it to the customer and get paid. Out of those 85 steps, only taking the order, picking the order, and shipping the order are VA steps within the confines of the order fulfillment process to the external end customer. In the accounts payable process, from the supplier standpoint, the company receiving their invoice, cutting the check, and putting it physically in the mail are all VA. This is juxtaposing to the fact it has nothing to do with assembling and shipping the physical product to the end customer.

Other examples of VA within the context of the process being studied include landscaping, where the initial interview process with the customer, while not physically changing the plant beds, may be the most VA part of the process. It is all information, that is, the brainstorming, which is the creation of a connection and subsequent relationship with the end customer. In an emergency room, as stated before, the communication of the words you are going to be fine and a nurses' touch are considered VA.

Transactional Wastes

Listed in the following are the wastes most found in transactional processes:

Examples of Transactional Wastes

1. Waste from overproduction of goods or services—waste of excess reports, both paper and electronic, batch copying, too many brochures printed, information duplicated across forms or not needed. Gathering, sorting, and saving more information than is really needed.
2. Waste from waiting or idle time—is either the information itself or the person waiting for it, time to secure (rubber stamped) approvals for contracts, equipment ordering, repairs in the office, unplanned interruptions, unbalanced workflow, lack of capacity for volume, etc.
3. Waste from transportation (unnecessary)—document flow/movement between offices for processing, routing, and poor office layout placement of adjacencies, travel time, unnecessary copying/approval of information to people who do not use it.
4. Waste from over-processing (inefficiency)—multiple, redundant, and undefined approvals; and multiple reviews and inspections. Elaborate filing systems for documents that have information already contained in the ERP system.
5. Waste of motion and effort—rework of requests, calls for following up on approvals if multiple people are involved, searching for information, centralized printers, etc. Waste driven in computer systems by:
   a. Keeping transactions up to date that could be automated.
   b. Sometimes entering the same information into different computer systems.
   c. Waste created because the IT department is too busy to change the screens to make people's jobs easier. After all, it is more important not to change the system so we can upgrade it later!
   d. Waste created because we don't have time to train the users.
6. Waste of inventory; unnecessary stock on hand—too many supplies, duplicative files, multiple file storage, just in case storage, etc.
7. Waste from defects lack of training documents, completion of company errors in capturing data, errors in transferring data, supplies and equipment ordered incorrectly or in the wrong quantities, missed deadline, rework, clarifications, etc.
8. Waste of talent—frustration of employees, no one listens to their input, right person in wrong position, talented people spending time on rework, lack of empowerment to correct processes, lack of training on process improvement, unclear roles, task interruptions, multitasking, underutilization of talent, etc.
9. Corporate staff waste—creating report-out presentations and ongoing requests for data. Sometimes we receive the same requests from various positions corporate staff. These people create no value yet justify their positions by creating work for people already busy.
10. Waste driven by centralizing processes.

Other types of information waste include redundant input and output of data, incompatible IS, manual checking of electronically entered data, data dead ends (data never used), reentering same data, converting data formats, unavailable or missing data, and unclear or incorrect data definitions.

Beginning the Transactional Change Process

The first step in the process is to define an owner, project leader, and a cross-functional team. Make sure you have all the key functions that participate in the process on the team and include a fresh eyes person who does not know the process but understands process improvement. Their job is to provide perspective by asking, "Why do we do it that way?" on a regular basis.

Lesson Learned: In larger organizations, which have processes spanning multiple locations with global interaction, it is important to include an IT member and possibly a finance team member. This will help them to understand Lean principles. Larger companies tend to use workflow tools to implement some of their transactional processes. The features and functions of the workflow tool should be introduced during the process discussion and not at the end of the process. Many times, the tool can facilitate process improvements the team members would not know are even available without the IT member available to introduce the concepts.

Using the BASICS® Process for Transactional Processes

BASICS® - Baseline

The next step in the process is to define the problem and establish the baseline. It is important to understand the scope, goals, and problem statement prior to starting the analysis phase. If not, it will create a high amount of confusion and frustration involved for the team. Typical baseline metrics would include the following:

- Current throughput time of the process
- Listing of major sub processes and cycle times
- Number of people that touch it
- Number of approvals required
- Distance traveled
- Total labor time required
- Total number of steps
- VA%, RW% (i.e., NVA but necessary), storage%, inspect%, and transport%

Sometimes, there are no procedures, much less metrics. At other times, if there is a procedure, it is either so high level or so out of date that it is virtually of no value in helping the team coordinate their activities. It can be beneficial for the project leader or the consultant leading the project to let the team vent and hear the issues and complaints the team is experiencing. This way, everyone feels their concern has been captured and will be addressed. Our goal at this stage is to look at the problem from as many different points of view as possible and try to get all the issues out in the open. Part of basic Lean theory is for the team to understand identifying problems is a good thing. If the project leader does not do this in the beginning, there can be multiple instances where the problem-solving will get derailed because someone needs to tell a war story about how the process failed. It is best to get these stories out early and increase the ability of the team to stay on track once solutions are being proposed. It is important to distinguish between a discussion and a dialogue. According to Deming, a discussion is where:

- I believe that I know the right answer and I want to convince you that my position is correct.

Six thinking hats

White—Facts, figures, and objective information

Red—Emotions, feelings and intuition

Black—Caution and critical judgement

Yellow—Feasibility and benefits

Key point: Understand the source of the data or feeling. What is the source of the data or the background of the emotion. The source gives a subjective "weight" to the information.

Key point: Eliminate the "ping pong" game and arguments. Get people into roles different from their norm. Keep everyone on the same page.

Green—Creativity, new ideas and alternatives

Blue—Control of the other hats and thinking about thinking

Key point: Make time for creativity. Control of the dialogue process; determine which hat the team should be wearing and for how long.

Figure 5.3   Edward de Bono's Six Thinking Hats.

where a dialogue is:

■ I do not know the right answer and I want to reach an optimum conclusion through our interaction and exploration of the options.

It is not that dialogue or discussion is inherently correct or incorrect; they both have their place in the overall interaction. What is very important is that we are clear about whether we are engaged in a dialogue or a discussion. Edward de Bono's Six Thinking Hats[7] (see Figure 5.3) is an excellent brainstorming tool to keep people focused on:

■ What is wrong with the process?
■ What is right with the process?
■ What data do we have on the process?
■ What does your gut feel on why things are not working?
■ What are your out of the box ideas on how we can fix the process?

This is a big picture look at the process and will allow everyone time to explain what they feel is wrong with the current process. Before moving to our BASICS® assess step, please take note of the following:

■ Background of the problem conveyed.
■ A written problem statement.
■ Definition of terms in the scope.
■ Good understanding of input and output boundaries.
■ What is not included in the scope.

- The baseline metrics are written down (may have to be gathered manually since they normally don't exist or they exist in strange forms). Note: There must be a plan in place to make sure they can be captured after the kaizen to ensure improvement is realized.
- The takt time for the process.
- A business case is developed for solving the problem.
- A compelling need to change is felt by the team. Remember we must also walk through the change equation CxVxNxS>Rchange as we work through the kaizen.

Also included in the project plan must be a concept of how we will measure the new process. This will be utilized in the check phase of the BASICS® model. It is rare to find any company that tracks cycle times or overall lead times or their transactional processes. This will be a new concept for many people working with transactional processes. If the company has a workflow tool, it can be used to gather this data, but smaller companies will not be using these tools to implement the process. There must be a plan on who will gather the data. And how they will analyze the metric and define a corrective action if required (see Figure 5.4).

The quality of the process output or work product should also be measured. This is usually done by tracking the number of times a process has to be repeated (rework loops) due to errors or questions. In our experience, these types of failures are usually addressed through multiple phone calls, e-mails, or physically walking to the area to get the problem solved. If the process is to be continually improved, these failures need to be captured and tracked. The root cause for the mistake is usually lack of definition, unclear standard work, or lack of training. All these issues can be addressed but not without properly implementing active metrics.

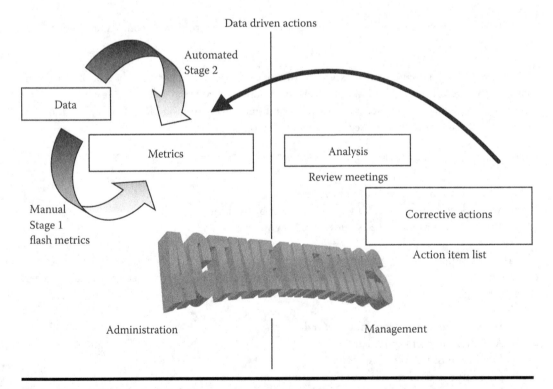

Figure 5.4   Act on facts not data.

BASICS®: Assess

If there is more than one process making up the problem statement, it may be necessary to use a Group Tech Matrix to understand which one to map first. The top priority may be the one with the most volume. In some cases, it can be the most representative process and sometimes it's a combination of the two. In certain situations, a Product Process flow map may also be required to understand the linkages between subprocesses. This can also help determine priority (see Figure 5.5). Next, the current state should be mapped using value stream or process mapping techniques. The team should walk the process to find out what happens versus what people think occurs. During this step, you can focus on each detailed step of the process and ask people what goes wrong during each step. These concerns are captured with kaizen bursts, which are improvement suggestions that can be documented as the team walks through the process. It is good to introduce the wastes before the mapping process, and then review the wastes again with the team after the mapping. This is because the wastes will be more obvious after the team has carefully gone through the details of the entire process.

Conducting Value Stream Mapping on Transactional Processes

We have found value stream maps in the office environment (see Figure 5.6) to be unsurpassed as a continuous improvement tool. The office environment could be any administrative office, that

Group Tech—Process Family Matrix

COUNTRY OF ORIGIN	LOG IN	TAKE COPIES	PROCESS	REVIEW	APPROVE	PAY	FILE	%
LATIN AMERICA	X	X	X		X	X	X	30
EUROPE	X		X	X	X	X		15
USA	X		X		X	X	X	40
ASIA			X		X	X		15

The Process Family Matrix is a tool that's used in the transactional space to help determine where to focus when faced with multiple processes or process types. It's a simple form of Group Technology and is usually applied in advance of a mapping exercise or product flow analysis activity. The process steps are documented on the matrix together with any relevant quantitative data therefore enabling the user to factor in to their decision how representative a process may be.

In the above table, the Accounts Payable department in Company X receives invoices from all over the world. Unfortunately as the business has grown the method of processing each type of invoice has evolved slightly differently. The Process Family Matrix shows the different processes that the invoice will follow depending on it's origin along with the percentage of total invoices made up by that country. The USA has the highest percentage of invoices with 40%, but Latin America is the most representative. Mapping the USA will cover 55% of the total invoices since process steps in the USA are also present in Asia. Mapping Latin America, on the other hand, will encompass both the USA and Asia making up 85% of the total number of invoices. In this example this is clearly the place to start.

Of course quite often there are other factors to consider when selecting a process and common sense must always be applied in conjunction with the application of this tool.

Figure 5.5 Group Tech Office example.

is, executive, government, congressional, life insurance, and bank. Is very difficult to see an office process because all you can see are cubicles, computers, and paperwork. In addition, the data package will morph as it moves through the process. For example, a quote turns into a requisition, then a purchase order, and finally an acknowledgment. In the human resources department, the process steps are: a job opening, to a posting, to an interview, to interview feedback, to the new hire and then the new hire orientation. Administrative processes embody in themselves waste. The waste might be more streamlined now (i.e., e-mailed, texted, and twittered versus paper documents in inboxes or in file cabinets) but it is still there. The process may pass through many people, floors of a building, across buildings, counties, states, or even across countries. VSMs are a great way to map, review, and discuss linkages between your customers and suppliers' processes and yours. This is discussed at length in Jim Womack's book, Seeing the Whole.

Therefore, a VSM is a great way to get your arms around the process using the process boxes (see Figure 5.7 and be able to visualize the entire system that's at work on one sheet of paper). Note: One must be careful about mapping an information-based process against information boxes at the top of the map but we find it works extremely well.

■ If one follows the entire process of VSM, one will complete the following steps:
  – Create a current state (and if it is the first map, baseline state) map with data.
  – Brainstorm the ideal state map.
  – Look for opportunities to eliminate, simplify, and combine steps and activities.
  – Create a list of potential ideas/improvements and sort into projects and tasks.

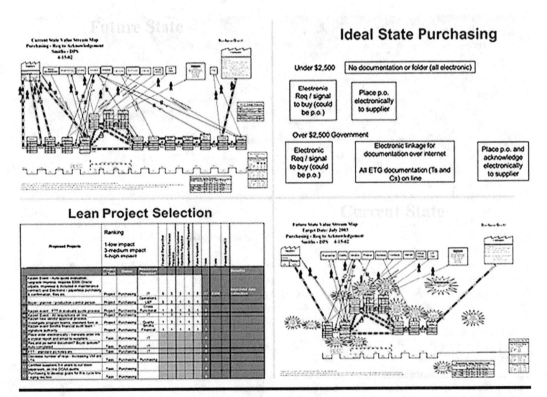

Figure 5.6 Purchasing VSM example, current, ideal, future states along with the project prioritization matrix aligned with the strategic business plan goals.

- Assign the tasks.
- Evaluate what projects can be completed within the next year.
- Create a future state map based on the projects that can be completed within a year.
- Prioritize all the tasks and projects based on the main objectives or goals in their strategic plan.
- Time phases the future state projects for the year along with responsibilities and expected results.
- Make the time phased list, part of each process owner's objectives for the year, upon which they are evaluated. If not held accountable for making the changes needed to achieve the improvements, the Lean implementation will fail and Lean will quickly become another flavor of the month type initiative.

Again, this same process is used in manufacturing environments. You are still collecting all the steps along with the time required to accomplish them, followed by attempting to eliminate or reduce all the NVA steps. This results in linking together the remaining VA steps as closely as possible just like in a Lean assembly line.

What Is Customer Value Added in the Office?

As the team works through the current state, they should ask themselves the following question: is what I am working on right now adding value for the customer? It must meet the same criteria:

1. Does the customer care?
2. Does it physically change the data package? In the healthcare world, we say, does it physically or emotionally change the patient (who is the product) for the better?
3. Is it done right the first time?

In general, most transactional processes, by default, do not add value[8] (see Table 5.1). The customer doesn't care what it takes to get them the product or service; they just want it when they want it, and, in most cases if asked, will tell you they don't want to pay for administrative costs. In many cases, the paperwork is required by some internal manager, government regulation, or someone's perception of what is necessary to meet an ISO requirement, none of which the customer generally cares about.

Think about the paperwork you must complete when buying a house, applying for a loan, or purchasing a car, making travel arrangements, applying for insurance, opening a bank account, or going in for surgery. Although some of the components might be VA to get you the correct outcome, most of the information requested is not VA and not necessary from the customer point of view.

Table 5.1 Production versus Office VA Percentages

Activity Type	Production Environment (%)	Office Environment (%)
Value adding	5	1
Not value added	60	49
Necessary but not value added	35	50

Sources: Typical waste proportions seen in companies before Lean efforts; Lean Enterprise Research Centre, Cardiff Business School, 2000 Public Domain.

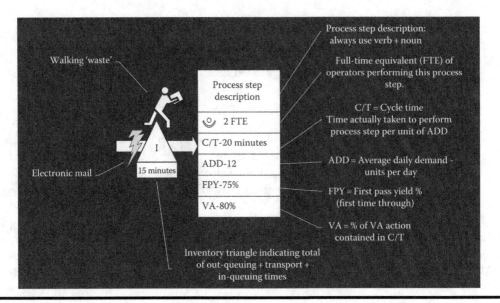

Figure 5.7 Process data box example.

Additionally, one often finds the paperwork is filled with requests for redundant information (creating rework and inefficiency).

In the order entry to release cycle, the only VA step is taking the order from the customer. Negotiation, design, engineering, CAD[9] drawings, etc. are not considered to be VA but are certainly necessary! Our main goal is to reduce the waste and simplify the job as much as possible with a goal of eventually eliminating the job itself, where it makes sense. Obviously, we will not be able to eliminate the need for marketing, strategy setting, design engineering, etc.; some processes can be automated or greatly simplified with technology. Just like in manufacturing, we should always be working to reduce the labor in the process while maintaining or improving the quality of the process deliverables.

During the ideal state brainstorming, we ask the team if it was their business or company how they would set up the process to be as close to an assembly line as possible and make money! During the Ideal state brainstorming, we force people to think out of the box. The first thing to pop out will be all types of IT systems-based ideas. In some cases, with many plants involved in the process, one may want to introduce the workflow tools here. Capture these IT suggestions and record them as options. While these are normally very good long-term suggestions, they tend to get expensive quickly, involve training hurdles, and can take a long time to implement. This does not mean they should be discouraged. Next, ask the team for creativity versus capital ideas. What can we do to fix the process first and then look at automating the solutions?

The Car Dealer

We purchased a car recently from a well-known and respected car dealer. By all accounts, it went as smooth as every other car dealer that did not have fixed pricing. The entire process took from 10:30 am until 4:30 pm before we left the dealership, over 6 hours! The longest time cycles were the back and forth by the salesperson to the manager's office over the small amount of negotiating we did, and the rest of the time was the hours spent in the finance office. The whole process should have taken less than 1 hour! The only steps that were VA to us were agreeing on a price, signing for the loan, and driving the car home.

Conducting Process Flow Analysis on Transactional Processes

Just like in manufacturing, every second counts and every second we waste threatens our company's competitiveness. When we follow the product (TIPS) in administrative processes, 95% of steps are NVA with the majority being storage and inspection. This may sound harsh, but in virtually every process, we have mapped less than 5% of the steps, and 1% of the time is VA to the end customer. Most administrative jobs are support jobs for the factory and service industry and, while necessary, do not fit the classic definition of VA (i.e., physical change, done right the first time, and does the customer care about the step?).

Results: We have yet to run into a process we could not take at least 50% or more out of the overall internal lead time (or throughput time) of the process just by eliminating the storage steps in the process. (This would not include a process with a significant amount of external time like an outside supplier lead time.)

Administrative process should flow, flow, flow just like the factory. When analyzing the information-based process, we must determine the following:

- What is the product?
- Who are the operators?
- Are there any changeovers? Or opportunities where we can apply the concept of internal versus external work? For instance, if something must be sent out for customer approval, we have an opportunity to continue to work on the process that essentially is on external time.

All information flows are part of the process and will experience significant improvement, typically 75% or more throughout the Lean journey. Just like the factory, after the VSM, we conduct a PFA to identify each step for the product and an operator flow analysis where we video the operators. Then we review each step for eliminating, rearranging, simplifying, and combining (ERSC).

Homework: Have accounting figure out what a second is worth every process. People can relate to dollars per second saved in cycle time or throughput time.

PFAs work on informational/transactional processes products, but they can be a bit more challenging. To do a transactional process, one must become the piece of paper or information that is being followed. It is very important to make sure you understand what you are following, or as the product morphs, it can get very confusing. Figure 5.8 shows the order entry to cash receipt for the entire company with every paper/electronic form pasted on the wall. For instance, when following the account payable process, it may start with the receiver. The receiver then gets matched with an invoice and then with the purchase order line item. It then turns into a check that is mailed to the supplier.

Improving the Accounts Payable Process

When working on an accounts payable process, we started with a process wall map. We then went out and walked and videoed the process. We started with the receiving department. The first thing we found was that several steps were left out of the process. For instance, our wall map says it receives material.

Figure 5.8   Entire order entry to collect process took up three walls in the conference room. Every piece of paper/electronic form was printed and put on the walls.

This turned out to be:

1. Material unloaded from truck.
2. Material waits to be received.
3. Material is moved to the receiving computer station.
4. Packing list is removed from one of the boxes (material waits).
5. Operator enters the packing list (material waits, but since we are following the packing list, it is a transport from the box to the computer).
6. Wait while the operator enters the information into the system.
7. Then we are set down to wait again while the operator prints out a bar-coded label and attaches one to the box.
8. Then we are stapled to the bar code label and put in a folder.
9. Then we are carried to the stock room and added to another folder where the water spider will pick us up and take us to accounting.

So, one sticky note in the conference room turned into nine steps when we went and followed the process. This process generated two questions from the group. Why do we staple the bar code label to the packing list? The answer was, we have always done it that way. But when probing further, we found from the process owner that the step was put in many years ago to keep track of the account charge in accounting, but the process was changed 4 or 5 years ago by the MRP system, negating the need for the label to be attached to the packing list. However, the process was never changed and the operator was never told. So, for 5 years, receiving has been printing out these rather expensive duplicate bar code labels and attaching them to the packing list for no reason. Think of the material costs of the bar code label and thermal printer ribbon, the labor cost to print them, wear and tear on the bar code printer, the labor cost to attach them to the box, and then the extra space taken up in file cabinets in accounting where all the packing lists are stored. We determined there was 8 seconds of labor per label. This doesn't sound like much, but if this is multiplied by 100 packages per day, it is 800 seconds per day and by 250 working days per year, it turns into 278 wasted hours over the last 5 years.

The next thing we questioned was why we took the packing list to the stockroom. When you first see this step on a yellow sticky, it doesn't look like a big deal, but when we walked the process, we found it was 165 ft to the stockroom desk from receiving, which was in the opposite direction from accounting! So, it had to travel another 165 ft just to get back to receiving, which it passed on its way to accounting with the water spider. This is 330 ft total × 2 trips per day × 2 receiving team members. It took 1 minute to go to the stockroom desk and another minute of wasted travel back to the receiving department on the way to accounting. This turned into over 65 miles per year of wasted travel for the packing list and over 16 wasted labor hours per year. When we asked why it was taken to the stockroom, we were first told that the packing lists were added in alphabetical order to the packing list folder in the stockroom. When we asked why the folder was in the stockroom, we found out that the stockroom moved 8 years ago and the folder moved with the stockroom. No one ever gave it a second thought as to why we carried it all the way over there. This is the boiled frog syndrome at work. Now our 16 hours multiplied by 8 years is 133 hours of wasted time. We immediately stopped both attaching the bar code label to the packing list and hiking over to the stockroom twice a day by two people, and the water spider now takes the folder from receiving to accounts payable. So, we identified all these opportunities and savings prior to even getting to the accounts payable department just by mapping and asking why or using the five whys tool on each step!

In transactional processes, people entrenched in the environment are used to things being done and often have not been empowered to change. If you inquire as to why things are done a certain way, you often hear "it has always been done that way or that is the way Mr. 'X' wants it done." To overcome the boiled frog syndrome, we must put our waste glasses on and see things through a new waste lens or perspective. When you walk the floor, everyone always looks busy, but if you really stand and watch what's going on, you will see that everything is not going that smoothly. The boiled frog embodies complacency, which has no place in our business.

Toyota uses the story of Newton. Newton discovered gravity by lying under an apple tree and watching the fruit fall. He probably spent a lot of time pondering why this was happening. He was a disciplined observer of nature. This attitude, alertness, and awareness allowed him to observe things that others may take for granted. The goal here is for you to develop your own eye for waste. Expand your own awareness of the problems around you. If you have always done it this way, there is a good chance there is waste involved and it can be improved. The only way to overcome the boiled frog syndrome is to question the present way of doing things the way it has always been done. Look for problems and opportunities for kaizen events. Always know there is a better way to do it; you just must figure out how. Until you develop this ongoing dissatisfaction with how things are done today, you cannot create the compelling need to change. Fight complacency at every turn; it is our ultimate and quite formidable foe.

You Must Walk the Process

We had a young Padawan[10] (Lean apprentice) doing a transactional map from order entry until the order was sent and received on the floor. We explained that he needed to walk the process with each person that was involved to fully understand it. We happened to be walking in the cafeteria to get a cup of coffee and noticed the young Padawan sitting by the windows in the cafeteria with a young lady sitting next to him. We went over to say hello and noticed he was vigorously typing in steps to the computer provided by the young lady as to her order entry duties. We asked him what he was doing. He said, "Oh, I am doing the PFA." We said, "how can you possibly do the PFA here in the cafeteria?" He proceeded to tell us why it was just as good there as to having to get up and exert himself to walk the process.

We invited him and the order entry person back to the order entry person's desk and started to walk through the steps with her. After she started showing us her job by entering an order, his first step turned into five steps. He said he was now convinced and understood why he had to walk the process. When we completed the walkthrough of the order entry person, we offered our help and were told it was not needed. He then went to get the engineer who was the next person in the process. Once again, we found him in the cafeteria with the engineer. We asked him what he was doing. He said the PFA. We said we thought he was convinced it couldn't be done in the cafeteria. He said he thought that was just for order entry. He quickly stood up and walked with the engineer to his desk. The final PFA was over 200 steps.

Lesson Learned: You must go to the workplace to truly understand what is going on; often you will find silos of information about a process even in their own work area. It is not surprising to find the people doing the job don't even realize how many steps they are doing in the process. Additionally, videoing is a valuable tool to engage people in the process and to identify opportunities to eliminate, simplify, and combine steps.

Inputs versus Outputs Diagram on Organizational Processes

When conducting an organizational process review, have the participant list on yellow Post-it notes what they feel are the major functions or processes within the high-level organization (company as a whole) or department level depending on the area being worked (see Figure 5.9). These steps are then placed on the diagonal of the map. Once everyone agrees on these steps

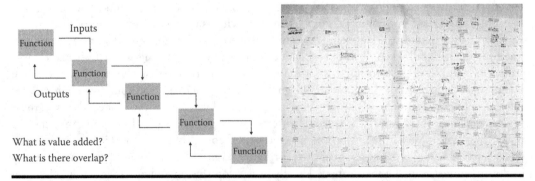

Figure 5.9 Process inputs on top and outputs on the bottom. Great way to find duplication in processes.

(don't be surprised if they change over the course of the exercise), the next step is to have each person list out the inputs each box provides to the other boxes, one per sticky, and place it on the chart. Then list the outputs each process provides to the other processes. Then question each input and output. Are there multiple inputs from one process to another? For instance, is quality supplying the same data to purchasing and manufacturing engineering? Is this necessary? Are purchasing and quality supplying the same input to finance? These duplications and overlapping inputs and outputs become immediately visible when utilizing this tool. The tool also starts to force everyone to see the inputs and outputs as processes, and they start to question which ones are VA and to what departments they are VA. What may be VA to one department may be NVA to another.

Another tool that can be used in conjunction with the input versus output diagram is the functional allocation diagram (FAD) (see Figure 5.10a and b). The input versus output diagram is used to see the big picture and determine where there are overlaps and gaps in information needed and provided. The FAD can be used to detail each step in the process regarding inputs, outputs, metrics, documents, and issues for every step. The input versus output diagram can be used to eliminate steps in the entire process; therefore, the FAD should only be used after the input versus output analysis has been completed.

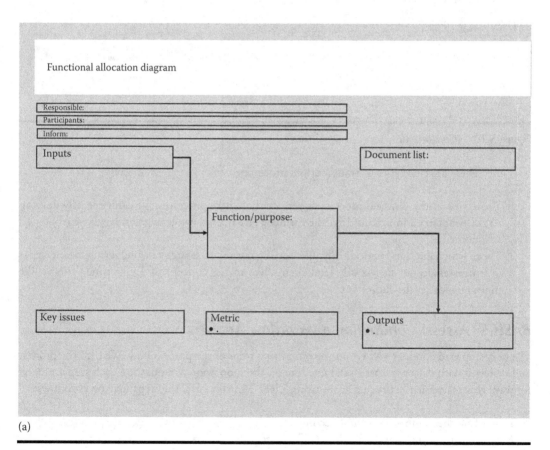

(a)

Figure 5.10 **(a) Functional allocation diagram and (b) Functional allocation diagram example.**

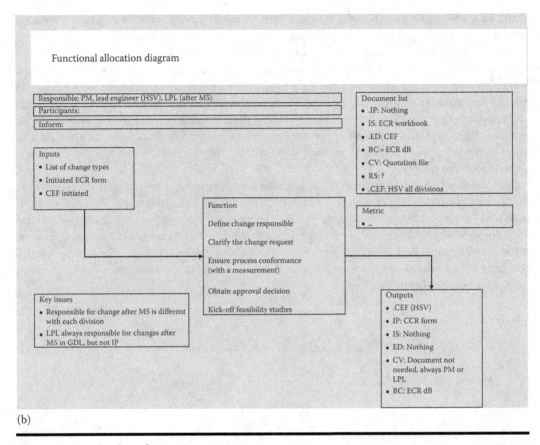

Functional allocation diagram

Responsible: PM, lead engineer (HSV), LPL (after M5)

Participants:

Inform:

Inputs
- List of change types
- Initiated ECR form
- CEF initiated

Function

Define change responsible

Clarify the change request

Ensure process conformance (with a measurement)

Obtain approval decision

Kick-off feasibility studies

Key issues
- Responsible for change after M5 is different with each division
- LPL always responsible for changes after M5 in GDL, but not IP

Document list
- .IP: Nothing
- IS: ECR workbook
- .ED: CEF
- BC = ECR dB
- CV: Quotation file
- RS: ?
- .CEF: HSV all divisions

Metric
- ..

Outputs
- .CEF (HSV)
- IP: CCR form
- IS: Nothing
- ED: Nothing
- CV: Document not needed, always PM or LPL
- BC: ECR dB

(b)

Figure 5.10 *(Continued)*

Note: There are two types of transactional processes:

1. Those tied to the physical product or service. For these processes, we can generally develop a takt time. Even in accounting, the number of payables or receivables per day can be tied to a takt time.
2. Those which are done periodically, like setting corporate strategy or budgeting. These types of processes do not necessarily lend themselves to the concept of a takt time. This is like maintenance on the shop floor.

BASICS® Assess: Conducting a Workflow Analysis

The next step is to conduct a WFA on the remaining steps of the process flow. We film the process and review it with the operators (staff) just like on the shop floor. We question each step and look for ways to streamline the process again using ERSC. In this case, the steps may be as follows:

1. Turn on the computer—RW 1 second
2. Wait for the computer—idle time (IT) 76 seconds
3. Login to the computer—RW 5 seconds
4. Wait for computer—IT 10 seconds

5. Login into application—RW 1 second
6. Wait for computer—IT 5 seconds
7. Enter part number into the screen—RW 3 seconds
8. Wait for computer—IT 2 seconds.

So far, we have zero VA, RW 10 seconds and idle time 91 seconds!

Note: Seconds add up and every second counts. Think about it. The previous steps seem time consuming and detailed because they are. But keep in mind, in many companies, the previous steps are necessary every time the person wants to update or make a change in the system because IT logs them out automatically after 5–10 minutes. If you add up the idle time people lose sitting and waiting for their computers each day, times the number of people using computers, in this type of environment each day, it adds up to millions or billions of seconds of waste every day!

While somewhat tedious, it is critical to go through each step and document it. It can be done by hand or in spreadsheets. The person doing the process has to go through each step so it is only fair to that person to accurately reflect what they must go through. Going through this analysis on video with the team and questioning each step help to build that compelling need to change.

Following a Customer Order

We followed a new customer order from opening the e-mail to generating the work order (a total of over 100 steps) only to get to the end of the process and find out there was a shortage on one of the major parts of the assembly. It turned out there were two inventory locations: one was the warehouse that had the correct amount parts and the other was on a quality hold. The supplier quality engineer (SQE) had dispositioned the parts to be returned to the supplier but found out there was a problem with the drawing. The parts had to be scrapped. However, the transaction was never entered into the MRP system; so, the system still thought the parts were there. We could not start the order short parts as the customer needed the entire quantity. The other problem with the order was the waste of overproduction because they were building it before it was needed to keep the workshop busy. The main problem was that the order went through the entire process only at the end to be had. We could not release the order, and we could not leave the order open in the system as parts were allocated to it. This meant if there was another finished good item they could have built and it happened to have the same parts, it would show up short because the parts were already allocated to order. So, we had to cancel the order off the MRP system to free up the parts. So, in this case, it was like scrapping a unit on the floor. We put all the labor into this work order only to have it cancelled (or scrapped) at the end.

Many times, we find all kinds of opportunities to improve transactional processes. Most of the steps we find were probably necessary at one time but with the changes in technology, and new procedures are no longer necessary. We find corrective actions that were put in place which were removed 2 years ago but we are still doing the paperwork for it. This is because there was no feed-back loop from the close out of the corrective action to eliminate the paperwork associated with it. We find many approval loops that can be eliminated or handled quickly on workflow tools.

We find many times it helps to try to do the process yourself or with members of your team that are not familiar with the process. This prompts many questions as to why we do it this way. It is important to really challenge the status quo. Unfortunately, many times we run into roadblocks with IT. In large companies, this means generating a work ticket, assigning a priority, and, after waiting a year, maybe actually getting something done. We find it helps to put an IT person on the team. Please keep in mind though there are lots of non-IT problems that can be fixed as well.

Once you assess the existing process, you must figure out and agree on what the new process will be and then compare the cycle times and other metrics you have chosen to forecast the improvement. Once we have finished analyzing the process, we must determine the new process and create and document the standard work. The standard work must include the sequence of operations and cycle times (based on takt time) for each process. It is important to follow up a check to make sure the improvements are and taught to the rest of the users. It is not unusual to have to create or modify the roles and responsibilities matrix when working on transactional processes. Many times, the owners of the processes are unclear and need to be assigned revised by who has the most stake in the process being improved.

The Role of Automation in Transactional Processes

When using Automation in the manufacturing environment, equipment should be "right sized" and compliant with the Lean principle of flow. In general, this means avoiding batch production machines in favor of "single piece flow" designed equipment. However, there are situations that are just not suitable for automation. For example, in the Packaging business, human beings are more than capable of making boxes and cartons and filling them with objects and containers of product. Why then do companies capitulate to the will of engineers seduced by the automation drug and spend hundreds of thousands of dollars on automated carton erectors and filling machines, justifying their existence with business cases based on labor savings? The main reason is there are hidden costs that are not taken into account. Expensive spare parts and maintenance contracts together with technical resources to carry out maintenance and oversight of machine operations can easily offset any labor savings. Add to this, the cost of equipment downtime (up to 40% is not unusual) and you have a financial meltdown on your hands.

In the transactional world, one of the most common forms of automation is computer software. As with the manufacturing example quite often during the business case stage little or no attention is paid to its running costs which include annual licenses, annual maintenance, and administrative labor to oversee and troubleshoot. Like the packaging line there are some situations that don't need to be solved with software. E-mail is one of the best examples of this where it has become the default method of communication across the globe, overriding the ancient custom of "talking" and forcing the computer terminal into every situation imaginable whether it's required or not. Another common mistake with software is to assume that it's a total solution instead of first designing an improved process and then applying the appropriate software infrastructure to match. MRP and ERP systems that push unnecessary functionality in the form of bolt on modules and Project Portfolio management solutions with bloated workflow designs are examples of this.

Throwing Away the Key

During a recent visit to a well-known theme park, I was lining up to experience one of their most popular thrill rides. As we entered the attraction, we stumbled over a locker room. A great idea I thought since I was the official pack mule for the day. A place to unload, decant, and disassemble myself with security and peace of mind! I quickly realized as I was making my locker selection that this was no ordinary locker room. Instead of the archaic, medieval, simplistic key, there was a modern, high tech, state of the art booth ready to accept fingerprints and the credit card of choice! Always willing to experiment and experience new gadgets, I jumped at the opportunity of playing secret agent. Unfortunately, after several tries the fingerprint scan failed to read my profile and I was left helpless with a line of technology hungry tourists impatiently growling behind me. Before I had time to fret, along came a theme park employee ready to assist. He politely darted in-between me and the unit and proceeded to enter a series of "top secret" commands before flying over to the next booth like a grounded version of Superman to save another stranded member of humanity. I proceeded to repeat my bio-transaction, this time my indentations were in alignment and the locker popped open.

From a Lean thinking perspective, the fingerprint-controlled locker room is a step in the wrong direction! Let's examine the facts. In the stone age locker room where keys are used to open and close the cabinets the process for selecting and occupying the spaces was cheap, simple, reliable, and intuitive with no need for any kind of emergency hotline or on-the-ground technical support. In the advanced tech version of the same, the cost to purchase and install the lockers is dramatically higher and the unreliability of the technology requires a full-time troubleshooting technician to keep the area running! This is a classic example of how automation has increased the costs and decreased the efficiency of an operation where the initial goal was the complete opposite. We are always looking for ways to decrease labor content and human intervention but in this case the labor content required to run the process went up from zero to one, really an unforgivable step. Add to it the cost of maintenance and spare parts and the business case is dead and buried.

There are similar scenarios, however, that do increase productivity. The self-checkout process in the supermarket may seem analogous but in that case the ratio of machine operators (checkout attendants) was one to one when they were operating their own checkout. With the self-checkout kiosks in place, only one attendant is required to oversee four stations therefore reducing the labor content by 75%. In this situation, the improvement is viable even taking into account some maintenance load since three operators have been removed. By the way, world class is between 20 and 30 machines to one operator. To reach this bar, the thinking needs to be injected way up stream and Lean principles applied to equipment early in the design stage.

The default remedy of using automation and technology to solve problems is a powerful but very dangerous concept. When used appropriately, it can be effective but if it's applied in the wrong situation, it can quickly facilitate a deterioration in processes and services that can be extremely costly. The high-tech locker room sounds like a cool idea but it just isn't the right solution for the problem at hand. In this situation, the right answer is to redeploy the attendant and go back to the manual process.

Save it or Scrap it

At Company X, a small to medium sized company, they purchased a new MRP system many years ago. The MRP salesman was a good friend and neighbor of the then CEO. Anyone who knew this company would have known the MRP system was overkill and unnecessary due to the type of business this company was in. A year later, the CEO was replaced by a new CEO and the MRP project and investment continued. Two years later that CEO was replaced by yet another CEO. By this time, they had over 8 million in the MRP system and it still wasn't functional. Two of the MRP implementation team leaders had been let go. Meanwhile, since the new system was being capitalized, they now had 8 million on the books. Someone, no one knows who, proposed they spend another million, this year, on a study to see if the system still made sense. The CEO agreed.

Think back to the earlier statement, 8 years have gone by now and they still haven't used (or even needed this system). Now the system had so much money invested no one knew what to do with it. In addition, if they choose to scrap it, they must take the loss on the P&L. The system was on the books as assets (less some minimal depreciation). However, there is no salvage value to the system. You can't turn around and sell it to someone else. One of their junior executives suggested they scrap the study and the MRP system and save the million dollars. The exec told us, "It is just baffling how some companies function. Over time these projects get a life of their own." This is the boiled frog syndrome at work.

Standard Work and Ongoing Training

Another very important topic for the team will be a training concept. When the team understands standardized work, they will understand the process will be undergoing continuous improvement and therefore the standardized work will be undergoing revisions to capture those improvements. This means the team will need to consider how to communicate those changes to the organization and potentially how to train people on the changes. The training concept must be designed with a just-in-time (JIT) concept in mind.

Lesson Learned: The blanket e-mail describing updates or changes to a process should not be considered training. Not only would this be considered one of the worst ways to transfer new knowledge about a process update, but it is also unfortunately the primary method organizations use.

The process improvement team should see themselves as a core team that interfaces with other key participants in the process. This interface will provide two key functions:

1. Firstly, it allows everyone who participates in the process to have a clear avenue to communicate issues and problems. The core team should encourage this approach with everyone involved with the process. Finding problems is good!
2. Secondly, the improvements made can be communicated to the extended team by the core team to make sure they are understood and accepted by everyone. The core team must adopt the principle that if the student hasn't learned, the teacher hasn't taught. It is the core team's responsibility to make sure that all changes are understood and accepted by the people using the process.

Workload Balancing

Workload balancing is one of the root causes of waste. Some reasons for this are as follows:

- Work is not distributed equally for clerical/administrative positions.
- Often, there is a lack of clarity in roles and responsibilities/activities.
- Layouts create isolated islands and fractional labor.
- The person performing the transactional process may not have enough work to do; so, they will fill their time with NVA work to look busy.
- Then there is the opposite where people are extremely busy doing tasks that are not really needed but required in the process.

What we often see is when the staff person goes on vacation, there is no drop in productivity, no loss of customer orders, and no dissatisfied customers. However, there are some missions critical to staff positions where a huge void occurs when the person is out. Why does this disparity occur?

What would happen in a Lean production line that normally ran with four operators and experienced a week of production with only three operators? We likely would see production drop by approximately 25%. This is often not the case with staff positions in the management and office areas. We find organizations are not as tuned-in to looking for opportunities to identify and restructure administrative activities with relation to customer value and workload balancing. The next time you go into an office area, take the opportunity to stand in one spot for an hour, look around, and write down the waste you observe. This is waste you will never see just walking around on Gemba walks or management by walking around (MBWA) because everyone looks busy, especially when the boss comes around! But once you stop and take the time to really look at what people are doing, the searching, the copying, the inspection, walking all over to centralized printers, and waiting for their computers to respond, you will be amazed at what you find.

Lesson Learned: Generally, people are always busy but what are they busy working on? People are doing the best jobs they can with the tools management gives them. Instead of a Gemba walk, video them or sit with them and do their job for a day if you really want to learn the problems. While the people are busy, normally the things they are working on are sitting in storage. Just eliminating the storage steps and getting informational processes to flow like assembly lines will result in reducing the throughput time by 50% or more!

First to Market—Delayed by Transactional Process

Company X had recently launched a groundbreaking new product. There was a vacuum in the marketplace and customers were hungry for it. Factory Y, responsible for the manufacture, had more than 3 months (150 lots) of manufactured product in finished goods inventory but could not ship because the associated paperwork was not approved. An attempt had been made to address the situation by throwing labor at the problem. More than 30 contractors were hired over three shifts and crammed into two empty rooms and a hallway. The overall operation when viewed on a videotape closely resembled a cafeteria without food!

Each of the documents was an inch thick and contained approximately 12,000 entries. There was no flow, a lack of standardization and no teamwork, leaving reviewers to fend for themselves. The area was disorganized with reviewers randomly claiming empty desk space without access to the equipment they needed such as copiers, printers, and computer terminals. There were no performance metrics of any kind and due to the extensive lead time, there was no opportunity to provide feedback, preventing any chance of timely corrective action.

A project was chartered to shift the backlog and PFA and WFA analyses undertaken to understand the base condition. For each packet of paperwork, the reviewer experienced up to 14 interruptions, spent 35 minutes walking around looking for information and 25 minutes of idle time waiting for people or data to show up. A new process based on single piece flow was designed and implemented in a secure location, in less than a week, with all the necessary equipment in place. A single document was moved down the line using standard work and line balancing, each document was split into four separate sections and each section assigned to a separate reviewer. The total amount of time required to review the document in the base condition was approximately 12 hours but no changes were made to the content of the document to realize the benefits. In the Lean condition each reviewer had around 3 hours of work to complete and standard work was created for each person using a simple checklist. Two new flow lines were established and a daily meeting set up to review the appropriate performance metrics including Day By The Hour, Month By The Day, and Reject/Downtime tracking. Support staff were co-located with the operation avoiding the need for reviewers to leave their seats, thus maximizing the time spent focusing on the documents. Post implementation the output increased 387% from 18 documents per week to 84 per week on the two new flow lines. The lead time for a document to be reviewed went down 73% from 60 hours to 16 hours and the production rate from 18 documents per week to 57 per week in the Lean state. The backlog was eliminated in 2 weeks and shortly after it was possible to reduce the two lines to one to meet the demand.

BASICS® Model: Implementation

In working through the transactional process improvement, we have used the tools of brainstorming, VSM, PFA, and input versus output diagrams to both baseline and assess the current state of the process. We have used the future state mapping tool to suggest solutions. Now it is time to move to implementation.

As pointed out in the VSM section, we must capture improvement ideas and prioritize them using the Lean project selection tool (see Figure 5.6). An important aspect for the team to realize is that many of the tasks listed on the sheet will not be simple tasks that can be completed by a person in an hour or 2. Some tasks are just done in nature and can be completed the next day. However, some very key tasks common to transactional process improvement teams will be sub-projects and will take time and resources to complete. Implementing a metric system in a part of the organization that is not used to tracking their lead times and quality is a good example. Developing good, standardized work is a task that most people will have very little background or experience in putting into place. Without standard work, our improvements cannot sustain, and without it we have nothing to audit or train our team members. A training concept must be implemented to communicate changes as the standard work goes through improvement iterations. If you want the changes to last, you must consider topics such as these for a sustainable change. Each topic that needs to be implemented may require some training for the person responsible for the task.

While some of the tactics may be put in place immediately after a workshop or event, others will need to be tracked like any other project. This is an excellent place to introduce the team to the A3 thinking method. It allows the person responsible an opportunity to demonstrate that their project is aligned to higher level strategic goals. It also requires that person to think about the problem-solving tools they have or should use to address their sub-project. The project leader can ask that each sub-project leader put a small set of next steps together as part of the sub-project roadmap. The project leader can use each of these sub-project roadmaps to put together their own A3 that shows how the sub-projects interact and who needs to coordinate with whom to make sure the implementation is harmonized.

The A3 is a great method to help the sub-project leaders understand the importance of coordinating with a small extended project team to ask about other problems with the process and coordinate updates or changes to the process. As each sub-project leader reaches out to parts of the organization that are engaged with implementing the process, asking questions, and providing updates, the team will be part of the implementation of a learning organization. In this way, the changes should be sustainable and continuously improving.

The Matching Process in AP

In addition to the wastes that were identified in the accounts payable process story earlier, it was also discovered there was a very complex paper matching (packing slip, receiver, and invoice) process which consumed the labor of a full-time accounting resource in addition to a temporary resource that was working approximately 20 hours per week to help catch up. This paper matching process fed into a sea of filing cabinets that consumed a huge amount of floor space in the office in addition to a tremendously large storage area in the plant for all the documents held from previous years. All this activity seemed to be NVA at first glance; but it was stressed to us that it had to be this way in case someone needed to look at one of these documents in the event of a discrepancy. After a little more investigation, it was determined that it was only once or twice every couple months, if that, where anyone needed to find these documents. In summary, this company was spending approximately 12 hours per day of labor to save less than an hour of searching or requesting new documentation once a quarter. Eventually, the team came up with a solution that involved scanning the invoices daily, recycling the packing slips after the receiving transaction was completed, and never printing the receiver since all the info on it was already maintained in the computer. The new process for accounting became a simple verification of the receipt in the system when an invoice was received and then scanning the invoices at the end of the day. The hours and hours of wasted labor was thought to be VA to the purchasing department but was not adding any value to the accounting department. What can be done with all the office and plant square footage that would be freed up from not saving all this paperwork?

Once the tool is completed, it becomes much easier to put together roles and responsibilities by function. This tool can also provide a starting point for discussions as to what should be considered value streams in the organization.

Lesson Learned: Walking the actual process or reviewing video of the actual process is the only way to truly identify all the waste in a process. This provides the granularity necessary to drive change within the organization.

BASICS®: *Check and Sustain*

Just like the shop floor processes, we must build in checks to make sure the new process is meeting our expectations and to continue looking for additional improvement opportunities. We need to make sure we have active metrics in place that surface any problems within the process. Many times, we can use similar tools to the day-by-hour chart in the office as well as the +QDIP board to monitor the process real time and implement counter measures and root cause corrective action as necessary. It is also important, as stated earlier, to build as much of the documentation and standard work for the resulting transactional processes into ISO 9000 type systems or configuration control systems to ensure the new processes become part of the system. This way, as leadership changes, the system will not. This is part of the learning organization we are ultimately striving to create.

Remember, metrics should be created to highlight problems, not make people feel good. We must set our standards high to achieve world class. At one company, they put a plus or minus 5% on their cycle times. When we reviewed their standard work, we questioned why this was in place. "Well, we wanted to put something in place the employees would consider reasonable." We immediately objected to this and said the standard should be set to the lowest verifiable cycle time. If it can be met once, it can be met again. This forces us to strive for perfection and to train everyone in the proper motions to meet the times. We received the comment back "but it is only 5%, who cares?" So, we told the person the following analogy. Let's say I owe you a hundred dollars but I decide I am going to lower the standard and only pay you $95. He said, "Well that is ok as long as you pay me 105 next time!" I replied, no way we agreed to lower the standard. I am paying you $95 from now on.[11] We must have standard work to sustain and we must have high standards to force the problems to the surface and strive for perfection.

Lean in the Office: Batching Example

Most offices batch just like manufacturing. Office processes are now referred to as transactional Lean.

Office processes tend to be segmented by function just like manufacturing. Consider the following example: to ship out a spare or aftermarket part Company X had:

- 17 steps in customer service
- 22 steps in shipping
- 9 steps in inventory control
- 19 steps in traffic
- 18 steps in credit

and the customer request spent:

- 87% of its time in storage
- 9.2% in process
- 0.09% VA
- Over half a mile being transported

Of the 85 steps, only 3 were VA:

1. Take the order.
2. Pick the order.
3. Ship the order.

Throughout each area, each batch of requests (normally a day's worth) was sent from department to department for notification, approvals, reports, and various documentations that had built up over the years. In most companies, these steps evolve as problems or mistakes in the process are incurred. Instead of fixing the process, we add inspection steps and approval levels. Over time, the processes become very bureaucratic and go from hours to days or weeks. To Lean out the processes, we must go back through each step and question why it exists and what can be done to eliminate, rearrange, simplify, or combine it with another step. Think of the frustration that occurs by staff that must continually call for updates, approvals, and rework, not counting the wasted man hours and costs that go essentially unnoticed.

Homework: Look at any office process in your company and see if you can find batching somewhere in the process.

HR at Company X versus Company Y

Company X and company Y both have similar world-class employee performance review processes. Company Y is structured such that their evaluations are due each year on the anniversary of the employee's hiring date. Company X does all their evaluations each December. Which company do you think has a better overall review system?

The system for company Y naturally staggers their reviews; this level loads the employee evaluations so each supervisor has maybe one or at most a couple of reviews a month. Much thought and time can be put into each one. Each employee fills in their evaluation and has a 360-feedback review process. Each employee reviews their evaluation one on one with their supervisors and discusses their role in the succession plan and their strengths and weaknesses in their ongoing development plan and their hard and soft goals for the next year along with how it is linked to the strategic plan. Company X batches their evaluations. Every supervisor is sent a reminder at the end of November that their evaluations are due prior to the Christmas holiday. Not only are they all due at once, but it is a short month. Someone had the bright idea that this would make it easy for the company to keep track of evaluations and make sure they were completed, not recognizing the potential impact to quality.

Each supervisor rushes through the process so they can check off the box at the end of the month. Imagine the chaos that ensues. Supervisors trying to make the end of the month and end of the year now scramble to get all their evaluations done, reviewed, and presented to the employees, and most don't always make the deadlines. Employees generally have a rushed one-on-one review if they even have it all! As a result, they don't really understand their current or future role in the company. When employees don't understand how they contribute to the organization or their future development plans, they are more likely to leave to pursue other options. This negatively affects the overall attrition and retention rate. What are the repercussions of this system companywide? The evaluations are hurried, mistakes are made, employees don't receive good feedback, and development plans are not thought out if they exist at all. Can you see the potential long-range implications?

Author's Note: This is where making it easy for one department (HR) by batching the process has a huge undesirable effect on the rest of the company. However, as characteristic of systems thinking, most of us would never even question this decision or consider it a bad one.

If employees are our biggest asset, should we batch all their evaluations up at the end of the year? How does this impact our employees' overall growth and development? How does this impact the succession plan? How does this impact our long-range strategic plan? What you often find is managers are hidden in their offices for a week or more trying to get all the evaluations done in a batch form. It is often difficult to expect a manager to perform the high-quality evaluation that the employee deserves when he or she is required to complete all staff evaluations in bulk, over a short period of time, along with their daily operational work.

Lesson Learned: There is a big difference between saying employees are our most important asset and treating them that way. Batching gets in the way and can impair the long-term health of our business. However, what is easy for the company isn't always what is best for the company or the employee.

Author's Note: The Lean principle of Level Loading or Production Smoothing is often misunderstood. Lean processes are designed to meet known demands and it's very important to do everything possible to level those demands for the process to be successful. It's true that Lean solutions can flex to demand changes, but those increases/decreases should be planned and predictable thus allowing time for line re-balancing to be implemented in a controlled fashion. It's critical that the source of the fluctuation be investigated and rectified for the improvement to be sustained.

Homework: Where else do these systems apply? How about all our taxes being due on April 15 in the United States?

Debit Card Story

William Hopper, a former investment banker, who has lived in Flask Walk for 20 years, said: "I ended up £300 better off and humorously hoping the same thing would happen to me every day. I decided it was not taxable since I was the beneficiary of a fraud and it would not come under income tax." "Although I was embarrassed at falling for it, I ended £300 up which cheered me up no end." The author, who is currently penning a sequel to his highly respected work The Puritan Gift, also recovered the £1,000 from his bank.

More than 100 elderly and vulnerable people across Camden have been hit by the scam losing hundreds of thousands of pounds, with a 92-year-old and a cerebral palsy sufferer among the victims. The conmen contact their targets masquerading as police or bank fraud investigators, alerting them to an alleged fraud on their account. They ask the victims to call their bank using the number on their card. But when the victims put the phone down, the conmen do not hang up, leaving the line open and then posing as bank staff, persuading the victims to reveal their PIN and other information. The gang then sends a courier to the victim's address to collect their bank cards and empty their accounts. Mr. Hopper, who helped found the Institute of Fiscal Studies, was defrauded last September when he was persuaded to hand over his bank cards. When he called the fraudsters the following day to request some spending money, the scammers sent him a stack of 15 used £20 bank notes to spin out the confidence trick. Mr. Hopper said: "These people are intelligently evil and they use that intelligence in this acting and deceit." A special police unit in Camden has made dozens of arrests in relation to the fraud, but officers warn it will be a complex crusade. Police recently seized a Ferrari in Camden after officers swooped on three men suspected of masterminding a similar scam worth £56,000. Detective Alex Stavrou said: "We have made arrests and we're trying to link as many cases as we can to the gangs who have been lifted."[12]

Many companies have had problems with P cards or purchasing cards where employees have taken advantage of the debit or credit cards and racked up thousands of dollars of fraudulent expenses (see Figure 5.11). Since this story, Mr. Hopper, the victim in the story earlier, has worked with a company to prevent this type of fraud in the future. As a staunch believer in mistake proofing, this company has created a debit card that contains integrated transaction control, enhanced reporting, data feed monitoring, and controls. It has real-time control of the entire transaction process from the moment you spend through to transaction tracking, billing, and reconciliation at the end.[13] It eliminates the chance for fraud or overspending and makes the P card solution viable once again.

Change in the Office

Do You Know What You Need to Know?

We have sat in meetings and listened while managers outright lied to their executives about things happening on the factory floor or in the office. So, we ask you the reader; if the manager never leaves their office, how will they ever know about the actual problems on the floor or in the office, the lack of progress being made, or if what is reported is even the truth? How reliable is the information transferred from layer to layer up to the CFO, CEO, or board of directors? How many layers do you have? How many layers are required? Begin to challenge the status quo at every opportunity to drive change.

Lesson Learned: Beware! There is only one way to know what you need to know. You must leave your office and go to the floor! Occasionally, a company ends up with a high-level executive that wants to look good. He or she chooses which information to pass up and down the chain becoming a cog in the wheel of progress and decision-making. Good people that work for him/her get frustrated and leave while yes men/women get promoted. Every organizational layer is in essence a process step in the organizational communication process and hence an opportunity for defects. How effective is that organizational communication in your organization?

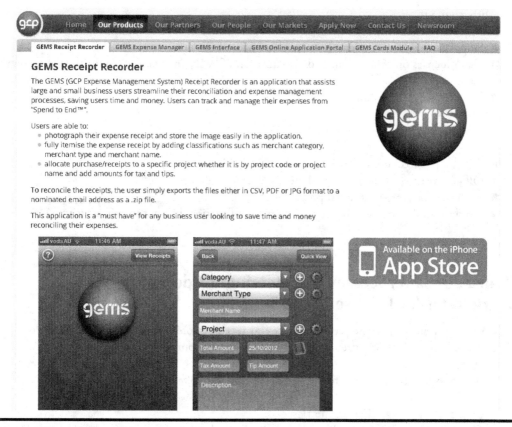

Figure 5.11 GCP Limited, gems App --new service provides real time checking of debit cards. https://itunes.apple.com/us/app/gems-receipt-recorder/id577263269?mt=8. (From William Hopper, Bestselling author of The Puritan Gift.)

Example of Results

Listed in the following are results from a joint supplier/customer cross-functional team over a 2-year period:

- Heijunka box between steps—made the bottleneck visible.
- Workflow manager limited in MS Excel.
- Improving turnaround already visible in a 70% engineer-to-order environment.
- Process efficiency improvement = orders÷# of people.
- Process efficiency:
  - One can see flow.
  - Walking between departments is avoided.
  - Search for lost files avoided.
  - Non-value-adding communication between departments is eliminated.
  - Non-value-adding reports eliminated.
  - Process issues are discussed and addressed immediately cross functional.
  - The process is transparent and measurable and visualization of standards for sustainability in place.
  - Elimination of mixed workflow and introducing standardized work instructions.

Turnaround time:

- Single piece flow of files creates a common pace or rhythm.
- Team focuses on throughput and visualization of WIP, and the team pulls the file through the process.
- Elimination of inbox and outbox waiting.

Conclusions:

- Equally possible improvements in the office and in production.
- Office processes are less visible, therefore need proper VSM.
- Focus on the cross-functional process is crucial.
- Fundamental improvement requires change of functional layout to process team.

Transactional Processes (Engineering) Order Entry to Order Release to the Shop Floor

At Company X, we scoped the previous process as receipt of order-to-order release to the floor for custom products (which require drawings with customer approval). We followed the BASICS® model (Figure 5.12).

The goal of the process was to cut the cycle time by 50%:

1. Step one was to baseline the metrics.
   One might think this would be simple but it took all day. The metric being tracked was the number of orders that spent over 3 days in engineering prior to release. The department felt they were doing well with 60% of the orders under 3 days, which was the metric being tracked. However, this is not the metric identified in the goal. To meet the goal, we had to determine the actual cycle time it was taking to get the orders through engineering. This metric did not exist. Since the steps in this metric were not tracked in the MRP system, we had to take a random sampling of orders and manually build the data matrix. There was a great reluctance initially to fill in the matrix since it required manually pulling the information from file cabinets. However, forcing the team to revisit the engineering packages was elucidating. We learned there were many other problems in the process that we documented. We also discussed the problem statement and business case for the kaizen. It took much discussion to agree on these, and again, just getting customer service, engineering, and production in the same room resulted in everyone learning what the other players in the organization were doing. We also found the cycle time for the last part of the process done by one engineer wasn't even included in the original less than 3-day metric. In the end, we found the actual number of orders meeting the 3 days was closer to 40% versus the 60% being reported. We also found there were three categories of orders which needed to be considered. These were new orders, new orders that already had a proposal, and existing orders. This is because new orders with proposals had engineering work done up front, prior to receipt of the order, some of which was not included in the scope. After much discussion, we finally all agreed on the baseline metrics.

No. of Steps	OMIT	Flow Code	Flow Symbol	Description	Alt. Start Time (Optional)	Cumulative Time	Baseline Time	Post Lean Estimate Time	Distance (in feet)	Distance Post (with omits)
1		va	O	Receive Order	000000	000001	1	1	16	16
2		RM	□	Wait in queue (3 to 5 days)	000000	043000	16200	28800		0
3		i	◆	check website	000000	000300	180	180		0
4	x	I	■	wait to check rest in queue		001800	900	0		0
5	x	nv	O	print po		001850	50	0		0
6	x	t	◉	to printer		001851	1	0		0
7	x	I	■	wait on printer for rest to print	000000	000500	300	0		0
8	x	t	◉	from printer to desk		000600	60	0	100	0
9	x	b	□	wait for up to a day	000000	043000	16200	0		0
10		I	◆	review order	000000	000230	150	150		0
11	x	L	■	Wait to review rest of orders	000000	001000	600	0		0
12	x	b	□	wait for up to a day	000000	043000	16200	0		0

Figure 5.12 Omits process in order entry to cash PFA. This PFA was 196 steps and 64 were omitted.

2. Step two is assess/analyze.

We outlined to the group that we needed to follow the process (product), the operator, and setups. We decided there were no major setups in the process. We conducted the TIPS analysis by first having everyone in the room write down each step in the process on a yellow sticky and code each step with the TIPS category, that is, is it a transport, inspection, VA or NVA process, or storage step. In addition, they had to add who did the step and how long it took. We then used the total quality (TQ) affinity tool to build our process wall map. We find this to be a much easier process than trying to walk it through the first time. Then we validate the map by walking the process and interviewing the folks to see what we missed and what issues they have. We have never had a time where we caught every step in the initial process mapping.

During this process, a lot of discovery happens. We always start with what is the first step. Someone reads off their first step. Then someone else says "Well that's not my first step?" and now the fun begins. The next issue is what level of detail we go to when doing TIPS. (Remember, this tool is a level down from the VSM. Now you must be detailed, down to the second, to really capture VA versus NVA steps.) We remind everyone of the three criteria for value added. As far as the level of detail, we try to make sure we don't have more than one of the TIPS categories on one sticky note. This is the easiest way to do it.

The other issue is remembering that if we send it to your inbox and you don't retrieve it immediately, then because you are the e-mail, you are sitting in storage for that time. So, you always must ask: "do you work on me right away or do I sit for a while?" Make sure you are entering transport distance on every transport step. We don't necessarily record the transport distance for e-mails but you could. Sometimes it helps to ask, how did we used to do it? What did we do before ERP or MRP? You must keep asking why for every process step. Does the customer really care about this step? If they don't, it is not value added.

Then customer service asked, "How come you guys (engineering) never include the sales order number? I must look it up every time!" Engineering says, "I need approval, and if no one is there, I just leave it in their rack. Sometimes it waits for a day! And I go work on something else." The engineering director says, "What? You wait a day for it? Well, we need to change that to minutes!" We constantly must remind the team that "you are the thing" going through the process, not the person doing the process and that all our focus is on the process not the person, etc. What are we now? Are we an e-mail, a quote, a drawing, etc.? Sometimes, it helps to write up on the minutes what you are since you keep changing as you progress through the process.

We get a lot of discussion over value added or not or how long it takes since the times vary so much. So, we recommend you put a range of time and go with the 80% of the time what happens.

Normally, this process wall map extends over an entire wall or walls! It is amazing. We then typed the steps into our PFA (TIPS) spreadsheet to calculate the number of steps by category and the times for each. Once we built the wall map, we physically walked the process to see if we missed any steps. Then we added up the total lead time and compared this to our baseline data to sanity check the data. Next, we looked for steps we could eliminate. We walk through each sticky and use the omits process ERSC (can we eliminate, rearrange, simplify, or combine). The first time we ran through each step, we were told why each step could not be changed. Then we started challenging each step. When we examined the data and found 85% of the time was storage, it would seem easy to meet our 50% targeted reduction in cycle time. But it turned into a slow and painful process filled with excuses (and very real objections) of why it couldn't be done (see Figure 5.11).

Lo and behold as we finally started to brainstorm ideas, we started to eliminate steps and -followed up with questions as to how we are going to justify and mitigate the perceived risk with the removal of each step. This put to rest the valid objections voiced by the engineers. Later in the discussion, one of the engineers said we could justify the removal of a certain step because we capture each part of the process on a whiteboard (visual controls). One of the team said, "We don't even have that step up there on the map." So, we had to add that step into the whole flow taking our 80 steps to 88. Then we started again to work on eliminating steps.

At the end of 4 hours, we had removed 20 of the 88 steps with half the steps left to go. By the end of the project, we were down to 40 steps.

Then we filmed each operation to use for the WFA. We decided since there is so much variation to film an easy, medium, and complex custom product. We then determined the percentage of each and used the weighted average tool to arrive at the average times for each step. We then compared this to our baseline data to sanity check the data.

3. Step three is suggest solutions.

The team first came up with a workflow type solution, which would have cost around $50,000 to implement. We then challenged the team with a question? If we purchase this software, will it, by itself, solve all the problems and allow us to reach our goal of cutting the process time by 50%? The answer was a resounding no.

So, the team noted it as option 1 and had an action to do an ROI for it after the kaizen. We then challenged the team to come up with some creativity before capital ideas. The team came up with 26 opportunity bursts for the PFA, all of which could be implemented immediately. We then mapped out the new flow and brought in all the customer service and design engineers to review and critique the new process. After several changes, they developed a visual control in the form of a whiteboard to track the movement of the order through the design and customer approval process. Many times, we would ask if we could change a process, and the first comment from the engineering director was no! It cannot be done. However, after sleeping on it, he figured out ways it could be done. We then ran a dry run of the process and documented the new positions and new procedures with times for each step.

4. Step four is implement.

The process was implemented with a plan to use the new whiteboard visual control tracking as the future metrics for the process since there was no automated way to measure the process. This new system tracked the design requests in real time and made any abnormalities immediately obvious. One problem was how to make sure the request was picked up within the 15 minutes allotted for the design engineer. A simple timer was purchased and pressed when customer service dropped off the request. Kind of like a chess clock. The design engineer was to pick up the request and note the time on the board and reset the clock. The alarm sounded at 15 minutes if it was not picked up. We also set up daily 5 minutes stand up meetings with the entire team to make sure the process was working and to make necessary adjustments.

5. Step five is check and sustain.

The plan to check and sustain the process was to build the metrics into the monthly reporting review process with corporate.

Results:

- Storage time was cut 93%.
- The overall cycle time (throughput time) was cut between 62% and 83% depending on the complexity of the drawing change for the custom parts.
- 88 steps were reduced to 49 steps (7 of those being logging in the information on the tracking board).
- 4.7 days plus or minus 3.8 days was reduced to 0.6–1.8 days easily surpassing the 50% goal of 2.35 days set for the kaizen.
- Four additional kaizens were also identified.

These results were obtained for a minimal investment in 3.5 days of time for the cross-functional team and the minimal cost of some tape for the whiteboard and a stopwatch. By increasing the velocity of time through the system, it should result in additional sales dollars as well.

6. Step six is presented in the following table, showing possible Lean transactional kaizens within a manufacturing company.

High-Level Processes	Order Entry to Collect			
Order Entry	Manufacture/ Operations	Ship	Invoice/AP	Collect
Contract/PO review	Acquire staff	Order completed to order stock	Order ship to order invoice	Order invoice to order collect
RFQ to quote Inside sales Outside sales	Initiate material Pos	Order completed to order ship	Accounts payable	Cash management
	Line layout/factory setup/tooling		Accounts receivable	PO closeout
	QA/QC		Month end closing	

Supplier RFQ to receipt of materials	Order receipt to order release			
Marketing Strengths, weaknesses, opportunities, and threats (SWOT) analysis Strategy Forecasting	Order release to order completed		Payroll	
	Kanban		Inventory	
	Vendor-managed inventory (VMI)			
	Total productive maintenance (TPM)			
Sales configuration process	Environmental health and safety			
Budgeting/finance process Department budgeting Cost control Capital budgeting Financial reporting				
Engineering processes Research and development Concepts of operations/use Systems requirements Concept design Detailed design Engineering change Configuration control Engineering change Engineering test and evaluation Engineering transition to production E&M and sustainment End of life part process				

Case Study: Experience with Lean in an IT Technical Support Environment[14]

The IT help desk was experiencing low customer satisfaction. We didn't have a customer assessment tool to measure how we were doing, but complaints found their way to my desk. The IT director was continually defending his staff to irate customers and the term helpless desk was bantered about.

IT was supporting well over 1,000 users and an equal number of devices (servers, routers, telephones, workstations, handheld devices, etc.). In addition to providing end-user troubleshooting and support, they worked on hospital-wide projects, building new servers, updating software, decommissioning equipment, etc. There were four employees in the department and they were busy indeed. We had recently implemented new systems to achieve stage I meaningful use, and that meant hundreds of nurses for the first-time using carts connecting wirelessly into our main health IS. Another hundred doctors needed access to the network to enter medication orders. It was a period of transition and there were connectivity and device problems. No matter how much we tested the hardware and computer programs, it seemed that we couldn't come up with the exact keystrokes or order of keystrokes used by end users who would constantly crash the system. The phones rang off the hook. There was a lot of repeat work.

We brainstormed hundreds of things we could do to keep up with the volumes of calls. Adding staff was mentioned numerous times. Intuitively, staff thought they could accomplish more in less time if they could avoid interruptions. Just let support calls go to voice mail and then resolve them in an uninterrupted batch process. But it wasn't working. Throughout all this time, we began to study Toyota principals and Lean concepts: observation, continuous processes, standardization of processes, and identification and elimination of waste. Could we do things differently and achieve our objectives of quality services and customer satisfaction?

We began our journey using observation, spending several sessions in the computer room recording activity: how often did the phone ring? What was the nature of the call? Could it be resolved over the phone or did someone have to be dispatched to the site of the problem? Was it a new call or a repeat call? What about those voice-mail messages when the phone was tied up or not answered? What about e-mail requests for help?

Yes, we found that the staff was extremely busy and yes, the phone seemed to ring constantly. Checking the voice mail and e-mail system was the responsibility of all four technicians, and they gave a higher priority to fixing a problem they were already aware of than listening to voice mail, knowing they would most likely just add another problem to the list of things to do. When they did listen to the voice messages, we observed a tendency for technicians to prioritize responding to what they perceived as quick or easy fixes over other messages before even talking to the customer. We have order tracking software but observed that it was not consistently being used. The technicians were too busy. Our count of calls, new voice-mail messages and e-mail end-user support requests during our observation period, totaled, on average, ten calls per hour.

A quick analysis of the types of support calls showed that 75% of those calls could be resolved over the phone and most of them in less than 5 minutes. But every time one of those calls went to voice mail, we added time to problem resolution. Since most of our customers are clinical people who move around the hospital, the likelihood of reaching them in a call back was low. There was great variability in time to make those connections. It often took days. At an average reconnect time of 5 minutes per call, we identified 40 hours per week of waste. We quickly realized that the more often we could answer the call, the more waste would be eliminated.

In March, we changed to a continuous process. We assigned two of our technicians to staying in the computer room, answering the phones, and resolving those problems that could be fixed immediately. One technician had primary responsibility and the second picked up when the first was on a call, while performing project work when not on the phone. Other staff members in the vicinity were also instructed to answer calls when both first-level technicians were on the phone. The goal was to prioritize answering the phone, speak to the customer, assess the urgency of the call, fix the problem, if possible, set an expectation when someone would call back in response to the problem if that was necessary, and inquire as to whether that expectation was acceptable to the end user. All calls were logged into the work order system as the phones were answered. Keeping up that continuous process was not effortless. Whenever a technician would be out on sick leave, the tendency was to let the calls go to voice mail and focus on uninterrupted technical work. But we persevered, insisting that responding to the calls and setting expectations were the top priorities. So, what did we accomplish and what do we know today, 9 months after making that change from batch to continuous flow?

Results:

- I have not received even one complaint about the technical support department and, indeed, have received comments indicating improved customer satisfaction.
- We learned that 50% of the ten requests per hour we counted during our on-site observation were people calling back because they hadn't yet received a response to their first contact. We average five new calls per hour, not ten.
- With the help of our order tracking system, we can assess the number of work orders being created and compare that to the number being closed during a period. Prior to our process change, we saw more work orders created each month than were completed, ranging from 2% up to 12%. That trend reversed itself immediately when we began our continuous process, and we have worked down the backlog without overtime by closing 2%–3% more work orders each month than are being created.

Lesson Learned: Batching in transactional processes can have significant consequences, particularly in areas that receive multiple orders or drop-offs of documents or items. Errors occur when people are trying to batch such as in order processing or as information, documents, or materials are received. Processing items in batch can lead to incomplete documentation when entering in a system and mismatching between orders, resulting in delays in processing as rework will be needed and first in, first out (FIFO) will not occur.

Summary

In every transactional environment, there is the opportunity to apply Lean concepts and tools. Transactional processes are generally NVA but necessary to run an effective and efficient business. Transactional processes have steps that are NVA and can and should be eliminated, combined, or changed to support better process flow. Transactional processes will be very different for different types of companies. Large global firms that are coordinating processes across multi-location, multifunction, and multicultural entities will have different issues from a smaller company dealing with one or two locations in proximity. Transactional processes are both directly in support of the manufacturing floor or service location daily and indirectly associated, such as strategy development, sales and marketing, program management, and budgeting.

Being able to provide tools that assess value in the process, address flow, apply standard work to ensure repetition of best practice for operating procedures, identify opportunities to mistake proof and decrease the number of defects, and measure the lead time of key processes are common goals that all organizations strive for as they work to improve their bottom line and provide a competitive advantage to remain in business. In every organizational environment, it is important that the support areas also engage in Lean deployments to fully benefit the organization and provide the most value for the customer.

Chapter Questions

1. Why are transactional processes many times the most inefficient processes in the value stream?
2. Why is it important to eliminate the waste in the transactional and administrative process?

3. Are most transactional processes value added?
4. What is the most important tool for analyzing an office process?
5. What is the best way to see all the steps of a process?
6. What should the evaluation team become during the transaction PFA, noting we often want to be the part during a process flow review in a manufacturing process?
7. What are the VSM steps in a transactional process? How does a VSM integrate into the strategic plan and personnel evaluation process?
8. List and describe five transactional wastes.
9. Where are transactional costs in the profit and loss statement of a firm? Are the costs fixed or variable?
10. What did you learn from this chapter?

Discussion Questions

■ Why do so many leaders think Lean is only for the shop floor? How would you convince them otherwise?
■ When should we start the office implementations?

Notes

1. http://www.brainyquote.com/quotes/quotes/p/peterdruck163694.html#rzA2pKx6L6uxaOdb.99
2. Industry Week, April 2013, p. 26, A Penton Media Publication, http://www.industryweek.com
3. Jim Womack and Dan Jones, Seeing the Whole (Boston MA: LEI), 2002.
4. A workflow management system is a computer system that manages and defines a series of tasks within an organization to produce an outcome or outcomes. Workflow management systems allow the user to define different workflows for different types of jobs or processes. For example, in a manufacturing setting, a design document might be automatically routed from designer to a technical director to the production engineer. At each stage in the workflow, one individual or group is responsible for a specific task. Once the task is complete, the workflow software ensures that the individuals responsible for the next task are notified and receive the data they need to execute their stage of the process. Workflow management systems also automate redundant tasks and ensure that uncompleted tasks are followed up. Workflow management systems may control automated processes in addition to replacing paperwork order transfers. For example, if the previous design documents are now available as AutoCAD but the workflow requires them as Catia, then an automated process would implement the conversion prior to notifying the individual responsible for the next task. This is the concept of dependencies. A workflow management system reflects the dependencies required for the completion of each task.
5. Competing against Time, Stalk and Houk, need to finish.
6. GAAP is generally accepted accounting principles, http://www.investorwords.com/2141/GAAP.html
7. Edward De Bono, Six Thinking Hats, 2nd edition (New York: Back Bay Books), August 18, 1999.
8. Typical waste proportions seen in companies before Lean efforts; Source: Lean Enterprise Research Centre, Cardiff Business School, 2000.
9. CAD is a three-letter acronym (TLA) for computer-aided design. This is a software program used by designers.
10. Star Wars. Movie Director: George Lucas, Writer: George Lucas, Stars: Mark Hamill, Harrison Ford, Carrie Fisher.
11. Contributed by Casey Weems.
12. Story used with permission, http://www.hamhigh.co.uklnews/court-crime/former_hampstead-.roliticjan_enjoys_ni... July 2, 2013 © 2013 Archant Regional Ltd. All rights reserved. Furnished by William February 7, 2013.

13. Based on personal correspondence from William Hopper October 31, 2012, and February 7, 2013, also used their website http://www.gcpgroup.com/
14. Prepared by Dianne Emminger, Vice President, Information Services, ACMH Hospital.

Additional Readings

Lareau, W. 2002. Office Kaizen: Transforming Office Operations into a Strategic Competitive Advantage. Milwaukee, WI: ASQ Quality Press.

MCS Media. 2005. The Lean Office Pocket Guide. Chelsea, MI: The Lean Office Pocket Guide.

MCS Media. 2008. The 5S for the Office User's Guide. Chelsea, MI: MCS Media.

Tapping, D. and Shuker, T. 2003. Value Stream Management for the Office. New York: Productivity Press.

Appendix A - Study Guide

Chapter 1 Questions and Answers

1. **Describe some of the various Lean implementation methods.**

   Hit and Miss Method
   This method was deployed by a big eight accounting firm and consists of assembling a team, maybe providing some basic Lean training for a 1/2 day, or so, and then sending the team to the floor to make an improvement. There is no formal data collected, and participants make observations and pick one to improve. This is a ready-fire-aim approach.

   Point Kaizen Events
   This method is used by virtually 95% of consultants and professional organizations today. It typically involves a day of training, 3 days of observation and implementation of the team's agreed-upon changes, and a report out and celebration lunch on Friday. This method is often implemented similar to the hit and miss method. They emphasize a ready-fire-aim approach.

   Demand Flow
   This method involves following the product, following the operator, creating a sequence of events that merges the two together, and then developing a layout. The layouts are usually characterized by a middle conveyor line fed by individual branch conveyor lines. The main unit is assembled down the middle as subassemblies are completed on the branch lines. These are normally sit-down lines with a focus on station balancing. It is more of a ready-aim-fire approach.

2. What is the difference between a point kaizen event and a system level kaizen?

   Point Kaizen Events
   This method is used by virtually 95% of consultants and professional organizations today. It typically involves a day of training, 3 days of observation and implementation of the team's agreed-upon changes, and a report out and celebration lunch on Friday. They emphasize a ready-fire-aim approach.

   System Kaizen Implementations
   This process involves following the product and the operator and then analyzing any setups or changeovers for the overall value stream. We then create a block diagram where the

product flow is aligned such that required assembling or machining the part is in order of assembly. Then we create the layout with a focus on baton zone balancing versus station balancing. This is a ready-aim-fire approach with some layout advantages over the demand flow approach.

Each of these implementation methodologies will realize improved results. It is the degree of result realized that makes the big difference.

– Point kaizen events have a 50% or less chance of sustaining.
– The system kaizen implementation approach has the best chance of sustaining as the entire product line or machining area is reviewed and analyzed versus just a piece of an area.

3. What are some of the pros and cons behind point kaizen events?

There can be problems with this point kaizen approach when implementing, large-area projects or conversions, from batch to flow. Point kaizen events are an easy sell to company management as they only tie up four to eight people for a week. Management is initially amazed at what a dedicated, cross-functional team can accomplish in a week. The team appears, based on the closing PowerPoint™ presentation, to achieve great initial results. Point kaizens can be leveraged to achieve quick wins but should be used with caution as discussed in the succeeding text. In many cases, the results are great, but after several months, management determines the gains are difficult to sustain and can't understand why.

Many point kaizen events don't sustain the improvement.

Point kaizen events are designed to make small and large improvements within the week and rarely lead to organizational cultural transformations. On larger lines, only a small part of a line can be attacked in a point kaizen event. Therefore, if you don't target a process that is on the critical path, or roll it out, area or system wide, and sustain it, the results don't go to the bottom line.

This does not mean the point kaizen approach cannot work. A fundamental cornerstone of Lean employs a scientific approach as demonstrated by Deming and the Shewhart PDSA cycle or the CCS PDCA cycle used many years before, not only for improvements but also for coaching and mentoring. This provides for both a planning and execution phase to obtain desired results.

4. Why do a lot of companies start with 5S? What can be some of the shortcomings with this approach?

Starting with 5S seems to be a straightforward approach with five processes to follow and many companies start with a 5S initiative. While sometimes this can be successful, most find they do not have the accountability or discipline in their organizations to sustain even the simplest area that has undergone 5S. This can be discouraging and sometimes significantly delays moving on to other Lean initiatives or converting product lines assembly or machining from batch to flow. They figure if they can't sustain 5S, why bother going forward. While this has some merit, the BASICS® approach is to start with a final assembly line and to do 5S as part of the implementation. This provides a chance to get all the workers in the area involved and makes sense because we can't implement standard work until 5S is in place.

5. What is the best way to implement a Lean line? What do we have to work off first?

A cardboard is a simple, inexpensive, quick, and effective way to help people visualize what the line will look like. Many times, this becomes the heart of the product preparation process (3P) or layout design kaizen. We recommend using Lean pilots. We start off with small pieces within the project, apply the Lean tools, and work out the kinks prior to converting the entire area. A phased approach provides everyone time to voice their opinions and secure the necessary staff buy-in from the area. We also suggest involving the engineering/maintenance and health safety and environmental departments on the team either full time or part time.

6. What are some of the guidelines for a Lean group leader/supervisor? How do they differ from a traditional supervisor?
   - Be a leader and lead the work area
   - Create an atmosphere that encourages adherence to standard work
   - Run the daily huddle with the team
   - Prioritize and delegate
   - Make timely and effective decisions
   - Be the role model
   - Make the numbers and schedule
   - Embrace quality
   - Ensure Lean tools and methods, such as day-by-hour charts are used
   - Keep area clean and ensure 5S is followed

7. What is the importance of a team charter?
   The significance of the team charter is not just to provide a road map for the team but also to create a pull for the team, provide a structured approach for leadership interventions, and create a vehicle for leadership follow-up and sustaining during and after the initial Lean implementation. The charter is a symbol of management commitment and provides an escalation process and ultimate ownership for the team and its results in the event they run into any resistance to change.

8. What role does variation play when implementing a Lean system?
   Most assembly lines have variation. It has been our experience that it is virtually impossible to remove all the variation in a line when it is first implemented; however, we do address the lack of standardization and training and many of the test and equipment issues as part of the implementation. Tuning and tweaking generally involve engineering which is why Lean needs to be an overall company effort and not just a pursuit of the shop floor. There needs to be a variation reduction or mitigation action plans assigned to the appropriate individuals who are held accountable to resolve the problems. As the problems are resolved any necessary changes will need to be incorporated into the standard work.

9. Why is conducting anFMEA important before rolling out a Lean implementation?
   Failure mode and effects analysis (FMEA) is a structured approach to assess the magnitude of potential failures and identify the sources of each potential failure. When planning your implementation, take the time to brainstorm with the team everything that could go wrong. Then consider each item as to the probability it could go wrong, the severity if it went wrong, why it might go wrong, how you will determine if it does go wrong, and what to do if it does go wrong.

10. What are two of the implementation guidelines?
    - Include a strategy for accountability and sustaining as part of the continuous improvement road map
    - Listen to your lean consultants/experts
    - Reasons not to try Lean immediately on your own without a sensei
    - Adopt and integrate standard work and create a suggestion and reward system
    - Continue videoing after the consultant leaves
    - Don't leave managers in place who aren't going to get it
    - Don't lay people off after Lean implementation

- Don't shortcut the tools
- Encourage Lean architectural designs
- Include a go forward person on the team
- When implementing multiple sites or campuses, it works best if the prior campus team contains a person from the next campus to be implemented. We call this a go forward person. This is a great way to load the next team for success.
- Train, train, train

11. What role does SWIP play in implementing a new line? Why is it so difficult for people to figure it out?

SWIP is a key part of implementing Lean synchronous flow lines and is a very difficult concept for operators and supervisors to understand. Once the SWIP level is determined, the line has to be run until all of the excess WIP is worked off and the SWIP is in place and we call this wetting the line and sometimes this can take several days. The operators will naturally want to finish these pieces. This requires the lead (Lean practitioner) to be there with the operators to teach them about SWIP and to help them get the line wet. The Lean practitioner must stay with the line for at least a week or two, sometimes longer, depending on the line complexity, to ensure the line continues to run properly. It is a very counterintuitive process, and if operators are left to their own discretion, they will not run the line properly and could revert to their previous ways.

12. What was your favorite lesson learned in the chapter?

13. What is the problem with the cookie cutter approach to Lean implementation?

While many areas across different companies are similar, we have found none exactly the same. We highly discourage cookie cutter-type approaches. It is important to go through the analysis steps (BASICS®) in each implementation to obtain the buy-in from the existing staff. This does not mean that once the formula is created, it can't be implemented slightly quicker, but it is important not to try to implement it too quickly or it will not sustain. Lean requires people to think differently than they are used to. If they don't go through the process of actually seeing their wastes in the process for themselves, they will have difficulty in accepting any new process proposed.

14. What is the escalation process and how is it used?

It is critical to have an escalation process in place to help the improvement teams or supervisors remove barriers to improvement. Failure to have this process in place will force these issues to be hidden and not surface. The escalation process should go all the way up to the CEO.

15. How is TLT calculated?

Calculate the TLT from the WFA. The TLT is equal to the sum of the total VA and NVA labor time. It is the amount of time staff members spend to make "one" of the products or the activity taking place in the area.

16. What did you learn from this chapter?

Chapter 2 Questions and Answers

1. What is the simplest type of Kanban? How does it work?

The simplest type of Kanban is called a two-bin system that is composed of two separate bins containing the same parts, with one bin placed behind the other. When the first bin empties, the next full bin slides down. The empty bin becomes the Kanban signal or trigger visually indicating that the bin needs to be replenished. The empty bins are then collected, taken to the stockroom (or sent back to the supplier), and refilled. The new bin of materials is then returned to the original location in the area.

2. What are the two types of systems on which Kanban systems are based?

   Kanbans can be replenished in two ways:

      1. Constant time means they are replenished the same time each day or several times a day. This is referred to as breadman type replenishment, which is similar to grocery store shelves being restocked each night.
      2. Constant quantity is similar to the two-bin system. It may empty out at any time, and we refill it with the same quantity every time.

3. What is a gas gauge?

   A gas gauge comes in many forms but essentially is communicating when an item needs to be replenished.

4. How do you size a Kanban, that is, what is the Kanban formula to figure out how many to put in a bin?

   The Kanban formula is the number of parts required to cover the time to replenish the parts + buffer stock + safety stock divided by container size.

5. What are the rules of a Kanban system?

   Kanbans should only be used when we can't link processes directly together. Kanban cards should only be used when we can't use more simplistic systems such as an empty bin or space.

6. Can you explain the different types of Kanban systems?

   There are several types of Kanban. The main types are withdrawal (Toyota refers to this as retrieval) and production (Toyota refers to this as informative) Kanban. Withdrawal means a person goes to a shelf with an empty bin, obtains a full bin, and leaves the empty. The empty may be replaced by an area, a stock room, or a supplier.

7. How are JIT and Kanbans related?

   Kanban is a means through which JIT is achieved. The purpose of a Kanban system is to control the flow of material by providing inventory as a buffer to synchronize two disconnected processes. Kanban is a visual management tool to help prevent overproduction, the number one waste, and for detecting delays in the process or when processes are producing ahead of schedule (a pacemaker to prevent overproduction—i.e., produce only what is ordered, when ordered, and quantity ordered).

8. What is the simplest way to size a Kanban?

   The simplest way to consider sizing a Kanban is to think about a two-bin system.

9. What is a two-bin Kanban system?

   A two-bin system has two bins. When one empties, the next one slides down to be used by the operators. While the second bin is being used, the first bin is being filled. There must be enough parts in each bin to cover the time to refill one bin.

10. What are some of the failure modes for Kanban?

    Kanban systems have two major failure modes: First, the Kanban system was originally designed in the plan for every part (PFEP) to support a certain maximum volume or customer demand. If this volume is exceeded, there will be parts shortages. Second, if Kanban cards are lost, inventory will not be replaced. If there are too many cards in the system to begin with, it will create excess inventory.

11. Excess inventory is always the sign of a problem. What problem do Kanbans hide?

    Kanbans can hide excessive inventory in the value stream as Kanbans are inventory, thus we must constantly work to minimize the amount of materials.

12. How should Kanban bins be labeled? What is the difference between the front and rear labels?

    On an assembly line, the bins should be labeled by location and in the order the product is produced. The parts and tools must be placed on the line in order of assembly in correct orientation even if it means duplicating parts.

    They must be labeled with the part number, revision level if applicable, and description along with both the lineside location on the front and replenishment location on the back such as warehouse, stock room, or supplier on the back. The front of the bin should include the quantity per unit (where it makes sense) and the back of the bin should include the quantity necessary to refill the bin from the material warehouse or supplier if VMI.

13. Where did the name water spider come from? What does the water spider do?
    - The water spider comes from the water spider which is an insect that moves quickly, often seen running or skating in groups over the surface of a pond or stream.
    - Material handlers or water spiders replenish parts when the bin is empty or when triggered by a Kanban card so operators can continue to work on the product and not have to worry about replenishing their stock. In assembly, the water spider is used to replenish lineside materials from the materials warehouse and is also used to sometimes perform offline tasks or to relieve for restroom breaks.

14. What is the difference between lineside inventory bins and material warehouse inventory?

    Lineside inventory is at the line in bins (decentralized) ready for use on the line. Material warehouse inventory is inventory stored in a central warehouse that needs transport to the line that involves additional waste (transportation) and typically more storage space than lineside.

15. What did you learn from this chapter?

Chapter 3 Questions and Answers

1. What are two reasons station balancing does not work well?

   The major problem with station balancing is that people are not robots and we all work at different rates. A second issue is if an operator is absent, the line does not run well.

2. What hides problems on manufacturing lines?

   Excess material on the line hides problems.

3. What two things will point to a problem on a manufacturing line?

   Excess inventory and idle time point to problems on a manufacturing line.

4. What is a baton zone?

   A baton zone, or flex zone, is an area where handoffs occur between operators. The layout must be designed with short, easily shared steps around the zone. Long operations should be split into smaller steps.

5. What are three failure modes of baton handoff lines?
   - Most people want to bump to the SWIP, not the person.
   - They are not cross-trained and cannot bump.
   - Equipment is off the line requiring operators to leave the line disrupting the flow.

- Line is not stand-up and walking.
- Team leader or supervisor doesn't understand how to run the line.
- SWIP is dried up or not maintained in the line.
- All components for the product being built are not available when the order is released.

6. What are three advantages of baton handoff manufacturing lines?
   - Maximizing team member's efficiency
   - Maximizing output of the line by using the fastest person to create the pull
   - Minimizing the effect of absenteeism
   - The line does not have to be U shape
   - Drive cross-training
   - Ability to easily measure output
   - Quality improvements and mistake proofing opportunities surface from breaking the operations into small steps
   - Incorporation of subassemblies or other operations being performed off-line
   - Eliminates idle time (assuming SWIP is in place)

7. What are in-process Kanbans? Are they the same as SWIP?
   In-process Kanbans between operators are buffer inventory used to hide line imbalances and make it easy to balance a line. Standard WIP (SWIP) is a calculated buffer based on replenishment times utilized to link processes together.

8. Describe bumping.
   When a product is given to operator 3, operator 2 then moves down to take the part from operator 1, this is considered a handoff or what we call bumping. This bumping down the line causes a baton handoff and bump by each subsequent operator on the assembly line until the operator closest to the beginning of the assembly line no longer has a product to work on.

9. What is a mixed model matrix?
   A mixed model matrix is a table or chart. On the left side are all the different operations the product might see. On the top (x axis) is each of the model types. Then in each box contains the cycle time per model per operation. When the operations are summed up for each model, it yields the TLT. This can then be divided by the number of operators to figure out the average cycle time and output per hour and per day.

10. What is rabbit chase?
    The rabbit chase line balancing methodology has each operator make their own parts by working around the entire cell every cycle. So instead of one operator bumping back to another, each operator is continuously circling the cell working on making a complete product from start to finish.

11. What is meant by the Lazy Man's Balance?
    We call the "pull 3 or pull 1 or any system with WIP caps" the lazy man's balance. In effect, the line is being balanced by the WIP present between the operators. Also, in a lazy man's balance, the true work necessary to maintain the product flow and balance the operators is replaced with a Kanban square of material placed between the operators that hides the line imbalance.

12. What are five-line balancing rules?
    - Everyone must be cross-trained.
    - May have to duplicate tools, fixtures, or materials.
    - Standard WIP must be labeled and maintained at all times.

- On mixed model lines, since several orders could be running down the line at the same time, one has to figure out how to handle the paperwork. Normally, the paperwork travels with the first unit.
- Operators should rotate several times a day.

Chapter 4 Questions and Answers

1. What is a group tech matrix?

   The goal of the group tech matrix is to determine what, if any, families exist and to what extent of the parts they will cover. The chart has the machines used and part fabricated listed for all machines and parts.

2. Can Lean principles be applied to a machine shop with significant amounts of automated equipment?

   Yes, for example, in set up time.

3. When do we conduct a PFA?

   Once we do a group tech matrix and determine a cell can be created, we do a process flow analysis (PFA) on the part(s) in the cell to make sure we have the steps in the correct order.

4. What is a Yamazumi board? How is it used?

   The Yamazumi board has different uses and varies by company. In general, it visually displays the load on each machine or machining center compared to the available time. Sometimes it is used to compare cycle times for operations to the TT. This board breaks down process steps in time slices indicating value added, non-value added, periodic work and setup/change over time.

5. What is the PPCS?

   The PPCS is a part production capacity sheet (PPCS). This, along with the setup times and lot size, will provide the capacity for each machine and the overall process for the particular part we are following. In some cases, we will need a PPCS for each part, part type or family of parts. The PPCS along with standard work is a tool for the supervisor to use to manage their line

6. What role does setup reduction play in a machine shop?

   Reducing setup is important in a machine shop. Many times, the group tech matrix will help reduce and sometimes eliminate setups, due to the families of parts we are able to put together. By creating families of parts, we can often load all of the tools in the carousel for that family, thus eliminating the need for changeover.

7. Should we outsource our products?

   In general, an organization should avoid outsourcing. Focus attention on Lean and continue to perform the value-added work internally.

8. What is a paced line? Provide an example.

   A paced line is a line that continues at a steady rate or pace. A good example is a conveyor as the product moves through the system at a steady rate (or pace).

9. What is vendor managed tooling? Is there value in this process to the machine shop? Support your answer.

   Vendor managed tooling is used in many Lean machine shops. There are many vendors now, especially with consumable-type tooling (i.e., drill bits, inserts) that will manage your tooling for you whether it be at point of use (POU) or at a breadman or more central location. There is value as the organization can focus on the value-added activities and not the small support items (i.e., drill bits) needed to conduct the value-added operations.

Chapter 5 Questions and Answers

1. Why are transactional processes many times the most inefficient processes in the value stream?
   Transactional processes tend to be more inefficient than manufacturing as no one measures them and more over-processing waste occurs in offices than in manufacturing.
2. Why is it important to eliminate the waste in the transactional and administrative process?
   There are large gains to be made by applying Lean principles and eliminating waste in the transactional and administrative processes.
3. Are most transactional processes value added?
   No, all transactional processes fall into the category of non-value added but necessary steps.
4. What is the most important tool for analyzing an office process?
   When implementing transactional processes, we utilize all the same tools in the BASICS® and PDCA models.
5. What is the best way to see all the steps of a process?
   We have found value stream maps in the office environment to be unsurpassed as a continuous improvement tool.
6. What should the evaluation team become during the transaction PFA, noting we often want to be the part during a process flow review in a manufacturing process?
   The team should become the information, often a piece of paper or form.
7. What are the VSM steps in a transactional process? How does a VSM integrate into the strategic plan and personnel evaluation process?
   These VSM processes supply companies with the data necessary to make the strategic decisions required to stay in business and provide the customer with better products and services at a lower cost.
8. List and describe five transactional wastes.
   – Waste from overproduction of goods or services—waste of excess reports, both paper and electronic, batch copying, too many brochures printed, information duplicated across forms or not needed. Gathering, sorting, and saving more information than is really needed.
   – Waste from transportation (unnecessary)—document flow/movement between offices for processing, routing, and poor office layout placement of adjacencies, travel time, unnecessary copying/approval of information to people who do not use it.
   – Waste from over-processing (inefficiency)—multiple, redundant, and undefined approvals; and multiple reviews and inspections. Elaborate filing systems for documents that have information already contained in the ERP system.
   – Waste of inventory; unnecessary stock on hand—too many supplies, duplicative files, multiple file storage, just in case storage, etc.
   – Waste from defects—lack of training documents, completion of company errors in capturing data, errors in transferring data, supplies and equipment ordered incorrectly or in the wrong quantities, missed deadline, rework, clarifications, etc.

9. Where are transactional costs in the profit and loss statement of a firm? Are the costs fixed or variable?

   Transactional costs are shown on the P&L in both the labor overhead line and the G&A line. The costs should not be considered fixed as there is substantial waste in the overhead value stream that could be subjected to Lean (i.e., waste removal).

10. What did you learn from this chapter?

Appendix B - Acronyms

5Ws	when, where, what, who, why
5W2Hs	when, where, what, who, why, how, how much
5 whys	asking why five times in a row in order to get to the root cause
AGV	automatic guided vehicle
AI	artificial intelligence
AP	accounts payable
ASL	approved supplier list
AT	actual time
AT&T	American Telephone and Telegraph
BASICS®	lean implementation model for converting batch to flow: baseline, analyze (assess), suggest solutions, implement, check, and sustain
BFT	business fundamental table
BIG	Business Improvement Group LLC based in Towson, MD
BOM	bill of material
BPD	business process development
BRIEF	Baseline Risk Identification of Ergonomic Factors
BVA	business value added
C	Cold
CAD	computer-aided design
CAP	change acceleration process
CEO	chief executive officer
CM	centimeters
COGS	cost of goods sold
CQI	continuous quality improvement
CTP	cost to produce
CTQ	critical to quality
CV	coefficient of variation
CWQC	company-wide quality control
CYA	cover your ass
DBH	day by hour
DFA	design for assembly
DFM	design for manufacturing
DFMA˙	Design for Manufacturing and Assembly
DIRFT	do it right the first time
DL	direct labor
DMAIC	design, measure, analyze, improve, control

DMEDI	design, measure, explore, develop, implement
DOE	design of experiments
DPMO	defects per million opportunities
EBIT	earnings before interest and taxes
EBITDA	earnings before interest taxes depreciation, and amortization
ECR	engineering change request
ED	emergency department (emergency room)
EDD	earliest due date
EDI	electronic data interchange
EHS	environmental, health, and safety
ERP	enterprise resource (requirements) planning
ERSC	eliminate, rearrange, simplify, or combine
EHS	Environmental Health and Safety
ETDBW	easy to do business with
EV	earned value
EVA	economic value added
FC	full change
FG	finished goods
FIFO	first in, first out, replaced by EDD, earliest due date
FISH	first in still here
FMEA	failure modes and effects analysis
FPY	first pass yield
FT	feet
FTT	first time through (thru)
FWA	full work analysis
GE	General Electric
GM	general manager
GMS	global manufacturing system
GPI	global process improvement
H	hot
H	hour or hours
HBS	Harvard Business School
HEPA	high-efficiency particle absorption
HPWT	high-performance work teams
HR	human resources
HS&E	health safety and environmental
ICE	SMED formula, identify, convert, eliminate
i.e.	that is
IL	indirect labor
IN	inches
INFO	information
INSP	inspection
ISO	International Organization for Standardization
IS	information systems
IT	information technology (computing/networking)
IT	idle time
ITCS	intelligent tracking control system

JB	job breakdown
JEI	job easiness index
JI	job instruction
JIC	just in case
JIT	just in time
JM	job methodology
JUSE	Japanese Union of Scientists and Engineers
KPI	key process indicators
KPO	Kaizen Promotion Office
KSA	knowledge, skill, or ability
LB	pound or pounds
LBDS	lean business delivery system
LCL	lower control limit
LEI	Lean Enterprise Institute
LIFO	last in, first out
LMAO	laughed my butt off
LMP	lean maturity path
LP	lean practitioner
LP1	lean practitioner level 1
LP 2–5	lean practitioner level 2 through level 5
LRB	lean review board
Max	maximum
MBD	month by day
MBTI	Myers-Briggs Type Inventory—personality styles
MH	man hours
Min	minute or minutes
Min	minimum
MM	materials manager
MPS	master production schedule
MRB	material review board
MSA	measurement systems analysis
MSD	musculoskeletal disorder
MSE	manufacturing support equipment
MSE	measurement system evaluation
MT	meter
MTD	month to date
MVA	market value added
NIH	not invented here
NOPAT	net operating profit after taxes
NOW	not our way
NRE	Nonrecurring engineering
NTED	no touch exchange of dies
NVA	non-value added
NVN	non-value added but necessary
OCED	one cycle exchange of die
OE	order entry
OEE	overall equipment effectiveness

OEE	overall engineering effectiveness scale
OPBSF	one-piece balanced synchronized flow
OPER	operator
OPF	one-piece flow
OPI	office of process improvement
OPS	operations
OR	operating room
ORG	organization
OSED	one-shot exchange of dies
OTD	on-time delivery
OTED	one-touch exchange of dies
OTP	on-time performance
PC	production control
PCDCA	plan–control–do–check–act
PDCA	plan–do–check–act
PDSA	plan–do–study–act
PEST	political, economic, social, and technological
PFA	process flow analysis (following the product)
PFEP	plan for every part
PI	process improvement
PI	performance improvement
PIT	process improvement team
P/N	part number
PM	preventative maintenance
PO	purchase order
POU	point of use
POUB	point of use billing
PPCS	part production capacity sheet
PPF	product process flow, synonymous with PFA
PPM	parts per million
PPV	purchase price variance
Prep	preparation
PSI	pounds per square inch
PWI	perceived weirdness indicator scale (1–10) developed by Charlie Protzman
QC	quality control
QCD	quality, cost, and deliver
+QDIP	safety, quality, delivery, inventory, productivity
QTY	quantity
RC	running change
RCCA	root cause corrective action
RCCM	root cause counter measure
Rchange	resistance to change
REQ	requisition depending on the context
Reqmt	requirements
RF	radio frequency
RFQ	request for quote
RFID	radio-frequency identification

RM	raw materials
ROA	return on assets
ROI	return on investment
RONA	return on net assets
RR	railroad
RTC	resistance to change
RW	required work
S	second or seconds
SASL	signal acquisition source locator
SIPOC	suppliers–inputs–process–outputs–customer
SJS	standard job sheet
SMART	specific, measurable, attainable (achievable), realistic (relevant), timely
SMED	single-minute exchange of dies
SMG	strategic materials group
SOP	standard operating procedure
SORS	standard operation routine sheet, same as SWCS
SPACER	safety, purpose, agenda, code of conduct, expectations, roles
SPC	statistical process control
SPEC	specification
SQC	statistical quality control
ST	storage time
STRAP	strategic plan
SWCS	standard work combination sheet, same as SORS
SWIP	standard work in process
SWOT	strengths, weaknesses, opportunities, threats
TBP	Toyota Business Practice
TCWQC	total company-wide quality control
TH	throughput time
TIPS	transport, inspect, process, store
TL	team leader
TLA	three letter acronym
TLT	total labor time
TM	team member
TOC	theory of constraints
TPM	total productive maintenance
TPS	Toyota production system
TQ	total quality
TQM	total quality management
TT	takt time
UAI	use as is
UCL	upper control limit
UHF	ultrahigh frequency
USW	United Steelworkers
VA	value added
VMI	vendor-managed inventory
VOC	voice of the customer
VOP	Value of the Person

VS	value stream
VSL	value stream leader
VSM	value stream map
W	warm
WACC	weighted average cost of capital
WADITW	we've always done it that way
WE	Western Electric
WFA	Workflow analysis, following the operator
WIIFM	what's in it for me
WIP	work in process
WMSD	work-related musculoskeletal disorder
WOW	ways of working
YTD	year to date

Appendix C - Glossary

5 whys: Method of evaluating a problem or question by asking *why* five times. The purpose is to get to the root cause of the problem and not to address the symptoms. By asking why and answering each time, the root cause becomes more evident.

5 Ws: Asking why something happened—when, where, what, why, or who did the task.

5W2H: Same as the five Ws but adding how and how much.

5Ss: Method of creating a self-sustaining culture that perpetuates a neat, clean, and efficient workplace:

- **Shine:** Keep things clean. Floors swept, machines and furniture clean, all areas neat and tidy.
- **Sort:** Clearly distinguish between what is needed and kept and what is unneeded and thrown out.
- **Standardize:** Maintain and improve the first three *Ss* in addition to personal orderliness and neatness. Minimums and maximums can be added here.
- **Store:** Organize the way that necessary things are kept, making it easier for anyone to find, use, and return them to their proper location.
- **Sustain:** Achieve the discipline or habit of properly maintaining the correct procedures.

Absorption costing: Inventory valuation technique where variable costs and a portion of fixed costs are assigned to a unit of production (or sometimes labor or square footage). The fixed costs are usually allocated based on labor hours, machine hours, or material costs.

Activity-based costing: Developed in the late 1980s by Robert Kaplan and Robin Cooper of Harvard Business School. Activity-based costing is primarily concerned with the cost of indirect activities within a company and their relationships to the manufacture of specific products. The basic technique of activity-based costing is to analyze the indirect costs within an organization and to discover the activities that cause those costs.

Affinity diagram: One of the seven management tools to assist general planning. It organizes disparate language information by placing it on cards and grouping the cards which go together in a creative way. Header cards are used to summarize each group of cards. It organizes information and data.

Allocation: A material requirement planning (MRP) term where a work order has been released to the stockroom; however, the parts have not been picked for production. The system allocates (assigns) those parts to the work order; thus, they are no longer available for new work orders.

Andon: Andon means management by sight—visual management. Japanese translation means light. A flashing light or display in an area to communicate a given condition. An andon can be an electronic board or signal light. A visual indicator can be accompanied by a unique sound as well.

Assembly: A group of parts, raw material, subassemblies, or a combination of both, put together by labor to construct a finished product. An assembly could be an end item (finished good) or a higher level assembly determined by the levels in the bill of material.

Backflush: MRP term used to deduct all component parts from an assembly or subassembly by exploding the bill of material by the number of items produced. Backflushing can occur when the work order is generated or when the unit is shipped.

Backlog: All customer orders received but not yet shipped.

Balance on hand (BOH): The inventory levels between component parts.

Balancing operations: This is the equal distribution of labor time among the number of workers on the line. If there are four workers and 4 minutes of labor time in one unit then each worker should have 1 minute of work.

Batch manufacturing: A production strategy commonly employed in job shops and other instances where there is discrete manufacturing of a nonrepetitive nature. In batch manufacturing, order lots are maintained throughout the production process to minimize changeovers and achieve economies of scale. In batch manufacturing environments, resources are usually departmentalized by specialty and very seldom dedicated to any particular product family.

Benchmarking: Method of establishing internal expectations for excellence based upon direct comparison to the very best at what they do. Benchmarking is not necessarily a comparison with a direct competitor.

Bill of material: A list of all components and manufactured parts that comprise a finished product. The list may have different levels denoting various subassemblies required to build the final product.

Bin: A storage container used to hold parts. Bins range in various sizes from small to very large containers and can be made of plastic, wood, metal, cardboard, etc.

Bin location file: An electronic listing of storage locations for each bin. Generally, locations are designated to the work area, rack, and shelf, and location on the shelf, that is, 1—A—2 defines assembly area 1, rack A, and shelf 2 position on the shelf.

Blanket order: An order generally issued for a year or longer for a particular part number or group of specific part numbers. The blanket order defines the price, terms, and conditions for the supplier, thus allowing an authorized representative of the purchasing team to issue a release against the blanket order to the supplier.

Blanket order release: An authorization to ship from the customer to the supplier a specified quantity from the blanket order.

Block diagram: A diagram where the processes are represented in order of assembly by blocks denoting the process name, cycle time, utilities required, standard work in process (SWIP), etc.

Bottleneck: Generally referred to as the slowest person or machine. However, only machines can be true bottlenecks as we can always add labor. A true bottleneck runs 24 hours a day and still cannot keep up with customer demand.

Breadman: Centralized floor stock systems where the suppliers normally own and manage the material until it is used.

Budget: A plan that represents an estimate of future costs against the expected revenue or allocated funds to spend.

Buffer: Any material in storage waiting further processing.

Buffer stock: Inventory kept to cover yield losses due to poor quality.

Capacity: The total available possible output of a system within current constraints. The capability of a worker or machine within a specified time period.

Carrying costs: The cost to carry inventory, which is usually determined by the cost of capital and cost of maintaining the space (warehouse) and utilities, taxes, insurance, etc.

Catch ball: Communications back, forth, up, down, and horizontally across the organization, which must travel from person to person several times to be clearly understood and reach agreement (consensus). This process is referred to as *catch ball*.

Cause and effect diagram: A problem-solving statistical tool that indicates causes and effects and how they interrelate.

CEDAC: Anachronism for cause and effect diagram with the addition of cards. Problem-solving technique developed by Ryuji Fukuda. A method for defining the effect of a problem and a target effect statement. Through the development of a CEDAC diagram, facts and improvements will be identified that allow action.

Cellular layout: Generally denotes a family of product produced in a layout, which has the machines and workstations in order of assembly. Does not necessarily imply the parts that are produced in one-piece flow.

Chaku-Chaku: Japanese term for *load-load*. Refers to a production line that has been raised to a level of efficiency that requires simply the loading of parts by the operator without any effort required for unloading or transporting material.

Checkpoint: Control item with a means that requires immediate judgment and handling. It must be checked on a daily basis.

CNC: Acronym for computerized machining—stands for computer numerical control.

Consigned inventory: Normally finished goods stored at a customer site but still owned by the supplier.

Constraint: Anything that prevents a process from achieving a higher level of output or performance. Constraints can be physical like material or machines or transactional like policies or procedures.

Continuous flow production: Production in which products flow continuously without interruption.

Continuous improvement (kaizen): A philosophy by which individuals within an organization seek ways to always do things better, usually based on an understanding and control of variation. A pledge to, every day, do or make something better than it was before.

Contribution margin: Equal to sales revenue less variable costs leaving how much remains to be put toward fixed costs.

Control chart: A problem-solving statistical tool that indicates whether the system is in, or out, of control and whether the problem is a result of special causes or common system problems.

Control item: A control item is an item selected as a subject of control for maintenance of a desired condition. It is a yardstick that measures or judges the setting of a target level, the content of the work, the process, and the result of each stage of breakthrough and improvement in control during management activity.

Control point: Control item with a target. A control point is used to analyze data and take action accordingly.

Cost cutting: Eliminating costs in the traditional way, that is, reducing expenses, laying people off, requiring people to supply their own pens, making salary workers work much more overtime, etc.

Cost of capital: The cost of maintaining a dollar of capital invested for a certain period. Normally over a year.

Cost reduction: Reducing costs by eliminating the waste in processes.

Correlation: A statistical relationship between two sets of data such that when one brings about some change in the other it is explained and is statistically significant.

Cp process capability: Process capability is the measured, inherent reproducibility of the product turned out by a process. The most widely adopted formula for process capability (Cp) is

$$\text{Process capability } (Cp) = 6\sigma = \text{total tolerance} \div 6$$

where σ is the standard deviation of the process under a state of statistical control. The most commonly used measure for process capability within ASA is a process capability index (Cpk), which is

$$Cpk = \text{lesser of } Cpu \text{ or } Cpl$$

where

$$Cpu = (\text{upper specification} - \text{process mean}) \div 3$$

and

$$Cpl = (\text{process mean} - \text{lower specification}) \div 3$$

Interpretation of the index is generally as follows:

Cpk > 1.33	More than adequate
Cpk ≤ 1.33 but > 1.00	Adequate, but must be monitored as it approaches 1.00
Cpk ≤ 1.00 but > 0.67	Not adequate for the job
Cpk ≤ 0.67	Totally inadequate

CPIM: APICS—acronym for certified purchasing and inventory manager. Rigorous course material required with five modules of testing to be certified.

CPM: Acronym stands for certified purchasing manager—this is a NAPM (national association of purchasing managers) certification for purchasing professionals. Requires passing rigorous testing and experience criteria.

Cross-functional management: Cross-functional management is the overseeing of horizontal interdivisional activities. It is used so that all aspects of the organization are well managed and have consistent, integrated quality efforts pertaining to scheduling, delivery, plans, etc.

Cross-training: Training an employee in many different jobs within or across cells.

Customer relations: A realization of the role the customer plays in the continuation of your business. A conscious decision to listen to and provide products and services for those who make your business an ongoing concern.

Customer service: Any specifications required to meet the customer demands, needs, or requests for information and service. Everyone in the company should be a customer service representative.

Cycle: Completion of one whole series of processes by a part or person.

Cycle time: Available time divided by the factory capacity demand, the time each unit is coming off the end of the assembly line or the time each operator must hit, or the total labor time divided by the number of operators.

Cumulative: The progressive total of all the pieces.

Cumulative time: Is equivalent to adding up the total times as you progress. For instance, if step 1 is 5 seconds and step 2 is 10 seconds, the cumulative time is 15 seconds.

Daily control: The systems by which workers identify simply and clearly understand what they must do to fulfill their job function in a way that will enable the organization to run smoothly. These items are usually concerned with the normal operation of a business. Also a system in which these required actions are monitored by the employees themselves.

Data: Any portrayal of alphabetic or numerical information to which some meaning can be ascribed. Data can be found in a series of numbers or in an answer to a question asked of a person.

Data box: Term apportioned to a box in a value stream map that underlies a process box and contains elements such as process cycle time, number of persons, change over time, lot size, etc.

Demand flow: Material only moves to a work center when that work center is out of work. Subject of the book *Quantum Leap* by the World Wide Flow College of Denver. Layouts are typically a conveyor down the middle of the line with subassembly lines feeding in both sides.

Deming cycle: A continuously rotating wheel of plan, do, check, act.

Demonstrated capacity: Term to depict capacity arrived at by nonscientific means. Generally, it is arrived at by feel or observing actual output without determining what the process could generate if all the waste was removed.

Deviation: The absolute difference between a number and the mean of a data set.

Direct labor: Labor attributable specifically to the product.

Direct material: Raw material or supplied materials that when combined become part of the final product.

Distribution: Term generally refers to a supply chain of intermediaries.

Distributor: A company that generally does not manufacture material but is a middle man. They normally hold some finished goods but not always. Sometimes they may make some modifications to the finished goods.

Dock to stock: Process where suppliers are certified by the company's supplier quality engineers or purchasing and quality professionals that result in the supplier's products bypassing inspection or sometimes receiving to go directly to the stock room or shop floor where it is used.

Download: Transfer of information from a central computer (cloud) to a tablet, PC, phone, or other type of device.

Downstream operation: Task that is subsequent to the operation currently being executed or planned.

Downtime: Time when a scheduled resource is not operating.

Earned hours: Standard hours credited for actual production during the period determined by some agreed upon rate.

Economic order quantity: Model used to determine the optimum batch size for product running through an operation or a line. It is equal to the square root of two times the annual demand times average cost of order preparation divided by the annual inventory carrying cost percentage times unit cost.

Economy of scale: Larger volumes of products realize lower cost of production due to allocating fixed costs against a larger output size.

EDI: Acronym stands for electronic data interchange which is the ability for computer systems between supplier and customer to talk to each other without human involvement. In some cases, this requires programing of an interface between computers so they can talk to each other.

Effectiveness: Is the ability to achieve stated goals or objectives, judged in terms of metrics that are based on both output and impact. It is (a) the degree to which an activity or initiative is successful in achieving a specified goal and (b) the degree to which activities of a unit achieve the unit's mission or goal.

Efficiency: Production without waste. Efficiency is based on the *energy* one spends to complete the product or service as well as timing. For example, we all know of the *learning curve*. The more one performs a new task, the better they become each time the task is practiced. As one becomes more efficient, they definitely reduce stress and gain accuracy, capability, and consistency of action. A person has achieved efficiency when they are getting more done with the same or better accuracy in a shorter period of time, with less energy and better results.

Eight dimensions on quality: Critical dimensions or categories of quality identified by David Garvin of the Harvard Business School that can serve as a framework for strategic analysis. They are performance, features, reliability, conformance, durability, serviceability, esthetics, and perceived quality.

Elimination of waste: A philosophy that states that all activities undertaken need to be evaluated to determine if they are necessary, enhancing the value of the goods and services being provided and what the customer wants. Determining if the systems that have been established are serving their users or are the users serving the system.

Ending inventory: Inventory present at the end of a period. Sometimes validated by taking a physical inventory.

EPE: Acronym stands for every part every—this denotes batch size of lots running through the process.

Ergonomics: The study of humans interacting with the environment or workplace.

ERP: Acronym for enterprise resource planning system. It is a business management software to integrate all business phases to include marketing/sales, planning, engineering, operations and customer support the third generation of MRP systems usually used to link company plants locally, nationally, or globally. SAP, ORACLE, and BPCS are examples of these types of systems.

Excess inventory: More inventory than required to do any task.

Expedite: To push, rush, or walk a product (or information, signatures, etc.) through the process or system.

Expeditor: One who expedites.

External setup time: Time utilized and steps that can be done preparing for changeovers while the machine is still running. Example—prepping for a racing car pit stop like getting tires in place, having fuel ready, etc. Focus of changeovers or setups moving internal elements to external elements.

Fabrication: The process of transforming metals into a final product or subassembly usually by machine. Generally, a term to distinguish activities done in a machine shop versus manually assembling components into a final product.

Facility: The physical plant or office (transactional areas).

Failure analysis: The process of determining the root cause of a failure usually generating a report of some type.

Family: A group of products (or information) that shares similar processes.

FIFO: First in, first out inventory management system.

Flex fence: Purchasing term used in contracts to mitigate demand risk by having the supply chain capable of flexing production plus or minus 10%, 20%, or 30%. This is accomplished by identifying long lead items and developing plans to stock some of those parts at the buyer's expense.

Flexible workforce: A workforce totally cross-trained, capable, and allowed to work in all positions.

Floater: Cross-trained workers moved around throughout the day to different positions depending on the takt time or cycle time and the staffing requirements for the day.

Floor stock: Generally less expensive C-type parts stored centrally on the floor and owned by the company.

Flow: Smooth, uninterrupted movement of material or information.

Flow chart: A problem-solving tool that illustrates a process. It shows the way things actually go through a process, the way they should go, and the difference.

Flow production: Describes how goods, services, or information are processed. It is, at its best, one piece at a time. This can be a part, a document, invoice, or customer order. It rejects the concept of batch, lot, or mass producing. It vertically integrates all operations or functions as operationally or sequentially performed. It also encompasses pull or demand processing. Goods are not pushed through the process but pulled or demanded by succeeding operations from preceding operations. Often referred to as *one-piece-flow.*

FMEA: Failure mode and effects analysis. A structured approach to assess the magnitude of potential failures and identify the sources of each potential failure. Each potential failure is studied to identify the most effective corrective action. FMEA is the process of mitigating risk by looking at a process to determine what is likely to go wrong, the probability of it going wrong, the severity if it does go wrong, and the countermeasures to be taken in the event it does go wrong.

FOB: Free on board—logistics term used to designate where title passes to the buyer.

Focused factory: A plant or department focused on a single or family of products. Where everything can be done within the four walls. Does not necessarily mean cellular or one-piece flow.

Forecast: An attempt to look into the future in order to predict demand. Companies use techniques that range from historical statistical techniques to systematic wild ass guesses (SWAGs). The longer the forecast horizon, the less accurate the forecast.

FTE: Acronym standing for full-time equivalent. The formula is to take the total number of hours being worked by one or multiple people and divide by 2,080 hours (per year) and come up with the equivalent of one person's worth of labor per year.

Functional: Organized by department.

Functional layout: Layouts where the same or similar equipment is grouped together. These layouts support batch production.

GAAP: Acronym for generally accepted accounting principles.

Gain sharing: Method of compensating employees based on the overall productivity of the company. The goal is to give the employee a stake in the company and share based on productivity. Measures and participatory schemes vary by company and philosophy. There are many different methods of gain sharing. Normally differentiated from profit sharing, which is based on formulas relating only to company profits.

Grievance: Term refers to complaint (contract violation) filed by an employee (normally union based) against someone who is union or nonunion in the company.

Hanedashi: Device or means for automatic removal of a workpiece from one operation or process, which provides proper state and orientation for the next operation or process. In manufacturing, a means for automatic unloading and orientation for the next operation or process. In manufacturing, a means for automatic unloading and orientation for the next operation, generally a very simple device. Crucial for a *Chaku-Chaku* line.

Heijunka: Japanese term for level loading production. Necessary to support Kanban-based systems.

Histogram: A chart that takes measurement data and displays its distribution, generally in a bar graph format. For example, a histogram can be used to reveal the amount of variation that any process has within it based upon the data available.

Hoshin: Type of corporate planning, strategy, and execution in a setting where everyone participates in coming up with goals through a process called catchball and everyone down to the shop floor knows what they are doing is directly supporting the top three to five company goals.

Housekeeping: Keeping an orderly and clean environment.

Idle time: When a person is standing around with nothing to do, visible by arms crossed. Also known as pure waste.

Indirect costs: Traditional accounting costs that are not directly related or accounted to the product. Also known as overhead costs.

Indirect labor: Traditional accounting of labor required to support production without directly working on the product.

Indirect materials: Traditional accounting of materials used to support production but not directly used on the product.

Information: Data presented to an individual or machine.

Information systems: Term used to designate manual or computer-based systems, which convey information throughout the department or organization as a whole. Term used in value stream mapping for boxes located at the top of the map with lines to the process (information) boxes with which they interact.

Input: Work or information fed to the beginning of a system or process.

Inspection: The act of multiple (two or more) checks on material or information to see if it is correct. Can also refer to a department of humans that checks incoming materials (receiving inspection), WIP (in-process inspection), or final inspection before the product leaves the plant.

Internal setup time: Term used to designate time when machine or process is down (not running). Example is time when the racing car is in the pit stop having tires replaced and fuel added, etc.

Interrelationship diagram: A tool that assists in general planning. This tool takes a central idea, issue, or problem and maps out the logical or sequential links among related items.

It is a creative process that shows every idea can be logically linked with more than one idea at a time. It allows for *multidirectional* rather than *linear* thinking to be used.

Inventory: Purchased materials used to assemble any level of the product or to support production. Inventory can be in various stages from raw materials to finished goods.

Inventory turnover or turns: The number of times inventory cycles or turns over during the year. Generally calculated by dividing average cost of sales divided by the average inventory (normally three months). This can be a historical or forward-looking methodology. Can also be calculated by dividing days of supply into the number of working or calendar days.

Ishikawa diagram: Referred to as a fishbone used to graphically display cause and effect and to get to the root cause.

Item number: Normally a part number or stock number for a part.

Jidoka: Automation with a human touch or mind, autonomation. Automatic machinery that will operate itself but always incorporates the following devices: a mechanism to detect abnormalities or defects and a mechanism to stop the machine or line when defects or abnormalities occur.

Job costing: Where costs are collected and allocated to a certain job or charge number. Can be based on actual or standard costs.

Job description: List of roles and responsibilities for a particular job.

Job rotation: Schedule of movement from machine to machine or process to process. Used to support and encourage cross-training.

Job shop: Term used for factories that have high mix and low volume typically nonrepeatable or customized products.

Just-in-time manufacturing: A strategy that exposes the waste in an operation, makes continuous improvement a reality, and provides the opportunity to promote total employee involvement. Concentrates on making what is needed, when it is needed, no sooner, no later.

Kaizen (Kai = change; zen = good): The process improvement that involves a series of continual improvements over time. These improvements may take the form of a process innovation (event) or small incremental improvements.

Kanban: Japanese for a sign board. Designates a pull production means of communicating need for product or service. Originally developed as a means to communicate between operations in different locations. It was intended to communicate a change in demand or supply. In application, it is generally used to trigger the movement of material to or through a process.

Kit: Collection of components used to support a sub- or final assembly of a product.

Kitting: Process of collecting the components used to support a sub- or final assembly of a product.

Knowledge worker: A worker, who acquires information from every task, analyzes and validates the information, and stores it for future use.

Labor cost: Cost of labor, can be direct or indirect. In Lean, we look at total labor cost versus indirect or direct associated with traditional cost accounting systems.

Layout: Physical arrangement of machines and materials or offices.

LCL: Lower control limit, used on control charts.

Lead time: The time to manufacture and deliver a product or service. This term is used in many (often contradictory) contexts. To avoid confusion, lead time is defined as the average total lapse time for execution of the product delivery process from order receipt to delivery to the customer under normal operating conditions. In industries that operate in a build-to-order environment, lead times flex based on the influences of seasonal demand loads. In environments where production is scheduled in repeating, fixed-time segments or cycles, the lead time is usually determined by the length of the production cycle (i.e., days, weeks, months, etc.).

Lead time or throughput time: Time it takes to get through the entire process or time quoted to customers to receive their orders (from order to cash).

Lean production: The activity of creating processes that are highly responsive and flexible to customer demand requirements. Successful Lean production is evident when processes are capable of consistently delivering the highest quality (defect-free) products and services, at the right location and at the right time, in response to customer demand and doing this in the most cost-effective manner possible.

Learning curve: A planning technique used to predict improvement based on experience. Uses log charts to trend the data.

Level load: Process of leveling or equally distributing demand or products across a cell or plant. Also known as heijunka.

LIFO: Last in, first out inventory management.

Limit switch: Various electronic devices used to trigger an action when a particular limit is reached. Used to control machines or count parts, used to turn on or off machines, used often for poka yoke, etc.

Little's Law: Throughput time divided by cycle time = amount of inventory in the system.

Logistics: The art and science of shipping materials, distribution, warehousing, and supply chain management.

Lot: Refers to a group of parts or information generally batched together through the process.

Lot size: Number of parts in a batch to be produced.

LTA: Acronym for long-term agreement. An agreement negotiated with a supplier for a longer term and more complex than a simple blanket (pricing) agreement, normally three to five years with other conditions centering on the supplier's improvement, quality and delivery certification, and price reduction goals.

Machine hours: Total hours a machine is running. Can be value-added or non-value-added time normally used for capacity planning. May or may not include setup time or unplanned downtime.

Machine utilization: The amount of time a machine is available versus the amount of time the machine is being used. Includes setup and run time compared to available time. It used to be the *be all and end all* for traditional cost accounting measures. With Lean, it is not as important unless it is a true bottleneck machine.

Make or buy: Study of costs of purchasing a part versus purchasing the raw materials and making it in house.

Make to order: A product that is not started until after the customer orders it. In some cases, a Kanban or inventory of parts produced to a certain level may then be modified to fit the customer requirements.

Manufacturing resources planning (MRP II): A second-generation MRP system that provides additional control linkages such as automatic purchase order generation, capacity planning, and accounts payable transactions.

Master schedule: Schedule with customer orders loaded by due date or promised date.

Master scheduler: Person who enters sales orders into the master schedule.

Material requirements planning (MRP): A computerized information system that calculates material requirements based on a master production schedule. This system may be used only for material procurement or to also execute the material plan through shop floor control.

MBO: Management by objectives—a system where goals are handed down from manager to employee where the employee participates in the process.

Means (measure): A way to accomplish a target.

Min max: Refers to a type of inventory system where once the minimum level is reached or a reorder point is reached, a quantity is reordered, which brings the quantity back up to the maximum level. Some computer MRP systems (Oracle) have this as an option to manage inventory.

Milk run: Term used to identify the path water spider uses to replenish materials for a line.

Mistake proofing: Also known as poka yoke or foolproofing. A system starting with successive checks by humans to inspection devices built into or added to machines to detect and or prevent defects.

Mixed model production: The ability to produce various models with different levels of customization one by one down the production line.

Monthly audit: The self-evaluation of performance against targets. An examination of things that helped or hindered performance in meeting the targets and the corrective actions that will be taken.

MPS: Master production schedule.

MRO: Term used to designate maintenance repair and operating supplies.

MRP: Material requirements planning; a computerized system developed by Olie Wright using lead time offsets, bill of material, and various planning parameters used to predict when to release requisitions or work orders in order to schedule the production floor.

MRPII: Material resource planning; a more advanced MRP system, which ties various systems together within a single company, that is, manufacturing and finance.

MTM: Methods time measurement; system that has studied and determined times for various operations or movements by operators. Generally used with motion study.

Muda: Japanese term for waste.

Multiskilled or process workers: Description for individuals at any level of the organization who are diverse in skill and training. Capable of performing a number of different tasks providing the organization with additional flexibility.

Mura: Japanese term for uneven.

Muri: Japanese term for overburden.

Nemawashi: Refers to the process of gaining consensus and support prior to implementing a strategy.

Net sales: Total sales less returns and allowances.

Noise: Randomness within a process.

Nominal group technique: Process of soliciting information from everyone in the group.

Non-value added: Designation for a step that does not meet one of the three value-added criteria.

Non-value added but necessary (sometimes called business value added): Any step that is necessary but the customer is not willing to pay for it but it is done right the first time.

Normal distribution: Statistical term where most data falls close to the mean (± 1 sigma), less fall away from the mean (± 2 sigma), and even less fall even further away (± 3 sigma), where the distribution when graphed looks like a bell-shaped curve.

NTED: No-touch exchange of dies.

Objective: What you are trying to achieve with a given plan. The desired end result. The reason for employing a strategy and developing targets.

Obsolete: Loss of product value due to engineering, product life decisions, or technological changes.

Offset: Time entered into MRP systems to designate how long it takes to get through a part of the system, that is, purchasing time entered as two days. MRP uses this information to develop a timeline to predict when to release the order or purchase requirement. When added up, it equals the total lead time of the product in the system.

OJT: Acronym for on-the-job training.

One-year plan: A statement of objective of an organizational event for a year.

Operating system: Refers to the type of system computer is using, that is, DOS, windows, etc.

Operation: A series of tasks grouped together such that the sum of the individual task times is equal to the takt time (cycle time to meet product demand requirements). It is important to distinguish between operations and activities. Operations are used to balance work content in a flow manufacturing process to achieve a particular daily output rate equal to customer demand. An operation defines the amount of work content performed by each operator to achieve a balanced flow and linear output rate.

Opportunity cost: Return on capital, which could have been achieved had it been used for something else more productive.

Order policy: Term used in MRP to decide lot sizing requirements.

Organization structure: The fashion in which resources are assigned to tasks. Includes cross-functional management and vertical work teams. Also includes the development of multiskilled workers through the assignment of technical and administrative personnel to nontraditional roles.

Organizational development: Process that looks at improving the interactions within and between departments across the overall organization. Generally led by a consultant or company change agent.

Organizational tools: These provide a team approach in which people get together to work on problems and also get better at what they are doing. Organizational tools include work groups and quality circles.

OTED: One-touch exchange of dies. Uses a human touch to changeover one or more machines at the same time.

Overhead: Costs not directly tied to the product. Normally refers to all personnel who support the production process whether it is physical or transactional.

Overtime: Work beyond the traditional 40 hours usually results in a premium paid per hour.

Pareto chart: A vertical bar graph showing the bars in order to size from left to right. Helps focus on the vital few problems rather than the trivial many. An extension of the Pareto principle that suggests the significant items in a given group normally constitute a relatively small portion of the items in the total group. Conversely, a majority of the items in the total will, even in aggregate, be relatively minor in significance (i.e., the 80/20 rule).

Participative management: Employees collaborate with managers to work on improvements to the process. Basis for QC circles.

Pay for performance: Pay is tied to overall output by a team.

Perpetual inventory system: System designed to always have the correct amount of inventory in the system.

PFA: Process flow analysis, looks at the flow of just the product through the process using TIPS.

Phantom: A bill of material (BOM) or non-production work order used to determine if there are any parts shortages. How to create the phantom varies depending on the type of MRP or

ERP system. In general, a work order is created and then backed out of the system prior to MRP running again.

Physical layout: A means of impacting workflow and productivity through the physical placement of machinery or furniture. Production machinery should be grouped in a cellular arrangement based upon product requirements, not process type. In addition to this, in most instances, there is an advantage in having the workflow in counterclockwise fashion. Similarly, in an office environment, furniture should be arranged such that there is an efficient flow of information or services rather than strictly defined departments.

PDCA cycle: Plan-Do-Check-Act. The PDCA system, sometimes referred to as the Deming cycle, is the most important item for control in policy deployment. In this cycle, you make a plan that is based on policy (plan); you take action accordingly (do); you check the result (check); and if the plan is not fulfilled, you analyze the cause and take further action by going back to the plan (action).

Piece rate: Form of worker compensation based on individual output targets that vary by employee and process.

Pilot: Trying something out for one or several pieces in a controlled environment to test a hypothesis.

Plan: The means to achieve a target.

Planned downtime: Downtime that is scheduled for a machine or line.

Planner/buyer: Combines planning and buyer jobs.

Planner/buyer/scheduler: Combines planning, buying, and scheduling jobs.

Poka yoke: Japanese expression meaning *common or simple, mistake proof.* A method of designing processes, either production or administrative, which will by their nature prevent errors. This may involve designing fixtures that will not accept a defective part or something as simple as having a credit memo be a different color than a debit memo. It requires that thought be put into the design of any system to anticipate *what* can go wrong and build in measures to prevent them.

Policy: The company objectives are to be achieved through the cooperation of all levels of managers and employees. A policy consists of targets, plans, and target values.

Policy deployment: Hoshin Kanri—policy deployment orchestrates continuous improvement in a way that fosters individual initiative and alignment. It is a process of implementing the policies of an organization directly through line managers and indirectly through cross-functional organization. It is a means of internalizing company policies throughout the organization, from highest to lowest level. Top managers will articulate its annual goals that are then deployed down through lower levels of management. The abstract goals of top management become more concrete and specific as they are deployed down through the organization. Policy deployment is process oriented. It is concerned with developing a process by which results become predictable. If the goal is not realized, it is necessary to review and see if the implementation was faulty. It is most important to determine what went wrong in the process that prevented the goal from being realized. The Japanese name for policy deployment is Hoshin Kanri. In Japanese, Hoshin means *shining metal, compass,* or *pointing in the direction.* Kanri means *control.* Hoshin Kanri is a method devised to capture and concretize strategic goals as well as flashes of insight about the future and to develop the means to bring these into reality. It is one of the major systems that make world-class quality management possible. It helps control the direction of the company by orchestrating change within a company. The system includes tools for continuous improvement, breakthroughs, and implementation. The key to Hoshin planning is it brings the total organization into the strategic planning process, both top down and bottom up. It ensures the direction, goals, and objectives of the company are rationally developed, well defined, clearly communicated, monitored, and adapted based on system feedback. It provides focus for the organization.

POU: Point of use, designates location where product or tooling or information is used.

Preventative maintenance: Term given to duties carried out on machines in order to prevent a breakdown or unplanned stoppage.

Prioritization matrices: This tool prioritizes tasks, issues, product/service characteristics, etc., based on known weighted criteria using a combination of tree and matrix diagram techniques. Above all, they are tools for decision-making.

Problem-solving tools: These tools find the root cause of problems. They are tools for thinking about problems, managing by fact, and documenting hunches. The tools include check sheet, line chart, Pareto chart, flow chart, histogram, control chart, and scatter diagram. In Japan, these are referred to as the seven QC tools.

Process: A series of activities that collectively accomplish a distinct objective. Processes are cross-functional and cut across departmental responsibility boundaries. Processes can be value added or non-value added.

Process capability: See CPK.

Process control chart: Chart that represents tracking the sequence of data points over a number of or 100% samplings. It serves as a basis to define common cause versus special cause variation and to predict when a part or machine is likely to fail.

Process decision program chart: The process decision program chart (PDPC) is a method that maps out conceivable events and contingencies that can occur in any implementation plan. It, in time, identifies possible countermeasures in response to these problems. This tool is used to plan each possible chain of events that need to occur when the problem or goal is an unfamiliar one.

Process hierarchy: A hierarchical decomposition from core business processes to the task level. The number of levels in a hierarchy is determined by the breadth and size of the organization. A large enterprise process hierarchy may include core business processes, processes, subprocesses, process segments, activities, and tasks.

Process management: This involves focusing on the process rather than the results. A variety of tools may be used for process management, including the seven QC tools.

Process segment: A series of activities that define a subset of a process.

Product delivery process: The stream of activities required to produce a product or service. This activity stream encompasses both planning and execution activities to include demand planning, order management, materials procurement, production, and distribution.

Production control: Employee that tracks status of daily production; normally used in batch environments but sometimes in Lean environments.

Production schedule: Orders lined up in order of priority based on due date, promised date, or some other planning parameters.

Productivity: Productivity is the *amount* of products produced in a certain amount of time with a certain amount of labor. The products could be physical products or transactional such as processing an invoice or Internet blogs. Productive means getting things done, outcomes reached, or goals achieved and are measured as output per unit of input (i.e., labor, equipment, and capital).

Prototype: First piece on which new process is tried.

Pull production: In a pull process, materials are staged at the point of consumption. As these materials are consumed, signals are sent back to previous steps in the production process to pull forward sufficient materials to replenish only those materials that have been consumed.

Push production: In a push process, production is initiated by the issuance of production orders that are offset in time from the actual demand to allow time for production and delivery. The idea is to maintain zero inventory and have materials complete each step of the production process just as they are needed at subsequent (downstream) activities.

+QDIP: Acronym stands for safety, quality, delivery, inventory, and production. Ideally, parameters are set by the employees on the shop floor or in the workshop.

Quality: Refers to the ability of the final product to meet both the customers required specification and unspecified specifications.

Quality circles: Quality circles are an organizational tool that provides a team approach in which people get together to work on problems and to improve productivity. Their primary objective is to foster teamwork and encourage employee by involvement employing the problem-solving approach.

Quality function deployment: A product development system that identifies the wants of a customer and gets that information to all the right people so the organization can effectively exceed competition in meeting the customer's most important wants. It translates customer wants into appropriate technical requirements for each stage of product development and production.

Quality management: The systems, organizations, and tools that make it possible to plan, manufacture, and deliver a quality product or service. This does not imply inspection or even traditional quality control. Rather, it involves the entire process involved in bringing goods and services to the customer.

Queuing theory: Applies to manufacturing orders, people, or information that is waiting in line for the next process. Based on Little's law.

Queue time: Amount of time an order, people, or information is waiting for the next process.

Quick changeover: Method of increasing the amount of productive time available for a piece of machinery by minimizing the time needed to change from one model to another. This greatly increases the flexibility of the operation and allows it to respond more quickly to changes in demand. It also has the benefit of allowing an organization to greatly reduce the amount of inventory that it must carry because of improved response time.

Rate-based order management: This order management system employs a finite capacity loading scheme to promise orders based upon the agreed demand bound limits. These minimum and maximum demand bounds reflect potential response capacity limits for production and materials procurement.

Rate-based planning: A procedure that establishes a controlled level of flexibility in the product delivery process in order to be robust to anticipated variations in demand. This flexibility is achieved by establishing minimum and maximum bounds around future demand forecasts. The idea is that both the production facility and the material supply channels will echelon sufficient capacity to accommodate demand swings that do not exceed the established demand bounds. As future demand forecasts move closer to the production window, updated demand bounds are periodically broadcasted to the material suppliers. At the point of order receipt and delivery promising (within sales or customer service), demand bounding limits are enforced to insure that the rate-based production plan remains feasible.

Regression analysis: Statistical technique that determines or estimates the amount of correlation explained between two or more variable sets of data.

ROI: Return on investment, generally compares investment versus the return to determine the payback that is often stated in years and expressed as a percentage of earnings.

RONA: Return on net assets.

Root cause: The ultimate reason for an event or condition.

Run chart: A statistical problem-solving tool that shows whether key indicators are going up or down and if the indicators are good or bad.

Safety: Ensuring that the work environment is free of hazards and obstacles of which could cause harm.

Scanlon plan: A system of group incentives that measures the plant-wide results of all efforts using the ratio of labor costs to sales value added by production. If there is an increase in production sales value with no change in pricing, mix, or labor costs, productivity has increased and unit costs have decreased.

Scatter diagram: One of the seven QC tools. The scatter diagram shows the relationship between two variables.

Scheduled (planned) downtime: Planned shutdown of equipment to perform maintenance or other tasks or lack of customer demand.

Self-diagnosis: As a basis for continuous improvement, each manager uses problem-solving activity to see why he or she is succeeding or failing to meet targets. This diagnosis should focus on identifying personal and organizational obstacles to the planned performance and on the development of alternate approaches based on this new information.

Self-directed work team: Normally, a small group of employees that can plan, organize, and manage their daily responsibilities with no direct supervision. They can normally hire, fire, or demote team members.

Setup: The changing over of a machine or also the loading and unloading of parts on a machine.

Setup time: The amount of time it takes to changeover a machine from the last good part to and including the first good part.

Setup parts: Preparation, mounting and removing, calibration, trial runs, and adjustments.

Seven new tools: Sometimes called the seven management tools. These are affinity and relationship diagrams for general planning; tree systems, matrix, and prioritization matrices for intermediate planning; and activity network diagrams and process decision program charts for detailed planning.

Seven QC tools: Problem-solving statistical tools needed for customer-driven master plan. They are cause and effect diagram, flow chart, Pareto chart, run chart, histogram, control chart, and scatter diagram.

Seven wastes: Seven types of waste have been identified for business. They are as follows:

1. Waste from overproduction of goods or services
2. Waste from waiting or idle time
3. Waste from transportation (unnecessary)
4. Waste from the process itself (inefficiency)
5. Waste of unnecessary stock on hand

6. Waste of motion and effort
7. Waste from producing defective goods

The eighth waste: Waste of talent and knowledge

Shojinka: Means labor flexibility. The term means employees staffing the line can flex up or down based on the incoming demand, which requires employees to be cross-trained and multi-process/machine capable. It also means continually optimizing the number of workers based on demand. This principle is central to baton zone line balancing (bumping).

Shoninka: Means *manpower savings*. This corresponds to the improvement of work procedures, machines, or equipment to free whole units of labor (i.e., one person) from a production line consisting of one or more workers.

Shoryokuka[1]: Shoryokuka means *labor savings* and indicates partial improvement of manual labor by adding small machines or devices to aid the job. This results in some small amount of labor savings but not an entire person as in shoninka. Again this becomes a goal of all follow-up point kaizen events.

Simultaneous/concurrent engineering: The practice of designing a product (or service), its production process, and its delivery mechanism all at the same time. The process requires considerable up-front planning as well as the dedication of resources early in the development cycle. The payoff is in the form of shorter development time from concept to market, lower overall development cost, and lower product or service cost based upon higher accuracy at introduction and less potential for redesign. Examples of this include the Toyota Lexus 200 and the Ford Taurus.

SMED: Single-minute exchange of dies, 9 minutes 59 seconds or less setup time.

Smoothing/production smoothing: The statistical method of converting weekly or monthly schedules to level-loaded daily schedules.

SPC: Acronym for statistical process control.

Standard deviation: Statistical measurement of process variation (σ) which measures the dispersion of sample observations around a process mean.

Standard work: Standard work is a tool that defines the interaction of man and his environment when processing something. In producing a part, it is the interaction of man and machine, whereas in processing an invoice, it is the interaction of man and the supplier and the accounting system. It details the motion of the operator and the sequence of action. It provides a routine for consistency of an operation and a basis for improvement. Furthermore, the concept of standard work is it is a verb, not a noun. It details the best process we currently know and understand. Tomorrow it should be better (continuous improvement), and the standard work should be revised to incorporate the improvement. There can be no improvement without a basis (standard work).

Standard work has three central elements:

1. Cycle time (not takt time)
2. Standard operations
3. SWIP

Standard work (as a tool): Establishes a routine/habit/pattern for repetitive tasks, makes managing such as scheduling and resource allocation easier, establishes the relationship between man and environment, provides a basis for improvement by defining the normal and highlighting the abnormal, and prohibits backsliding.

Standard work in process: The amount of material or a given product that must be in process at any time to insure maximum efficiency of the operation.

Standardization: The system of documenting and updating procedures to make sure everyone knows clearly and simply what is expected of them (measured by daily control). Essential for application of PDCA cycle.

Statistical methods/tools: Statistical methods allow employees to manage by facts and analyze problems through understanding variability and data. The seven QC tools are examples of statistical tools.

Store, storage: Any time a product (part, information, or person) is waiting in the process.

Strategy: The business process that involves goals setting, defining specific actions to achieve the business goals, and allocating the resources to execute the actions.

Subprocess: A series of interrelated process segments that forms a subset of a total process.

Supplier partnerships: An acknowledgment that suppliers are an integral part of any business. A partnership implies a long-term relationship that involves the supplier in both product development and process development. It also requires a commitment on the part of the supplier to pursue continuous improvement and world-class quality.

System: A system is the infrastructure that enables the processes to provide customer value. Business systems comprise market, customer, competition, organizational culture, environmental and technological influences, regulatory issues, physical resources, procedures, information flows, and knowledge sets. It is through physical processes that business systems transform inputs to outputs and, thereby, deliver products and services of value in the marketplace.

Takt time: The frequency with which the customer wants a product or how frequently a sold unit must be produced. The number is derived by taking the amount of time available in a day and dividing it by the number of sold units that need to be produced. Takt time is usually expressed in seconds.

Target: The desired goal that serves as a yardstick for evaluating the degree to which a *policy* is achieved. It is controlled by a *control point, control item,* or *target item.*

Target costing: Method for establishing cost objective for a product or service during the design phase. The target cost is determined by the following formula:

$$\text{Sales price} - \text{target profit} = \text{target cost}$$

Target/means matrix: Shows the relationship between targets and means and to identify control items and control methods.

Target value: Normally a numeric definition of successful target attainment. It is not always possible to have a numeric target, and you must never separate the target from the plan.

Theory of constraints: A management philosophy first put forth in the book *The Goal* by Eliyahu Goldratt to identify bottlenecks in the process. In the book, he follows a young boy scout named Herbie. We call bottlenecks *Herbies* today in some cases. His approach was to identify the constraint, exploit the constraint, subordinate all non-constraints, elevate the constraint, and if the constraint is broken in step 4, then go back to step 1.

Throughput time: A measure of the actual throughput time for a product to move through a flow process once the work begins. Many people incorrectly label this measure as manufacturing lead time but it is actually a small subset and often has little to do with the total time from order inception to fulfillment.

TIPS: Acronym for parts of process flow analysis—transport inspect process store.

Total density: One of the eight Lean wastes is the *waste of motion*. One of the first things we advise when trying to identify wasted motions is do not confuse motion with work. In offices, this concept is revised slightly to the following: *do not confuse effort with results.*[2] Total density = work divided by motion.[3] Not all motion is work. It is important to separate needed motions versus wasted motions.

Total employee involvement (TEI): A philosophy that advocates the harnessing of the collective knowledge of an organization through the involvement of its people. When supported by the management, it is a means of improving quality, delivery, profitability, and morale in an organization. It provides all employees with a greater sense of ownership in the success of the company and provides them with more control in addressing issues that face the organization. TEI does not allow top management to abdicate its obligation to properly plan and set objectives. It does, however, provide more resources and flexibility in meeting those objectives.

Total labor time: The sum of labor value-added and labor non-value-added times.

Total productive maintenance: TPM is productive maintenance conducted by all employees. It is equipment maintenance performed on a companywide basis. It has five goals:

1. Maximize equipment effectiveness (improve overall efficiency).
2. Develop a system of productive maintenance for the life of the equipment.
3. Involve all departments that plan, design, use, or maintain equipment in implementing TPM (engineering and design, production, and maintenance).
4. Actively involve all employees—from top management to shop-floor workers.
5. Promote TPM through motivational management (autonomous small group activities).

The word total in *total productive maintenance* has three meanings related to three important features of TPM: total effectiveness (pursuit of economic efficiency or profitability), total PM (maintenance prevention and activity to improve maintainability as well as preventative maintenance), and total participation (autonomous maintenance by operators and small group activities in every department and at every level).

Transport: Any travel a part or information does throughout the process.

Tree diagram: The tree diagram systematically breaks down plans into component parts and systematically maps out the full range of tasks/methods needed to achieve a goal. It can either be used as a cause-finding problem-solver or a task-generating planning tool.

Value added: Must meet three criteria from the AMA video *Time The Next Dimension of Quality*: customer cares, physically changes the thing going through the process, and done right the first time. Value added was expanded for hospitals to physically or emotionally change the patient for the better in addition to the other two criteria.

Value-added work content ratio: The steps that actually transform and increase the value of the product or test requirements legislated by industrial licensing agencies. The value-added work content ratio is formed by simply dividing the sum of all value-added work steps by the product lead time for the total process. This ratio can also be used to evaluate waste only in the manufacturing process segment by dividing the numerator by the manufacturing flow time.

Vertical teams: Vertical teams are groups of people who come together to meet and address problems or challenges. These teams are made up of the most appropriate people for the issue, regardless of their levels or jobs within the organization.

Vision: A long-term plan or direction that is based on a careful assessment of the most important directions for the organization.

Visual management: The use of visual media in the organization and general administration of a business. This would include the use of color, signs, and a clear span of sight in a work area. These visuals should clearly designate what things are and where they belong. They should provide immediate feedback as to the work being done and its pace. Visual management should provide access to information needed in the operation of a business. This would include charts and graphs that allow the business status to be determined through their review. This review should be capable of being performed at a glance. To facilitate this, it is necessary to be able to manage by fact and let the data speak for it.

Water spider: New role for material handler. Water spiders can be a low-skill or high-skill job. The water spider job is to replenish empty bins on the line daily, plays a vital role in mixed model parts sequencing, should stay 15 minutes or more ahead of the line, can be utilized as a floater, can be utilized to release parts orders from suppliers, and should have standard work and walk patterns/milk runs.

Work groups: Work groups are an organizational tool providing a team approach in which people work together on problems to improve productivity.

World-class quality management: The commitment by all employees. It is a philosophy/operating methodology totally committed to quality and customer satisfaction. It focuses on continuous process improvement in all processes. It advocates the use of analytical tools and scientific methods and data. It establishes priorities and manages by fact. World-class quality management has perfection (world class) as its goal. We should benchmark to be better than the competition by a large margin, the best. To obtain this status, all employees must be involved, everyone, everywhere, at all times. The result will be products and services that consistently meet or exceed the customers' expectations both internal and external. This group is always passionate with respect to improving the customer experience.

Yo-i-don[4]: It means ready set go. It is used to balance multiple processes and operators to a required cycle time using andon. This means each station or line is station balanced to one cycle time. When each operator completes their work, they press the andon button. Once the count-down or count-up clock reaches the prescribed cycle time, any station not completed, immediately turns the andon light to red. At this point, the supervisor and other team members will come to help that station.

Yokoten[5]: It is a process critical for creating a true learning organization. Sharing best practices (successes) is critical across the entire organization. In kanji, yoko means beside, side, or width and ten has several meanings but here it would mean to cultivate or comment. Yokoten is a means of *horizontal or sideways transfer of knowledge*, that is, peer-to-peer across the company. People are encouraged to Gemba, to see the kaizen improvement made for them, and see if they can apply the idea or an improved idea in their area. At Honeywell, this is referred to as horizontal linking mechanisms (HLMs).

Notes

1. *Lean Lexicon*, John Shook, LEI, 2004.
2. Source unknown.
3. Kanban JIT at Toyota—Ohno, Japan Management Association.
4. Monden Yasuhiro, *Toyota Production System*, 3rd edition.
5. http://eudict.com/?lang=japeng&word=ten.

Index

Note: Locators in *italics* represent figures and **bold** indicate tables in the text.